Learn WinUI 3

Leverage WinUI and the Windows App SDK to create modern
Windows applications with C# and XAML

Alvin Ashcraft

BIRMINGHAM—MUMBAI

Learn WinUI 3

Group Product Manager: Kunal Sawant

Publishing Product Manager: Teny Thomas

Book Project Manager: Prajakta Naik

Senior Editor: Ruvika Rao

Technical Editor: Maran Fernandes

Copy Editor: Safis Editing

Proofreader: Safis Editing

Indexer: Tejal Daruwale Soni

Production Designer: Joshua Misquitta

DevRel Marketing Coordinator: Sonia Chauhan

First published: March 2021

Second edition: October 2023

Production reference: 1121023

Published by Packt Publishing Ltd.

Grosvenor House

11 St Paul's Square

Birmingham

B3 1RB, UK

ISBN 978-1-80512-006-3

www.packtpub.com

To my wife, Stelene, for her love and her continued support in our life together. I'm looking forward to the journey ahead of us. To my three daughters for working hard and growing into amazing, talented young women. I can't wait to see where life takes you all.

– Alvin Ashcraft

Contributors

About the author

Alvin Ashcraft is a senior content developer at Microsoft, working on the Windows developer documentation team on Microsoft Learn, with a focus on the Windows App SDK, .NET MAUI, Win32, and other desktop application technologies. Prior to this, Alvin spent over 25 years as a software developer and architect, most recently at Allscripts, a global healthcare software company, delivering **electronic health record** (**EHR**) software to healthcare systems across the world. He is the author of two previous books for Packt, the first edition of *Learn WinUI 3* and *Parallel Programming and Concurrency with C# 10 and .NET 6*.

I want to thank my family – especially my wife, Stelene, and my daughters – for supporting me in my writing journey, which has become my new career.

About the reviewer

Peter Foot is a Windows and IoT consultant at In The Hand Ltd, where he handcrafts apps and APIs for mobile and IoT devices. Peter has over 20 years' experience with .NET and Windows development, from the simple Pocket PC to the rich experiences of WinUI.

Peter has been awarded the Microsoft **Most Valuable Professional** (**MVP**) since 2003 for his involvement in the Microsoft .NET and Windows developer communities. Alongside involvement in other open source projects, Peter created and maintains the 32feet.NET library, which is a cross-platform .NET API for Bluetooth and other personal area networking technologies. Peter co-authored *Microsoft Mobile Development Handbook* and has written a host of technical articles and blog posts.

Table of Contents

2

Configuring the Development Environment and Creating the Project 29

3

MVVM for Maintainability and Testability 65

4

Advanced MVVM Concepts   87

5

Exploring WinUI Controls   111

6

Leveraging Data and Services   131

Part 2: Extending WinUI and Modernizing Applications

7

Fluent Design System for Windows Applications   155

Part 3: Build and Deploy on Windows and Beyond

11

Debugging WinUI Applications with Visual Studio   247

12

Hosting a Blazor Application in WinUI   269

13

Take Your App Cross-Platform with Uno Platform   295

14

Packaging and Deploying WinUI Applications   317

Preface

WinUI 3 is the newest desktop UI framework for Windows application development. It is part of Microsoft's Windows App SDK, providing developers with the tools to build beautiful apps with the Fluent Design System. This book will quickly get you up to speed with WinUI to build new Windows applications and to build apps across platforms with technologies such as Blazor and Uno Platform.

The book begins by exploring the history of Windows UI development frameworks to gain an understanding of how earlier frameworks influenced WinUI as it exists today. It covers the basics of XAML-based UI development and explores the controls available in WinUI before moving on to an examination of patterns and best practices for WinUI developers. To help reinforce these concepts, the early chapters in the book build practical skills by creating an application to organize a collection of books, music, and movies. Each chapter enhances the application, with new controls and concepts discussed.

Later chapters in the book explore how developers can leverage their WinUI knowledge to leverage open source toolkits, integrate web content in Windows apps, and migrate WinUI apps to Android, iOS, and the web. The book finishes by teaching some essential Visual Studio debugging techniques and discussing app deployment options to get your apps in the hands of consumers and enterprise users. At the end of every chapter, I've included a series of questions for you to attempt on your own, enabling you to gauge your level of understanding. Learn how WinUI can help you build and deploy modern, robust applications!

Who this book is for

This book is for anyone who wants to develop Windows applications with a modern **user experience** (**UX**). If you are familiar with Windows Forms, UWP, or WPF, and are looking to update your knowledge of Windows development or modernize existing apps, this book is for you. If you are just learning .NET development, you can take advantage of this book to learn the basics of XAML development in parallel with your C# and .NET journey.

What this book covers

Chapter 1, *Introduction to WinUI*, examines the history of UI frameworks in Windows and the origins of WinUI, and you will create your first WinUI 3 project in Visual Studio.

Chapter 2, *Configuring the Development Environment and Creating the Project*, explains how to install and configure Visual Studio for WinUI development, the basics of XAML and C#, and kicks off the hands-on with a project that will be enhanced throughout the book.

Chapter 3, MVVM for Maintainability and Testability, introduces the basics of Model-View-ViewModel (MVVM) pattern, one of the most important design patterns when building XAML-based applications.

Chapter 4, Advanced MVVM Concepts, builds on the basics you learned about the MVVM pattern in WinUI apps to handle more advanced techniques. You'll learn how to keep components loosely coupled and testable when adding new dependencies to your projects.

Chapter 5, Exploring WinUI Controls, explores some of the many controls and APIs that WinUI offers for developers building Windows applications. This chapter explores the brand-new controls and updated controls that were previously available in WinUI 2 and UWP.

Chapter 6, Leveraging Data and Services, looks at managing data, a core part of software development. This chapter covers some key concepts of data management, including state management and the service locator pattern.

Chapter 7, Fluent Design System for Windows Applications, explains the tenets of Microsoft's Fluent Design System and how to implement them in your WinUI applications.

Chapter 8, Adding Windows Notifications to WinUI Applications, covers how to leverage the Windows App SDK to support push notifications and app notifications in your WinUI applications.

Chapter 9, Enhancing Applications with the Windows Community Toolkits, introduces the Windows Community Toolkit and the .NET Community Toolkit – collections of open source libraries for Windows developers. You will learn how to leverage the controls and helpers from the toolkits in your WinUI projects.

Chapter 10, Accelerating App Development with Template Studio, shows how to leverage Template Studio to create a new WinUI project, which can be a daunting task, built on the best Windows development patterns and practices.

Chapter 11, Debugging WinUI Applications with Visual Studio, shows how to leverage the XAML debugging tools in Visual Studio to track down pesky bugs in your WinUI project – good debugging skills are essential for developers.

Chapter 12, Hosting a Blazor Application in WinUI, looks at the WebView2 control in WinUI and using it to host a Blazor application deployed to the cloud from inside your Windows application.

Chapter 13, Take Your App Cross-Platform with Uno Platform, explains how to migrate a WinUI project to Uno Platform, which allows developers to write XAML and C# code in a single code base and run it on any platform.

Chapter 14, Packaging and Deploying WinUI Applications, explores some of the multiple options WinUI developers have for packaging and deploying WinUI applications, looking at deploying through the Microsoft Store, WinGet, and side-loading apps.

To get the most out of this book

If you are familiar with Windows Forms, .NET MAUI, UWP, or WPF and are looking to enhance your knowledge of Windows development or modernize existing apps, you will find this book useful. Hands-on experience with C# and .NET is expected but no prior knowledge of WinUI is required.

Software/hardware covered in the book	Operating system requirements
WinUI 3	Windows 10 version 1809 or later or Windows 11
C#	Windows, macOS, or Linux
.NET 7	Windows, macOS, or Linux
Visual Studio 2022	Windows 10 or 11
Blazor	Windows, macOS, or Linux
Uno Platform	Windows, macOS, or Linux

The book covers how to get started with WinUI development, but you should have Visual Studio and .NET installed. Follow the instructions on Microsoft Learn: `https://learn.microsoft.com/visualstudio/install/install-visual-studio.`

If you are using the digital version of this book, we advise you to type the code yourself or access the code from the book's GitHub repository (a link is available in the next section). Doing so will help you avoid any potential errors related to the copying and pasting of code.

After you read this book, you can continue your Windows development journey by diving deeper into the documentation and samples on Microsoft Learn: `https://learn.microsoft.com/windows/apps/.`

Download the example code files

You can download the example code files for this book from GitHub at `https://github.com/PacktPublishing/Learn-WinUI-3-Second-Edition`. If there's an update to the code, it will be updated in the GitHub repository.

We also have other code bundles from our rich catalog of books and videos available at `https://github.com/PacktPublishing/`. Check them out!

Conventions used

There are a number of text conventions used throughout this book.

`Code in text`: Indicates code words in text, database table names, folder names, filenames, file extensions, pathnames, dummy URLs, user input, and Twitter handles. Here is an example: "In `INavigationService`, you can update the `namespace` to `UnoMediaCollection.Interfaces` and remove the `using System;` statement."

A block of code is set as follows:

```
using UnoMediaCollection.Enums;
using UnoMediaCollection.Interfaces;
using UnoMediaCollection.Model;
```

When we wish to draw your attention to a particular part of a code block, the relevant lines or items are set in bold:

```
using UnoMediaCollection.Enums;
namespace UnoMediaCollection.Model
```

Any command-line input or output is written as follows:

```
$ mkdir css
$ cd css
```

Bold: Indicates a new term, an important word, or words that you see onscreen. For instance, words in menus or dialog boxes appear in **bold**. Here is an example: "Right-click the **Enums** folder and select **Add | Existing Item**."

> **Tips or important notes**
> Appear like this.

Get in touch

Feedback from our readers is always welcome.

General feedback: If you have questions about any aspect of this book, email us at customercare@packtpub.com and mention the book title in the subject of your message.

Errata: Although we have taken every care to ensure the accuracy of our content, mistakes do happen. If you have found a mistake in this book, we would be grateful if you would report this to us. Please visit www.packtpub.com/support/errata and fill in the form.

Piracy: If you come across any illegal copies of our works in any form on the internet, we would be grateful if you would provide us with the location address or website name. Please contact us at copyright@packt.com with a link to the material.

If you are interested in becoming an author: If there is a topic that you have expertise in and you are interested in either writing or contributing to a book, please visit authors.packtpub.com.

Share your thoughts

Once you've read *Learn WinUI 3*, we'd love to hear your thoughts! Scan the QR code below to go straight to the Amazon review page for this book and share your feedback.

https://packt.link/r/1805120069

Your review is important to us and the tech community and will help us make sure we're delivering excellent quality content.

Download a free PDF copy of this book

Thanks for purchasing this book!

Do you like to read on the go but are unable to carry your print books everywhere?

Is your eBook purchase not compatible with the device of your choice?

Don't worry, now with every Packt book you get a DRM-free PDF version of that book at no cost.

Read anywhere, any place, on any device. Search, copy, and paste code from your favorite technical books directly into your application.

The perks don't stop there, you can get exclusive access to discounts, newsletters, and great free content in your inbox daily

Follow these simple steps to get the benefits:

1. Scan the QR code or visit the link below

https://packt.link/free-ebook/9781805120063

2. Submit your proof of purchase
3. That's it! We'll send your free PDF and other benefits to your email directly

Part 1:
Introduction to WinUI and Windows Applications

WinUI 3 is Microsoft's latest UI framework for Windows developers. This section will start by exploring the recent history of XAML and Windows UI frameworks and introduce you to WinUI. Throughout the chapters of this section, you will learn about WinUI concepts by building a simple project from scratch and adding controls and features, by following design patterns and best practices. These patterns and practices include the **Model-View-ViewModel (MVVM)** design pattern, building loosely coupled, testable C# classes, and using **dependency injection (DI)** to inject service dependencies into the application components.

This part has the following chapters:

- *Chapter 1, Introduction to WinUI*
- *Chapter 2, Configuring the Development Environment and Creating the Project*
- *Chapter 3, MVVM for Maintainability and Testability*
- *Chapter 4, Advanced MVVM Concepts*
- *Chapter 5, Exploring WinUI Controls*
- *Chapter 6, Leveraging Data and Services*

1

Introduction to WinUI

WinUI 3 is a set of **user interface** (**UI**) controls and libraries that Windows developers can leverage in their desktop applications. It is the UI part of the Windows App SDK, which was previously known as **Project Reunion**. UWP developers use the **Windows Software Development Kit** (**Windows SDK**) to build their applications and are required to select a target SDK version in a project's properties. By extracting the UWP controls and UI components from the Windows SDK, rewriting them for use with .NET, and releasing them as a set of libraries in the **Windows App SDK** under the name WinUI, Microsoft has been able to release versions at a faster cadence than Windows itself (as Windows SDK versions are linked to those of Windows). This separation also enables the controls to be used on older versions of Windows 10. While building desktop applications with WinUI is the current recommendation, it is important to learn where WinUI and the Windows App SDK fit into the larger Windows development landscape.

In this book, you will learn how to build applications for Windows with the WinUI 3 libraries. Throughout the course of the book, we will build a real-world application using the recommended patterns and practices for Windows application development.

Before we start building our WinUI app, it's important to have a good foundation in Windows client development, the different types of **Extensible Application Markup Language** (**XAML**) UI markup, and how WinUI compares to other Windows desktop development frameworks. Therefore, in this first chapter, you will start by learning some background on UWP and WinUI.

In this chapter, we will learn about the following topics:

- What UWP is and why Microsoft created yet another application framework
- How XAML can be leveraged to create great UIs on many device sizes and families
- Why WinUI was created and how it relates to UWP
- Where WinUI fits into the Windows developer landscape
- What WinUI 3 brings to the table

Don't worry! It won't take very long to cover the background stuff, and it will help provide some context as you start building your WinUI app. In the next chapter, you will get your hands on some code when you create your first WinUI project.

Technical requirements

To follow along with the examples in this chapter, the following software is required:

- Windows 10 version 1809 or later or Windows 11. You can find your version of Windows in **Settings | About**.

- Visual Studio 2022 version 17.0 or later with the following workload: .NET Desktop Development. On the **Installation details** tab of the **Visual Studio Installer**, ensure that **Windows App SDK C# Templates** is selected.

The source code for this chapter is available on GitHub at this URL: `https://github.com/ PacktPublishing/Learn-WinUI-3-Second-Edition/tree/main/Chapter01`.

> **Note**
>
> The Windows App SDK site on Microsoft Learn has up-to-date guidance on setting up a developer workstation for WinUI 3 development: `https://learn.microsoft.com/ windows/apps/windows-app-sdk/set-up-your-development-environment`.

Before UWP – Windows 8 XAML applications

Before UWP applications were launched with Windows 10 in 2015, there were XAML applications for Windows 8 and 8.1. The XAML syntax and many of the **application programming interfaces** (**APIs**) were the same, and they were Microsoft's next step to achieve universal app development across desktop, mobile, and other platforms (Xbox, mixed reality, and so on). A XAML app could be written for Windows 8 and Windows Phone. These projects would generate separate sets of binaries that could be installed on a PC or a Windows Phone.

These apps had many other limitations that modern UWP apps do not. For instance, they only ran full-screen, as shown in the following screenshot:

Figure 1.1 – Windows 8 full-screen app (sourced from Stack Overflow; reproduced
under CC BY-SA 4.0 – https://creativecommons.org/licenses/by-sa/4.0/)

Many other early restrictions on Windows 8 apps have been lessened or completely removed in UWP app development. *Figure 1.2*, which follows, documents these changes:

	Windows 8 XAML App	**Windows 10 UWP App**
Window Type	Full screen only	Resizable window
Device Type	Runs on PC only	Multiple Windows 10 device types
Number of Instances	1	1 (default) or Multiple
Console App Supported	No	Yes
File System Access	Sandboxed – local storage only	Sandboxed by default App can request additional access to user folders and removable devices

Figure 1.2 – Windows 8 and Windows 10 app comparison table

Windows application UI design

The term *Metro style* was used to define the design and layout of Windows 8 apps. Metro style apps were designed to be usable with touch input, a mouse and keyboard, or a stylus. Microsoft's introduction of the first Windows Phone was a driving factor for Metro style design. Metro style later became Modern UI design, with the introduction of Surface devices. Aspects of Metro live on today in UWP apps and Windows 10.

Live Tiles were born with Metro Style. These tiles on the user's Windows 8 home screen and Windows 10 Start menu can update to display live updates to users without having to open the app. Most of Microsoft's own apps for Windows 10 supported Live Tiles. The Weather app could show live updates to current weather conditions on the tile, based on the user's current location. Live tiles are no longer part of the operating system in Windows 11. They have been replaced by widgets, which app developers can also create. We will discuss widgets further in *Chapter 5, Exploring WinUI Controls*.

Windows Runtime (WinRT)

Another term that has its roots in Windows 8 app development is **WinRT**. The letters RT became a source of great confusion. WinRT was short for **Windows Runtime**, the underlying APIs used by Windows XAML apps. There was also a version of Windows 8 called Windows RT that supported Arm processors. The first Surface PC was the Surface RT, which ran the Windows 8 RT operating system.

Although WinRT can still be used today to define the WinRT APIs consumed by UWP apps, you will not see the term as often. We will also avoid using WinRT in this book and instead refer to the APIs as the UWP or Windows APIs.

User backlash and the path forward to Windows 10

While Microsoft pushed hard to win over users with Modern UI design, a new app model, Surface PCs, and Windows 8 and 8.1, the idea of a full-screen, touch-first app experience and a deemphasized Windows desktop was never embraced by customers. It turns out that Windows users really liked the Start menu experience they had used for years with Windows XP and Windows 7.

The next step in Windows app development was a big one—so big, in fact, that Microsoft decided to skip a number in their versioning, jumping straight from Windows 8.1 to Windows 10.

Windows 10 and UWP application development

While taking a leap forward with the launch of Windows 10, Microsoft also blended the best of what worked in previous versions of Windows. It brought back the start menu, but its contents look an awful lot like the Windows 8 home screen experience. In addition to an alphabetized list of all installed apps, there is a resizable area for pinned app tiles. In fact, when running Windows in Tablet mode, the start menu can transform into the Windows 8-style home screen experience for better usability on a touchscreen.

When Microsoft launched Windows 10, it also introduced UWP applications to Windows developers. While UWP apps have their roots in the XAML apps of Windows 8, some key differences give developers some major advantages when building apps for the platform.

A key advantage is the universal aspect of these apps. Microsoft builds versions of Windows 10 to run on different device families, listed as follows:

- Desktop (PC)
- Xbox
- Mobile (Windows Phone)
- HoloLens
- IoT
- IoT Headless
- Team (Surface Hub)

UWP developers can build apps to target any of these devices. There is a single base set of Windows APIs shared across all these targets, and specialized SDKs available for the device-specific APIs of some families—for example, there is a Mixed Reality Toolkit and SDK for HoloLens development. With UWP, it is possible to create a single project to target many device families—for instance, you can create a project that creates apps for Desktop, Xbox, and Team families.

Because the UWP XAML for building the app's UI is the same, the learning curve for cross-device development is lowered and code reusability is very high. The nature of XAML provides UI flexibility to adapt to different device sizes and aspect ratios.

Language choice with UWP development

While the underlying UWP APIs were written in C++, UWP developers can choose from several programming languages when building apps for Windows. UWP projects can be created with any of these popular languages:

- **C#**
- **C++**
- **F#**
- **Visual Basic .NET (VB.NET)**
- **JavaScript**

You may be surprised to see JavaScript on the list. During the Windows 8.x days, developers could create JavaScript apps with APIs known as WinJS apps. Today, Microsoft has created a branch of **React Native for Windows** developers, known as React Native for Windows. These JavaScript client apps have full access to the same Windows APIs as other UWP apps and can be packaged and deployed through the Windows Store.

> **Note**
>
> React Native for Windows is an open source project hosted by Microsoft on GitHub at `https://github.com/Microsoft/react-native-windows`.

While many of the UWP apps developed for Windows 10 and Windows 11 by Microsoft are created with C++, most other developers choose C#. We will also use C# when building our applications throughout the course of this book.

Lifting app restrictions

As discussed earlier, apps built for Windows 8 had several restrictions that have been either removed or relaxed with UWP.

First and foremost, modern UWP apps can run in resizable windows, just like any other Windows desktop application. The trade-off is that developers now need to test for and handle the resizing of their app to almost any size. The dynamic nature of XAML can handle a lot of the resizing very well, but below a certain minimum size, scroll bars will need to be employed.

For end users, one of the benefits of using UWP apps is the inherent security they provide due to the limited access of apps to the PC's filesystem. By default, each app can only access its own local storage. In 2018, the Windows developer team announced a new feature for UWP developers. By adding some app configuration declaring which additional types of access the app requires, applications can request access to additional parts of the filesystem. Among them are the following:

- User libraries, including documents, pictures, music, and videos
- Downloads
- Removable devices

> **Note**
>
> There are additional filesystem permissions that can be requested. See the Microsoft Learn documentation for an entire list: `https://learn.microsoft.com/windows/uwp/files/file-access-permissions`.

Any additional permissions requested will be declared on the app's listing on the Microsoft Store.

Some less-common scenarios are now available to UWP apps on Windows. Developers can add some configuration and startup code to enable multiple instances of their app to launch. While many believe the hallmark of a UWP app is the XAML UI, it was also possible to create a UWP console app. The app ran at the command line and had access to Universal C runtime calls. These are no longer supported, as developers can now create .NET console apps and package them with MSIX to provide them with package identity in Windows.

> **Note**
>
> We will discuss app packaging, MSIX, and package identity in detail in *Chapter 14, Packaging and Deploying WinUI Applications.*

UWP backward compatibility

No UWP app is compatible with any version of Windows before Windows 10. Beyond this, each UWP app must declare a **target version** and a **minimum version** of Windows with which it is compatible. The target version is your recommended version, which will enable all the app's features and functionality. The minimum version is, unsurprisingly, the minimum version of Windows that users must have to be able to install an app from the Microsoft Store.

Visual Studio will prompt you to select these versions when creating a new UWP project. If the two are the same, it keeps things simple. You will have all the APIs of that SDK version available to the app. If the target version is greater than the minimum version, you need to add some conditional code to light up the features of any versions greater than the minimum. The app must still be useful to users running the minimum version; otherwise, it is advisable to increase the minimum. If any of the newer APIs or controls are fundamental to the app, it is also recommended that the minimum version be increased to one where those are available.

> **Note**
>
> For more information on writing the conditional or version-adaptive code, see the Microsoft Learn documentation here: `https://learn.microsoft.com/windows/uwp/debug-test-perf/version-adaptive-code`.

If you are creating .NET libraries that will be referenced by your UWP project and you would like to share them across other platforms, perhaps by a .NET MAUI mobile app, a .NET Standard version should be targeted by the shared library project. The most common .NET Standard version today is .NET Standard 2.0. To reference a .NET Standard 2.0 project from a UWP project, the target version of the UWP project should be 16299 or later.

The primary benefit of WinUI over UWP is that it lessens the dependency of Windows apps on a particular version of Windows. Instead, the controls, styles, and APIs are maintained outside of the Windows SDK. At the time of writing, the minimum and target versions required for a WinUI

3 app must be set to 17763 or higher. Check the latest WinUI 3 documentation for the current minimum requirements.

The hope for WinUI is to bring a greater number of controls and features to more supported versions of Windows as the project matures.

What is XAML?

XAML is based on **Extensible Markup Language** (**XML**). This would seem like a great thing as XML is a flexible markup language familiar to most developers. It is indeed flexible and powerful, but it has some drawbacks.

The primary problem with Microsoft's implementations of XAML is that there have been so many variations of the XAML language created for different development platforms over the years. Currently, WinUI/UWP, **Windows Presentation Foundation** (**WPF**), and .NET MAUI (formerly Xamarin.Forms) applications all use XAML as their UI markup language, in addition to some third-party UI frameworks. However, each of these uses a different XAML implementation or schema, and the markup cannot be shared across the platforms. In the past, Windows 8, Silverlight, and Windows Phone apps also had additional.

If you have never worked with XAML before, you're probably ready to see an example of some UI markup. The following XAML is a fragment that defines `Grid` containing several other of the basic WinUI controls (you can download the code for this chapter from GitHub here: `https://github.com/PacktPublishing/-Learn-WinUI-3-second-edition/tree/master/Chapter01`):

```
<Grid Width="400" Height="250" Padding="2"
   HorizontalAlignment="Center"
    VerticalAlignment="Center">
   <Grid.RowDefinitions>
       <RowDefinition Height="Auto"/>
       <RowDefinition Height="*"/>
   </Grid.RowDefinitions>
   <Grid.ColumnDefinitions>
       <ColumnDefinition Width="Auto"/>
       <ColumnDefinition Width="*"/>
   </Grid.ColumnDefinitions>

   <TextBlock Grid.Row="0" Grid.Column="0"
           Text=»Name:»
           Margin=»0,0,2,0»
           VerticalAlignment="Center"/>
   <TextBox Grid.Row="0" Grid.Column="1"
         Text=»»/>
   <Button Grid.Row="1" Grid.Column="1" Margin="0,4,0,0"
```

```
                 HorizontalAlignment="Right"
                 VerticalAlignment="Top"
                 Content=»Submit»/>
    </Grid>
```

Let's break down the XAML here. The top level of a WinUI window is `Window`. WinUI 3 app navigation is Window-based (unlike UWP, which is Page-based), and the initial navigation happens in the `App.xaml` file in the project. You will learn more about navigation in *Chapter 4, Advanced MVVM Concepts*. A `Window` must contain only one child, and it will be some type of layout panel such as a `Grid` or `StackPanel`. By default, a `StackPanel` is inserted as that child. We will discuss other types of panels that serve as good parent containers in the next chapter. I made a few modifications and replaced the `StackPanel` with a `Grid`.

The `Height` and `Width` properties provide a static size for the example, and the `HorizontalAlignment` and `VerticalAlignment` properties will center the `Grid` within the `Window`. Fixed sizes are uncommon at this level of the XAML and limit the flexibility of the layout, but they illustrate some of the available attributes.

A `Grid` is a layout panel that allows developers to define rows and columns to arrange its elements. The rows and columns can have their sizes defined as fixed, relative to each other, or auto-sized based on their contents. For more information, you can read the Microsoft Learn article *Responsive layouts with XAML*: `https://learn.microsoft.com/windows/uwp/design/layout/layouts-with-xaml`.

The `Grid.RowDefinitions` block defines the number and behavior of the grid's rows. Our grid will have two rows. The first one has `Height="Auto"`, which means it will resize itself to fit its contents, provided enough space is available. The second row has `Height="*"`, which means the rest of the grid's vertical space will be allocated to this row. If multiple rows have their height defined like this, they will evenly split the available space. We will discuss additional sizing options in the next chapter.

The `Grid.ColumnDefinitions` block does for the grid's columns what `RowDefinitions` did for the rows. Our grid has two columns defined. The first `ColumnDefinition` has `Height` set to `Auto`, and the second has `Height="*"`.

`TextBlock` defines a label in the first `Grid.Row` and `Grid.Column`. When working with XAML, all indexes are 0-based. In this case, the first `Row` and `Column` are both at position 0. The `Text` property conveniently defines the text to display, and the `VerticalAlignment` in this case will vertically center the text for us. The default `VerticalAlignment` for a `TextBlock` is Top. The `Margin` property adds some padding around the outside of the control. A margin with the same amount of padding on all sides can be set as a single numeric value. In our case, we only want to add a couple of pixels to the right side of the control to separate it from `TextBox`. The format for entering these numeric values is `"<LEFT>,<TOP>,<RIGHT>,<BOTTOM>"`, or `"0,0,2,0"` here.

`TextBox` is a text entry field defined in the second column of the grid's first row.

Finally, we've added a `Button` control to the second column of the grid's second row. A few pixels of upper margin are added to separate it from the controls above. The `VerticalAlignment` is set to `Top` (the default is `Center`) and `HorizontalAlignment` is set to `Right` (the default is `Center`). To set the text of `Button`, you don't use the `Text` property as we did with `TextBlock`, as you might think. In fact, there is no `Text` property. The `Content` property of `Button` is used here. `Content` is a special property that we will discuss in more detail in the next chapter. For now, just know that a `Content` property can contain any other control: text, `Image`, or even a `Grid` control containing multiple other children. The possibilities are virtually endless.

Here is the UI that gets rendered by the preceding markup:

Figure 1.3 – WinUI XAML rendered

This is a very simple example to give you a first taste of what can be created with XAML. As we move ahead, you will learn how powerful the language can be.

Creating an adaptive UI for any device

In the previous example, `Grid` had fixed `Height` and `Width` properties. I mentioned that setting fixed sizes can limit a UI's flexibility. Let's remove the fixed size properties and use the alignment properties to guide the UI elements to render how we want them to appear at different sizes and aspect ratios, as follows:

```
<Grid VerticalAlignment="Top" HorizontalAlignment="Stretch"
Padding="2">
```

The rest of the markup remains unchanged. The result is TextBox resizing to fit the width of the window, and Button remains anchored to the right of the window as it resizes. See the window resized a couple of different ways here:

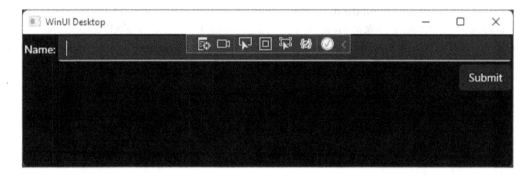

A narrower window

A wider window

Figure 1.4 – Resized windows

If you were using this app on a smaller PC such as the Surface Go Laptop, the contents would resize themselves to fit in the available space. That is the power of XAML's adaptive nature. When building a UI, you will usually want to choose relative and adaptive properties such as alignment to fixed sizes and positions.

It's this adaptive layout that makes XAML work so well on mobile devices with .NET MAUI, and this is why WPF developers have loved using it since its launch with Windows Vista.

Powerful data binding

Another reason why XAML-based frameworks are so popular is the ease and power of their data-binding capabilities. Nearly all properties on WinUI controls can be data-bound. The source of the data can be an object or a list of objects on the data source. In most cases, that source will be a `ViewModel` class. Let's have a very quick look at using WinUI's `Binding` syntax for data-binding to a property on a `ViewModel` class, as follows:

1. First, we will create a simple `MainViewModel` class with a `Name` property, like this:

    ```
    public class MainViewModel : INotifyPropertyChanged
    {
        public event PropertyChangedEventHandler
          PropertyChanged;
        private string _name;
        public MainViewModel()
        {
            _name = "Bob Jones";
        }
        public string Name
        {
            get
            {
                return _name;
            }
            set
            {
                if (_name == value) return;
                _name = value;
                PropertyChanged?.Invoke(this, new
                    PropertyChangedEventArgs(nameof(Name)));
            }
        }
    }
    ```

The `MainViewModel` class implements an interface called `INotifyPropertyChanged`. This interface is key to the UI receiving updates when data-bound properties have changed. This interface implementation is typically wrapped either by a **Model-View-ViewModel (MVVM)** framework, such as **Prism** or the **MVVM Toolkit**, or with your own `ViewModelBase` class. For now, we will directly invoke a `PropertyChanged` event inside the `Name` property's setter. We will learn more about `ViewModels` and the `INotifyPropertyChanged` interface in *Chapter 3, MVVM for Maintainability and Testability.*

2. The next step is to create an instance of the `MainViewModel` class and set it as `ViewModel` for our `MainWindow`. This happens in the code-behind file for the page, `MainWindow. xaml.cs`, as illustrated in the following code snippet:

```
public sealed partial class MainWindow : Window
{
    public MainWindow()
    {
        this.InitializeComponent();
        ViewModel = new MainViewModel();
    }
    public MainViewModel ViewModel { get; private set; }
}
```

We have added a `ViewModel` property to `MainWindow` and set it to a new instance of our `MainViewModel` class in the constructor.

> **Tip**
> Any code added to a window's constructor that interacts with any UI elements must be added after the call to `InitializeComponent()`.

3. Now it's time to add the data-binding code to the XAML markup for `TextBox`, as follows:

```
<TextBox Grid.Row="0" Grid.Column="1" Text="{x:Bind
    Path=ViewModel.Name, Mode=TwoWay}"/>
```

Some markup has been added to set the `Text` property using the `x:Bind` markup extension. The data-binding `Path` is set to the `Name` property on the `ViewModel`, which was assigned in the code-behind file in *step 2*. By setting the data-binding mode to `TwoWay`, updates in the `ViewModel` will display in the UI, and any updates by the user in the UI will also be persisted in the `Name` property of the `MainViewModel` class. Now, running the app will automatically populate the name that was set in the constructor of the `ViewModel`, as illustrated in the following screenshot:

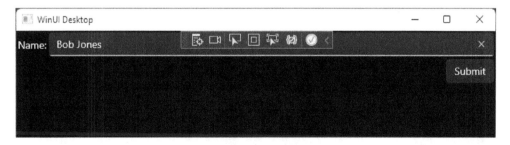

Figure 1.5 – Data-binding the TextBox

4. To illustrate data-binding to another property on another UI element on the page, we will first modify the grid to add a name, as follows:

```
<Grid x:Name="ParentGrid"
      VerticalAlignment="Top"
      HorizontalAlignment="Stretch"
      Padding="2">
```

5. Now add another `RowDefinition` to the `Grid` to fit the new UI element on the page:

```
<Grid.RowDefinitions>
    <RowDefinition Height="Auto"/>
    <RowDefinition Height="Auto"/>
    <RowDefinition Height="*"/>
</Grid.RowDefinitions>
```

6. Next, add a `TextBlock` element and use the `Binding` markup extension to bind its `Text` property to the `ActualWidth` of the `ElementName` set to `ParentGrid`. We are also adding a `TextBlock` to label this as **Actual Width**:

```
<TextBlock Grid.Row="1" Grid.Column="0"
           Text="Actual Width:"
           Margin="0,0,2,0"
           VerticalAlignment="Center"/>
<TextBlock Grid.Row="1" Grid.Column="1"
           Text="{Binding ElementName=ParentGrid,
                           Path=ActualWidth}"/>
```

7. Next, update the **Submit** button to appear in `Grid.Row 2`.

8. Now the new `TextBlock` control displays the width of `ParentGrid` when the page is loaded. Note that it will not update the value if you resize the window. The `ActualWidth` property does not raise a property change notification. This is documented in the `FrameworkElement.ActualWidth` documentation: `https://learn.microsoft.com/windows/windows-app-sdk/api/winrt/microsoft.ui.xaml.frameworkelement.actualwidth`:

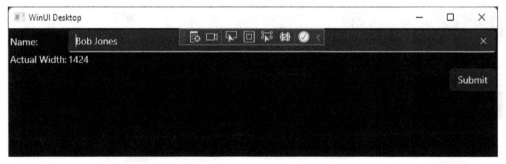

Figure 1.6 – Data-binding to another element

The **Submit** button does not function yet. You will learn how to work with **Events** and **Commands** with MVVM in *Chapter 5, Exploring WinUI Controls*.

Styling your UI with XAML

When working with XAML, styles can be defined and applied at almost any scope, global to the application in `App.xaml`, in the current `Window` inside a `Window.Resources` declaration, or inside any level or nested control on the page. The `Style` element specifies a `TargetType` property, which is the data type of the elements to be targeted by the style. It can optionally have a `Key` property defined as a unique identifier, like a class identifier in **Cascading Style Sheets** *(CSS)*. That `Key` property can be used to apply the style to only selected elements of that type. Only one `Key` property can be assigned to an element, unlike with CSS classes.

In the next example, we will modify the page to define a `Style` property for all buttons on the window, as follows:

1. Start by moving the **Submit** button to be nested inside a `StackPanel` element. A `StackPanel` element stacks all child elements in a horizontal or vertical orientation, with vertical being the default orientation. Some of the button's properties will need to be moved to the `StackPanel` element, as it is now the direct child of `Grid`. After adding a second button to the `StackPanel` element to act as a **Cancel** button, the code for the `StackPanel` and `Button` elements should look like this:

    ```
    <StackPanel Grid.Row="2" Grid.Column="1"
                Margin="0,4,0,0"
                HorizontalAlignment="Right"
                VerticalAlignment="Top"
                Orientation="Horizontal">
        <Button Content="Submit" Margin="0,0,4,0"/>
        <Button Content="Cancel"/>
    </StackPanel>
    ```

    A new `Margin` attribute has been added to the first button to add some space between the elements.

2. Next, we will add a `Style` block to a `Grid.Resources` section nested inside `Grid` before all its controls to style the buttons. Because no `Key` is assigned to the `Style` block, it will apply to all `Button` elements that do not have their styles overridden in an inner scope. This is known as an *implicit style*. The code for this is shown here:

    ```
    <Grid.Resources>
        <Style TargetType="Button">
            <Setter Property="BorderThickness"
                    Value="2" />
            <Setter Property="Foreground"
    ```

```
                          Value="LightGray" />
             <Setter Property="BorderBrush"
                      Value="GhostWhite"/>
             <Setter Property="Background"
                      Value="DarkBlue" />
          </Style>
        </Grid.Resources>
```

3. Now, when you run the app, you will see that the new style has been applied to both the **Submit** and **Cancel** buttons without adding any styling directly to each control, as illustrated in the following screenshot:

Figure 1.7 – Styled buttons

If we moved the `Style` block to the `Application.Resources` section in `App.xaml`, the defined style would get applied to every button in the entire app unless the developer had individually overridden some of the properties in the style. For instance, if the **Submit** button had a `Background` property set to `DarkGreen`, only the **Cancel** button would appear as dark blue.

We will spend more time on styles and design in *Chapter 7, Fluent Design System for Windows Applications*.

Separating presentation from business logic

We looked briefly at the MVVM pattern in the earlier section on data binding. MVVM is key to the separation of presentation logic from business logic in WinUI application development. The XAML elements only need to know that there is a property with a particular name somewhere in its data context. The `ViewModel` classes have no knowledge of the `View` (our XAML file).

This separation provides several benefits. First, `ViewModels` can be tested independently of the UI. If any WinUI elements are referenced by the system under test, the UI thread is needed. This will cause tests to fail when they're running on background threads locally or on a **Continuous Integration** (**CI**) server. See this Microsoft blog post for more information on unit testing WinUI applications: `https://devblogs.microsoft.com/ifdef-windows/winui-desktop-unit-tests/`.

The next benefit of View/ViewModel separation is that businesses with dedicated **user experience (UX)** experts will sometimes work on designing the XAML markup for an app while other developers are building the ViewModels. When it is time to sync up the two, the developer can add the necessary data-binding properties to the XAML, or perhaps the UX designer and developer have already agreed upon the names of the properties in the shared data context. Visual Studio includes another tool geared toward designers in this workflow, called **Blend for Visual Studio**. Blend was first released by Microsoft in 2006 as Microsoft Expression Blend, as a tool for designers to create UIs for WPF. Support was later added for other XAML languages such as Silverlight and UWP. Blend is still included with the .NET desktop development workload when installing Visual Studio.

A final benefit we will discuss here is that a good separation of concerns between any layers of your application will always lead to better maintainability. If there are multiple components involved in a single responsibility or if logic is duplicated in multiple places, this leads to buggy code and unreliable applications. Follow good design patterns, and you will save yourself a lot of work down the road.

Now that you have a good understanding of the history of UWP applications, it's time to look at WinUI: what it is, and why it was created.

What is WinUI?

The WinUI library is a set of controls and UI components that has been extracted from the Windows SDK and included in the Windows App SDK. After this separation, many controls have been enhanced and others have been added. The Windows App SDK is being developed in the open. Its issues are tracked on GitHub and with input from Microsoft and the Windows developer community.

So, if these WinUI libraries are based on UWP libraries in the Windows SDK, you may be wondering why you should choose WinUI as your UI framework instead of UWP. UWP has been around since the launch of Windows 10 and is quite robust and stable. There are several very good reasons to consider WinUI.

Choosing WinUI brings with it many of the benefits of **open source software (OSS)**. OSS is typically very reliable. When software is developed in the open by an active developer community, issues are found and resolved quickly. In fact, if you find an issue with an open source package, you can fix it yourself and submit a pull request to have the fix made available to the rest of the community. Open source projects can iterate quickly without having to remain in sync with product groups in a large enterprise such as the Windows team. Windows releases feature updates at a regular cadence now, but this is still less frequent than with a typical control library. Although the Windows App SDK and WinUI 3 are not yet open source, it is part of the product roadmap.

The best reason to use WinUI is its backward compatibility. When using a UWP control, the features and fixes in a specific version of the control cannot be deployed in apps to older versions of Windows. With WinUI, so long as you are targeting the minimum version of Windows supported by WinUI as a whole, you can use those new controls and features in multiple Windows versions. Controls not previously available to UWP developers in one version of Windows are now available there as WinUI controls.

For instance, Microsoft did not introduce the Fluent UI design to Windows until the Fall 2017 release (version 16299). However, WinUI controls can be included in apps targeting a minimum Windows version of Windows 10, version 1809, the Fall 2019 release. The controls in WinUI support Fluent UI styles. WinUI adds controls and other features that are not available at all in UWP and the Windows SDK.

The first WinUI release

The first version of WinUI was released in July 2018 as a preview release for Windows developers. It was released as the following two NuGet packages:

- `Microsoft.UI.Xaml`: The WinUI controls and Fluent UI styles
- `Microsoft.UI.Xaml.Core.Direct`: Components for middleware developers to access the `XamlDirect` API

3 months later, WinUI 2.0 was released. Despite the version number, it was the first production release of WinUI. The release included more than 20 controls and brushes. A few notable controls included the following:

- `TreeView`: A staple of any UI library.
- `ColorPicker`: A rich visual color picker with a color spectrum.
- `DropDownButton`: A button with the ability to open a menu.
- `PersonPicture`: An image control for displaying an avatar. It can fall back to displaying initials or a generic placeholder image.
- `RatingControl`: Allows users to enter star ratings for items.

> **Note**
> WinUI 2.x versions are libraries that are used by UWP projects. WinUI 3 is part of the Windows App SDK and is its own project type, although it shares the same XAML schema as a UWP project.

Let's add a few of these controls to our WinUI project and see how they look. Change the contents of `StackPanel` to look like this:

```
<StackPanel Grid.Row="1" Grid.Column="1" Margin="0,4,0,0"
            HorizontalAlignment="Right"
            VerticalAlignment="Top"
            Orientation="Horizontal">
    <PersonPicture Initials="MS" Margin="0,0,8,0"/>
    <DropDownButton Content="Submit" Margin="0,0,4,0">
```

```
        <DropDownButton.Flyout>
            <MenuFlyout Placement="Bottom">
                <MenuFlyoutItem Text="Submit + Print"/>
                <MenuFlyoutItem Text="Submit + Email"/>
            </MenuFlyout>
        </DropDownButton.Flyout>
    </DropDownButton>
    <Button Content="Cancel"/>
</StackPanel>
```

A `PersonPicture` control with the initials MS has been added as the first item in `StackPanel`, and the first of the two buttons has been replaced by a `DropDownButton` control. The **Submit** `DropDownButton` control has a `FlyoutMenu` serving as a drop-down list, and there are two `MenuFlyoutMenuItem` elements. Now, users can simply click the **Submit** button, or they can select **Submit + Print** or **Submit + Email** from the drop-down list. This is how the new window appears with the `DropDownButton` menu shown:

Figure 1.8 – Adding a PersonPicture and DropDownButton control

We're only scratching the surface of what WinUI can do for Windows developers. Don't worry, as we will dive much deeper in the chapters ahead. Let's briefly look at what was added in subsequent versions before WinUI 3.

The road to WinUI 3

There have been five additional minor releases of WinUI following version 2.0, in addition to many incremental bug fixes and pre-release versions.

WinUI 2.1

The WinUI 2.1 release brought several new controls and features to the library. These are some highlights:

- `TeachingTip`: Think of `TeachingTip` as a rich, context-sensitive tooltip. It is linked to another element on the page and displays informative details about the target element to help guide users with non-intrusive content as needed.

- `AnimatedVisualPlayer`: This hosts Lottie animations. Lottie files are a popular animation format created in **Adobe After Effects** used by designers across Windows, the web, and mobile platforms. There are libraries available to host Lottie animations for most modern development frameworks.

> **Note**
>
> Get more information about Lottie files on their website at `https://airbnb.design/lottie/` and check out this great repository of Lottie animation files: `https://lottiefiles.com/`.

- `CompactDensity`: Adding this resource dictionary to your app can provide the ability to switch between *Compact* and *Normal* display modes. `CompactDensity` will reduce the spacing within and between elements on the page, providing up to 33% more visible content to users. This Fluent UI design concept was introduced to developers at Microsoft's Build 2018 conference.

WinUI 2.2

This release brought many enhancements to existing features. However, the single new control added to the library is one that many Windows developers will find useful.

The `TabView` control creates a familiar tabbed UX on the screen. Each tab can host a page in your WinUI project.

WinUI 2.2 enhancements

A few of the notable updated controls and libraries in version 2.2 are listed here:

- **NavigationView**: The `NavigationView` control was enhanced to allow the back button to remain visible when the panel is collapsed. Other visual updates maximize the viewable content of the control.

- **Visual Styles**: Many of the WinUI visual styles were updated, including `CornerRadius`, `BorderThickness`, `CheckBox`, and `RadioButton`. The updates all make the WinUI visuals more consistent and in line with Fluent UI design guidelines.

WinUI 2.3

In the WinUI 2.3 release, `ProgressBar` received some updates, and a couple of new controls were added to the library.

There are now two modes available when creating a `ProgressBar` element in a WinUI application: **determinate** and **indeterminate**. A determinate progress bar has a known amount of the task to complete and a known current state of the task. An indeterminate control indicates that a task is ongoing without a known completion time. Its purpose is like that of a busy indicator.

New controls in WinUI 2.3

The following are a few new controls in this update:

- `NumberBox`: A `NumberBox` control is an input editor that makes it easy to support numeric formatting, up/down incrementing buttons, and inline mathematic calculations. It is a seemingly simple but practical and powerful control.

- `RadioButtons`: You might be thinking, *radio buttons have always been available. How is this a new control?* `RadioButtons` is a control that groups a set of `RadioButton` (*singular*) controls, making it easier to work with them as a single unit.

WinUI 2.4

When it was released in May 2020, two new features were made available in WinUI 2.4: a `RadialGradientBrush` visual and a `ProgressRing` control.

The brush is similar in use to the `RadialGradientBrush` used by WPF developers. It makes it easy to add a gradient to a visual element that radiates out from a central point.

The `ProgressRing` control, as it sounds, recreates progress bar functionality in a circular format. The control is available with a determinate state and an indeterminate state in version 2.4. An indeterminate `ProgressRing` control displays a repeating animation and is the default state of the control.

Several controls were updated in version 2.4. The `TabView` control was updated to provide more control over how tabs are rendered, including **Compact**, **Equal**, and **Size to Content** modes. `TextBox` controls received a *dark mode* enhancement to keep the content area of the control dark, with white text by default. Finally, the `NavigationView` control was updated with hierarchical navigation, with `Left`, `Top`, and `LeftCompact` modes.

WinUI 2.5

WinUI 2.5 was released in December 2020 and included a new `InfoBar` control. Several control enhancements and bug fixes were also included in the release.

The `InfoBar` control provides a way to display important status messages to users. The control can display an alert or informational icon, a status message, and a link or button allowing users to act on a message. There is also an option to display a close button to the right of the message. By default, the control includes an icon, message, and close button. Microsoft Learn provides usage guidelines for this new control. This is the documentation for the WinUI 3 version of the control: `https://learn.microsoft.com/windows/windows-app-sdk/api/winrt/microsoft.ui.xaml.controls.infobar`.

Several updates are also available in version 2.5. The `ProgressRing` control received enhancements to the determinate state of the control. The `NavigationView` control was updated to provide customizable `FooterMenuItems`. In previous versions of the `NavigationView` control, the footer area could be shown or hidden but not customized.

WinUI 2.x continued adding controls and features in versions 2.6, 2.7, and 2.8. For a complete listing of the new features in each version, see the following release notes pages on Microsoft Learn:

- WinUI 2.6 release notes: `https://learn.microsoft.com/windows/apps/winui/winui2/release-notes/winui-2.6`

- WinUI 2.7 release notes: `https://learn.microsoft.com/windows/apps/winui/winui2/release-notes/winui-2.7`

- WinUI 2.8 release notes: `https://learn.microsoft.com/windows/apps/winui/winui2/release-notes/winui-2.8`

We've seen what was available to UWP developers in WinUI 2. Now, let's see what you get with WinUI 3 and the Windows App SDK.

What's new in WinUI 3?

Unlike WinUI 2.0 and the incremental versions that followed, WinUI 3 is a major update featuring more than new and improved controls and libraries to use with Windows desktop apps. In fact, the primary goal of WinUI 3 was not to add new controls and features beyond its current UWP counterparts. The Windows App SDK team has made WinUI a complete UI framework that can sit atop the Windows desktop .NET platform.

Goodbye UWP?

So, what is happening to UWP? Will our UWP apps stop working?

As previously mentioned, the plan for the UWP UI libraries is to keep providing important security updates, but they will not receive any new features going forward. It is likely that WinUI 2.8 will be the final 2.x version. All new features and updates will be developed for WinUI and the Windows App SDK. New applications will be developed in WinUI with either .NET, written in C# or VB, or with native C++. These clients will sit on top of the Win32 platform. This is all possible because the Windows App SDK is developed completely in C++.

The fact that it is developed in C++ enables **React Native for Windows** client apps to interoperate with the Windows App SDK platform. Between React Native and Uno Platform, WinUI has some great cross-platform potential.

There will be multiple paths available for developers to create apps for Windows PCs and tablet devices. Other Windows devices, such as Xbox and HoloLens, will need to continue to develop UWP apps and use WinUI 2.x controls.

New features for WinUI 3 and the Windows App SDK

Are there any new features in WinUI 3?

While it sounded like the team was very busy creating a UI framework to replace the UWP UI libraries, they did find some time to add a few new features. The major new control available in WinUI 3 is the new `WebView2` control. It is a web browser host control based on the new Chromium-based **Microsoft Edge** browser. Compatibility is also a feature. All XAML and Composition features available in the Spring 2019 Windows SDK will be backward-compatible, back to the Windows 10 1809 update and later.

The Windows App SDK and WinUI

WinUI 3 is bringing desktop application developers together on a single set of UI libraries, but that is only the beginning. At Microsoft's Build 2020 conference, the Windows team announced **Project Reunion**, a long-term plan to bring all Windows developers together on a single platform. When WinUI was released in 2021, Project Reunion was renamed the Windows App SDK. WinUI 3 is focused on the UI layer, while the Windows App SDK will encompass WinUI and the entire Windows developer platform. In 2021, Microsoft released three versions of the Windows App SDK and WinUI 3.

To read more about the Windows App SDK and to follow its progress, you can check out the team's GitHub repository at `https://github.com/microsoft/WindowsAppSDK`. Now, let's see how WinUI compares to other Windows development frameworks.

WinUI 3 compared to other Windows development frameworks

Where does WinUI fit into the overall landscape of Microsoft's Windows development frameworks? Let's draw some comparisons to help answer that question, starting with those that are most like WinUI.

WinUI versus UWP

This is a tricky comparison because WinUI apps today share the same XAML schema as UWP apps. In fact, WinUI 2.x are controls for UWP applications. They share the same XAML schema, base visuals, and underlying Windows APIs. Any UWP app that has the same minimum and target versions of Windows specified can add the WinUI 2.x libraries to leverage the new and updated features. However,

UWP will not receive any feature updates beyond WinUI 2.8. Only security and bug-fix updates will be released as 2.8x minor releases.

A key difference between apps that use WinUI versus traditional UWP apps is access to new and updated controls and other visual elements without requiring an updated Windows SDK. This enables developers to bring apps with the same look and features to more users across multiple versions of Windows 10 or Windows 11. This differentiator makes for happier developers and users.

WinUI 3 also has the advantage of using the latest .NET version and C# language features. It will continue to benefit from these as new versions of .NET are released. As true .NET desktop apps, they are not constrained by the UWP sandbox. They have full access to hardware and the filesystem and can use most APIs. WinUI 3 apps also have more control over their Window size and appearance than UWP apps. However, developers who want to target platforms such as HoloLens or Xbox must stick with UWP development.

WinUI versus WPF

WinUI and WPF have many similarities. Both are application frameworks, and both types of apps rely on XAML to define UI elements. This means that they both offer the same separation of UI and business logic when implementing the MVVM pattern. WPF XAML has the same concepts of styles, resources, data binding, and adaptiveness as the UI layout.

WinUI advantages

A significant performance advantage of WinUI is the availability of **compiled bindings**. We will discuss compiled bindings in more detail later. For now, just know that using them offers a performance boost over traditional data binding in both UWP and WPF. Compiled bindings can be identified by spotting the use of `x:Bind` syntax in XAML, rather than `Binding`.

Unless your WinUI app is MSIX-packaged with `uap10:TrustLevel="appContainer"`, both WinUI and WPF have full access to users' filesystems and devices. Their access is only limited by the configuration of **Windows User Account Control** (**UAC**) on the PC. WinUI has the advantage of using GPU-accelerated features such as Mica and Acrylic brushes to support the latest Windows styles such as Microsoft's in-box apps. These styles are not available to WPF apps, making them feel less modern.

WPF advantages

The primary advantage of WPF applications is the fact that they are not directly tied to minimum versions of Windows. WPF apps target a .NET version. Any version of Windows that supports the target .NET version can run that WPF app. This significantly increases the potential user base of WPF apps. In fact, WPF apps can be deployed and run on Windows 7 with .NET Framework, something not possible with UWP or WinUI.

> **Note**
>
> There is a product called **Uno Platform** that enables WinUI XAML to run on iOS, Android, macOS, Linux, and even Samsung Tizen watches, and on the web with **WebAssembly**. These WinUI web apps can run in the browser on previous versions of Windows, including Windows 7. The Uno Platform goal and tagline is *WinUI Everywhere*.
>
> Learn more about Uno Platform at `https://platform.uno/`. We will create an Uno Platform project in *Chapter 13, Taking Your App Cross-Platform with Uno Platform*.
>
> Learn more about WebAssembly at `https://webassembly.org/`.

A new WPF advantage emerged with the releases of .NET Core 3.x and .NET 5 and later. .NET developers can now create WPF apps with .NET Core, bringing performance and deployment advantages of the modern .NET to WPF developers. For instance, applications targeting different versions of .NET can be deployed side by side on a machine without creating version conflicts. However, as mentioned previously, WinUI 3 apps also leverage the latest .NET features and performance.

The difference in deployment models can be debated as to which framework has an advantage. The easiest way to deploy a WinUI app is through the Microsoft Store. The easiest way to deploy a WPF app with .NET is via an installer package. WPF apps can be deployed through the Store by adding a Windows MSIX packaging project, and WinUI apps can be deployed without the Store with MSIX installers or **Windows Package Manager**. WinUI deployment will be covered in detail in *Chapter 14, Packaging and Deploying WinUI Applications*.

WinUI versus Windows Forms (WinForms)

WinForms is a .NET UI framework that was introduced with .NET Framework 1.0. Developers can easily create a WinForms UI with the visual design surface in Visual Studio, which generates C# or VB code that creates the UI at runtime. Most of the advantages and disadvantages of WPF also apply to WinForms: security, deployment, and .NET—WinForms apps can also be created with .NET Core 3.x and later.

WinUI advantages

Similarities between WinUI and WPF are their primary advantages over WinForms: data binding, adaptive layout, and a flexible styling model. These advantages all stem from the use of XAML for UI layout. Another advantage of XAML is offloading render processing from the **central processing unit** (**CPU**) to the **graphics processing unit** (**GPU**). WinUI controls inherit the Windows styles by default and have a more modern appearance than WinForms controls. WinUI applications also handle **dots per inch** (**DPI**) scaling and touch input well. The WinForms UI framework matured before touch input and DPI scaling were a concern for Windows developers. Localization and UI performance are also big advantages of WinUI 3 over WinForms.

WinForms advantages

In addition to the advantages that WinForms shares with WPF over WinUI—greater access to Windows, .NET app, and Windows compatibility—WinForms also has a well-deserved reputation for rapid UI development. If you need to create a simple Windows application in a minimal amount of time, the drag-and-drop WinForms designer is easy and intuitive. WinForms has also received some recent updates to improve its data binding support, and it now has ICommand support for MVVM. For more information about these enhancements, see this .NET blog post: `https://devblogs.microsoft.com/dotnet/winforms-cross-platform-dotnet-maui-command-binding/`.

Many experienced Windows developers still default to WinForms when tasked with creating a simple utility or UI test harness for a .NET library.

Summary

We covered a lot of the history of Windows application development in this chapter. We learned about the origins of UWP and its roots in Windows 8 apps and learned of the benefits of XAML when building Windows UIs. We had a taste of what some simple WinUI app code and UIs look like. Finally, we examined the recent history of WinUI versions and how WinUI 3 is a complete replacement for the UWP UI libraries and a viable option for WPF developers going forward.

This will give you a good foundation of what's to come as we start building an app with WinUI in the chapters ahead. In the next chapter, you will set up your development environment, learn about the app project that we will create throughout the book, and create your first WinUI 3 project. When we get to *Chapter 3, MVVM for Maintainability and Testability*, we will refactor the app to use the MVVM pattern. This will set us up with a solid, maintainable design as we later add to and extend the app throughout the rest of the book.

Questions

1. Which version of Windows first introduced UWP apps to developers?

2. What is the name of the pattern commonly used by WinUI and other XAML developers to separate the UI logic from the business logic?

3. WinUI and WPF apps can share the same XAML. True or false?

4. Which was the first Microsoft UI framework to use XAML to define the UI?

5. What was the version number of the first WinUI release?

6. What is one of the benefits of developing with WinUI over WinForms?

7. Can WinUI apps only be developed with .NET languages?

8. Challenge: create a style that will apply to `Button` elements.

2

Configuring the Development Environment and Creating the Project

To get started with WinUI and Windows App SDK development, it is important to install and configure Visual Studio for Windows desktop development. A WinUI developer must also understand the basics of application development with **Extensible Application Markup Language** (**XAML**) and C#, which we started learning in *Chapter 1, Introduction to WinUI*. However, the best way to understand the development concept is to get your hands on a real project. We will do that in this chapter.

After setting up your Visual Studio development environment, you will create the beginnings of a project that we will be building throughout the rest of the book.

In this chapter, you will learn the following topics:

- How to set up a new Visual Studio installation for Windows desktop application development
- How to create a new WinUI project, add a few controls, and run the project for the first time
- The anatomy of a new WinUI project and why each part is important
- How XAML can be used to build flexible, performant **user interfaces** (**UIs**)
- How WinUI fits with .NET and the role of each layer in the overall application architecture
- How to work with WinUI controls and customize them through changes in the XAML markup or C# code
- How to handle some basic UI events

If you are new to WinUI and other XAML-based development platforms, by the end of this chapter, you should be starting to feel comfortable working with WinUI projects.

Technical requirements

To follow along with the examples in this chapter, the following software is required:

- Windows 10, version 1809 (build 17763) or newer or Windows 11

- Visual Studio 2022 version 17.1 or later with the **.NET desktop development** workload and **Windows App SDK C# Templates** selected during installation

The source code for this chapter is available on GitHub at this URL: `https://github.com/PacktPublishing/Learn-WinUI-3-Second-Edition/tree/main/Chapter02`.

Installing Visual Studio and Windows desktop development workloads

The first step to follow when starting with WinUI development is to install Microsoft's Visual Studio **integrated development environment** (**IDE**). You can download the current version of Visual Studio 2022 from `https://visualstudio.microsoft.com/downloads/`. Visual Studio 2022 Community Edition is free for personal use and has all the features you will need to build WinUI applications.

> **Tip**
>
> If you want to try new Visual Studio features before they are released, you can install the latest Visual Studio Preview version from `https://visualstudio.microsoft.com/vs/preview/`. The Preview version is not recommended for the development of production applications as some features are unstable.

During installation, you can select workloads for any type of application that you want to create. For WinUI development, you must start by selecting the **.NET desktop development** workload. An overview of the **Workloads** section is shown in the following screenshot:

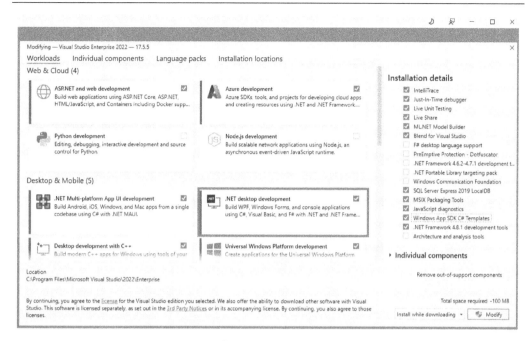

Figure 2.1 – Visual Studio Installer workload selection

After the **.NET desktop development** workload has been selected, select the **Windows App SDK C# Templates** component from the **Installation details** pane. These templates, required for building WinUI apps, are not installed by default with the workload.

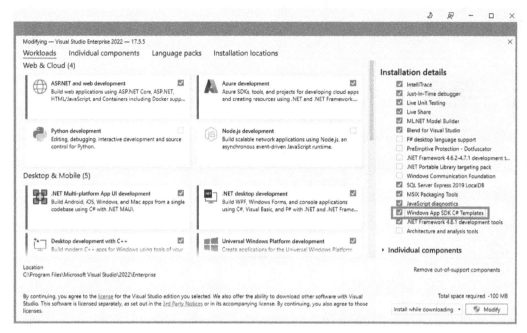

Figure 2.2 – Selecting the Windows App SDK C# Templates component for installation

> **Note**
>
> If you are a C++ developer and would like to build WinUI apps with C++, you must select the **Desktop development with C++** workload and the optional **Windows App SDK C++ Templates** component within the **Desktop development with C++** workload. However, building WinUI applications with C++ is beyond the scope of this book.

When continuing to the next step, the Visual Studio Installer will download and install all selected workloads and components. When setup is complete, launch Visual Studio. The first time you run Visual Studio, you will be prompted to sign in with a Microsoft account. Linking Visual Studio to your account will enable Visual Studio to sync your settings, link any available licenses, and link your Microsoft Store account after it has been created. We will discuss more about the Microsoft Store and application distribution in *Chapter 14, Packaging and Deploying WinUI Applications*.

Now, it's time to start building our WinUI application.

Introducing the application idea

The application we're going to build is a tool called **My Media Collection**. It's a simple utility that can catalog your entire media library. Because digital media is becoming more popular as time goes on, we can design the application to support the inclusion of both physical and digital media. The application will be able to catalog different types of media, including music, video, and books. We'll add some features that will only light up for certain media types. Physical media (books, DVDs, and CDs) are often loaned to friends. This application will help you remember who borrowed your favorite book at a recent family party.

Reviewing the application features

Before we dive in and create the new project, let's get organized. It helps to understand what you're going to build so that you can track your progress while progressing through each chapter. If you're tracking your development on GitHub, you could create an **Issue** for each feature. Let's start with a high-level look at the application's features, as follows:

- View all media
- Filter the media library by the following: **Media Type** (**Music, Video**, or **Book**), **Medium** (the available choices will vary by media type but will include **CD**, **Record**, **DVD**, **Blu-Ray**, **Hardcover**, **Paperback**, **Digital**), or **Location** (**In Collection** or **Loaned**)
- Add a new media item
- Edit a media item
- Mark an item as loaned or returned
- Application sign-in
- Back up (or restore) the collection data with OneDrive

The application will use features of the **Windows Community Toolkit**, which can simplify things such as Microsoft account authentication and file access on OneDrive. You can read more about the toolkit on Microsoft Learn: `https://learn.microsoft.com/dotnet/communitytoolkit/windows/`. The application's data will be stored in a local **SQLite** database, allowing for online or offline access to the media collection. You'll even be able to send email reminders if one of your friends is taking a little too long in returning one of the items in your collection.

WinUI in Desktop projects

In this chapter, we will be building a Windows App SDK application with the **WinUI in Desktop** project template. A **WinUI in Desktop** project targets the .NET runtime while using the same XAML schema as a UWP project.

A **WinUI in Desktop** project also includes a **Windows Application Packaging** project in the newly created solution. We will learn more about packaging WinUI applications in *Chapter 14, Packaging and Deploying WinUI Applications*. Now, let's get started with our first project.

Creating your first WinUI project

It's time to start building the project. To do so, proceed as follows:

1. Launch Visual Studio, and from the opening screen, select **Create a new project**, as illustrated in the following screenshot:

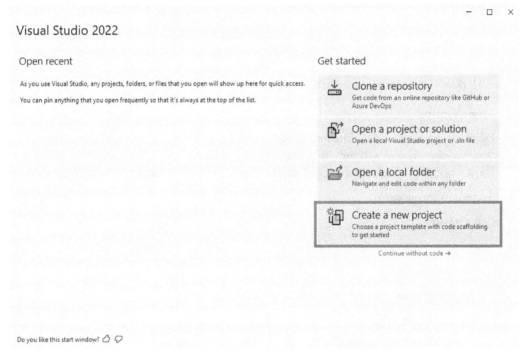

Figure 2.3 – The initial Visual Studio dialog

2. On the **Create a new project** screen, enter winui in the **Search for templates** field, select the **Blank App, Packaged (WinUI 3 in Desktop)** C# template, and click **Next**, as illustrated in the following screenshot:

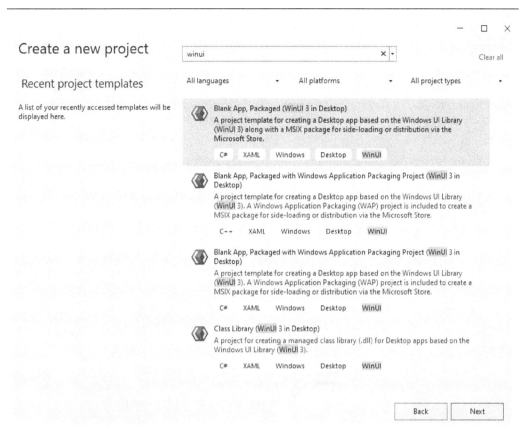

Figure 2.4 – Selecting the project template

Tip

Be sure to select the **C#** project template and not **C++**. You can filter the project types to show only C# projects by changing the **Language** filter from **All languages** to **C#**.

3. Name the project MyMediaCollection, leave the rest of the fields set to their default values, and click **Create**. You may be prompted to select the Windows versions to target with your app. You can leave these set to their default values for this project.

> **Note**
>
> It is up to you whether you want to change these versions for your app, but you will be limiting the versions of Windows that can install your app. If you are using a control or feature that you know is only available in specific versions of Windows, you must select that version as the **Minimum version**. The **Target version** must be equal to or greater than the **Minimum version**. If you are unsure of what to choose, you should stick with the default values.

4. Now, the project has been created and Visual Studio has loaded, it's always a best practice to build and run the project. Run the application and see what the template has provided for `MainWindow`. You should see an empty window hosting a few controls. Next, we will see what Visual Studio has created to get us started.

> **Note**
>
> To run and debug WinUI apps on Windows, you must update your Windows settings to enable **Developer Mode**. To do this, follow these steps:
>
> 1. Open **Settings** from the **Start** menu.
>
> 2. Type `Developer` in the search bar and select the **For Developers** settings from the search results.
>
> 3. On the **For developers** page that appears, switch the **Developer Mode** toggle switch on, if it is not already turned on. Enabling this allows developers to sideload, run, and debug unsigned apps, and enables some other developer-focused Windows settings. You can get more information here: `https://learn.microsoft.com/windows/apps/get-started/enable-your-device-for-development`.

Anatomy of a WinUI in Desktop project

Now that we have a new empty WinUI project loaded in Visual Studio, let's examine the different components. In **Solution Explorer**, you will see two XAML files, named `App.xaml` and `MainWindow.xaml`. We will start by discussing the purpose of each of these. Both files can be seen in the following screenshot of **Solution Explorer**:

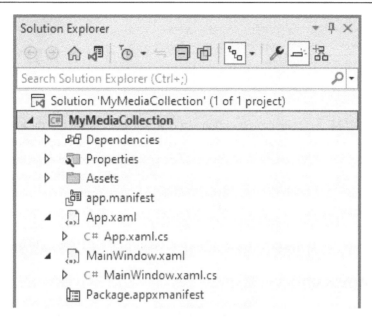

Figure 2.5 – The new WinUI solution in Solution Explorer

Reviewing App.xaml

The App.xaml file, as its name implies, stores resources available across the entire application. If you have any templates or styles that will need to be used across multiple windows, they should be added at the Application level.

The new project's App.xaml file will contain some initial markup, as illustrated in the following code snippet:

```
<Application
    x:Class="MyMediaCollection.App"
    xmlns="http://schemas.microsoft.com/winfx/2006/xaml/
    presentation"
    xmlns:x="http://schemas.microsoft.com/winfx/2006/xaml"
    xmlns:local="using:MyMediaCollection">
    <Application.Resources>
        <ResourceDictionary>
            <ResourceDictionary.MergedDictionaries>
                <XamlControlsResources
                  xmlns="using:Microsoft.UI
                    .Xaml.Controls" />
                <!-- Other merged dictionaries here -->
```

```
            </ResourceDictionary.MergedDictionaries>
            <!-- Other app resources here -->
        </ResourceDictionary>
    </Application.Resources>
</Application>
```

We will cover some XAML basics in the next section. For now, you should know that the Application. Resources section will contain all the resources to be shared across an application. Within this section, the ResourceDictionary.MergedDictionaries section contains references to other XAML files whose resources will be shared with the entire application. This allows developers to organize shared content into multiple resource files, leading to better-organized and more maintainable XAML. This also enables the sharing of third-party resources across the application. For example, this file merges XamlControlsResources from the Microsoft.UI.Xaml.Controls namespace. These are the resources for the WinUI controls that we will be using to build our app.

Reviewing App.xaml.cs

In **Solution Explorer**, expand the App.xaml file's node, and you will see there is another file named App.xaml.cs nested underneath. This is referred to as a **code-behind file**. It is a partial C# class that, in tandem with the XAML file, defines the Application class. If you open the C# file, you will see that it already contains some code. This is where you will handle any application-wide events. This is the event handler added by default: OnLaunched. If you need to execute any specific logic when your app is first launched, it should be added here. This is also where any application arguments passed to the app can be handled.

Reviewing MainWindow.xaml

The MainWindow.xaml file contains the MainWindow WinUI window that will be displayed when the application launches. You can see this in the OnLaunched event handler in App.xaml. cs, as illustrated in the following code snippet:

```
m_window = new MainWindow();
m_window.Activate();
```

In a new blank WinUI app, Window will contain an empty StackPanel layout control. Try replacing StackPanel's child controls with TextBlock with a Text property of Media and replace StackPanel with Grid. The result should look like this:

```
<Window
    x:Class="MyMediaCollection.MainWindow"
    xmlns="http://schemas.microsoft.com/winfx/2006/xaml/
```

```
        presentation"
    xmlns:x="http://schemas.microsoft.com/winfx/2006/xaml"
    xmlns:local="using:MyMediaCollection"
    xmlns:d="http://schemas.microsoft.com/expression/blend/
        2008"
    xmlns:mc="http://schemas.openxmlformats.org/
        markup-compatibility/2006"
    mc:Ignorable="d">
    <Grid>
        <TextBlock Text="Media"/>
    </Grid>
</Page>
```

To prevent exceptions at runtime, remove the event handler for the Button.Click event in MainWindow.xaml.cs. Now run the app with the **Debug | Start Debugging** menu item or the **Start Debugging** button on the Visual Studio toolbar, and you should see something like this:

Figure 2.6 – MainWindow with TextBlock added

We'll make this window a bit more functional later in the chapter. For now, let's finish our review of the project structure.

Reviewing MainWindow.xaml.cs

The code-behind file for the MainWindow.xaml.cs window now contains only a call to InitializeComponent() in the constructor because we removed the event handler for the original Button control. Later, we will add some code here to populate some sample data and handle events on the page. In a well-designed MVVM app, the code-behind files for your pages will have very little code. Most of the code will reside in the ViewModel classes.

Reviewing the project references

All your project's references to **NuGet** packages, **dynamic link libraries (DLLs)**, and other projects in the solution will appear in the `Packages` folder under **Dependencies** in **Solution Explorer**. Your WinUI project will reference the following NuGet packages:

- `Microsoft.WindowsAppSDK`: The Windows App SDK components, which include WinUI

- `Microsoft.Windows.SDK.BuildTools`: The Windows SDK components required to build a WinUI solution

> **Note**
> Do not modify or remove any of these references.

Reviewing the project properties

If you right-click the project in **Solution Explorer** and select **Properties** from the context menu, you can view and modify the project properties. You won't often need to make any changes here. These are a couple of properties you might need to modify from time to time:

- **Assembly Name**: You can change the name of the output assembly that is compiled by the project

- **Min Version** and **Target Version**: The Windows versions that were selected when creating the project can be modified here

The primary difference between a new UWP project and a new WinUI 3 project is the controls and other objects that are referenced in the `Windows.UI.Xaml.*` namespaces are now referenced in the Windows App SDK's `Microsoft.UI.Xaml.*` namespaces. One other difference is that in the `App.xaml` file of the UWP project, it's not necessary to import the controls' resources. The remaining differences are mostly hidden from app developers in the project file.

Now that you've become familiar with the WinUI project, let's start building the UI for `MainWindow`. We will start with some of the more common XAML controls and concepts.

XAML basics

It's time to start building the main screen of the **My Media Collection** application. The focal point of the application will be the media items in the collection. To display that list, we are going to need a few things, as follows:

- A `Model` class that defines an item in the collection

- Some code to bind the collection of items to the UI

- A XAML control to display the items

Building the model

We will start by building the model for the **My Media Collection** application. A **model** defines an entity and its attributes. Earlier in the chapter, we discussed some of the items' attributes we want to display in the UI. To display and (eventually) persist this information, we must create the model.

The initial version of our model will consist of two enumerations (`ItemType` and `LocationType`) in an Enums folder, and two classes (`Medium` and `MediaItem`) in a `Model` folder, as illustrated in the following screenshot:

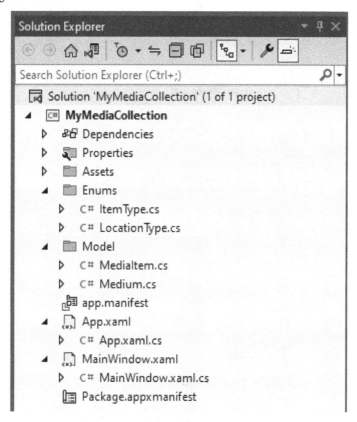

Figure 2.7 – Solution Explorer displays the new Model and Enum files

1. To add a new folder to the project, right-click on the **MyMediaCollection** project in **Solution Explorer** and select **Add | New Folder**. Enter Enums as the folder name and hit *Enter*. Repeat this process to add a Model folder.

2. Next, right-click the project file and select **Add | Class**. In the **Add New Item** dialog that
    appears, the **Class** file type will be selected. Because Visual Studio does not have a template for
    a new enum, keep this selection, change the name to ItemType, and click the **Add** button,
    as illustrated in the following screenshot:

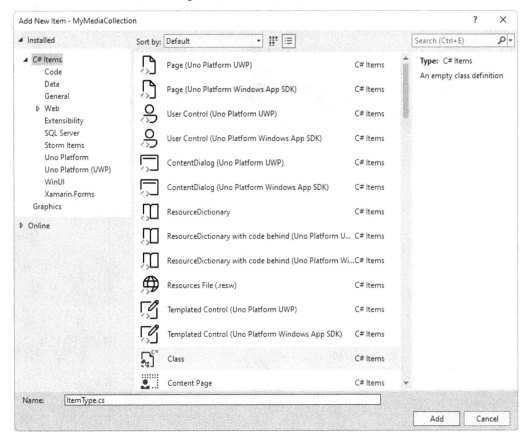

Figure 2.8 – The Add New Item dialog

3. The code for ItemType is created and displayed. Change the class definition to enum
    and change the internal keyword to public. The ItemType enum contains three
    possible values named Music, Video, and Book. When you're finished, the definition of the
    ItemType enum will look like this:

```
public enum ItemType
{
    Music,
    Video,
```

```
        Book
    }
```

4. Repeat the steps to create a `LocationType` enum, defined as follows:

```
public enum LocationType
{
    InCollection,
    Loaned
}
```

5. Using what you have learned, create two classes named `Medium` and `MediaItem` in the
    `Model` folder. The `Medium` class represents a specific medium such as *hardcover* or *paperback*,
    while the `MediaType` property assigns an `ItemType` to which the `Medium` class belongs.
    For these, the valid `ItemType` would be `Book`. When you are finished, the two new classes
    will look like this:

```
public class Medium
{
    public int Id { get; set; }
    public string Name { get; set; }
    public ItemType MediaType { get; set; }
}
public class MediaItem
{
    public int Id { get; set; }
    public string Name { get; set; }
    public ItemType MediaType { get; set; }
    public Medium MediumInfo { get; set; }
    public LocationType Location { get; set; }
}
```

> **Note**
>
> To reference the enum types in the Enums folder from the two classes, a `using` declaration
> will need to be added at the top of each new class, like this: `using MyMediaCollection.`
> `Enums;`.

In addition to the properties discussed earlier in the chapter, an `Id` property has been added to the
`MediaItem` class to uniquely identify each item in the collection. This will be useful later when we
start persisting data.

Creating sample data

With the model classes in place, we're ready to add some code that will create three media items to display in the UI. This will help us visualize things as we start creating our list of items on the main screen. When this step is complete and we're ready to move on to enabling the ability to add items through the app, this code will be removed.

For now, we are going to add this code in the `MainWindow.xaml.cs` code-behind file. Later, in *Chapter 3, MVVM for Maintainability and Testability*, this type of code will be added in a `ViewModel` file. The `MainWindow` will contain only presentation logic and will not be responsible for creating or fetching the data that populates the UI:

1. First, open `MainWindow.xaml.cs` and create a method named `PopulateData`. This method will contain the code that creates three `MediaItem` objects (a CD, a book, and a Blu-ray) and adds them to a private `List` named `_items`, as illustrated in the following code snippet:

```
public void PopulateData()
{
    if (_isLoaded) return;
    _isLoaded = true;
    var cd = new MediaItem
    {
        Id = 1,
        Name = "Classical Favorites",
        MediaType = ItemType.Music,
        MediumInfo = new Medium { Id = 1,
          MediaType = ItemType.Music, Name = "CD" }
    };
    Var book = new MediaItem
    {
        Id = 2,
        Name = "Classic Fairy Tales",
        MediaType = ItemType.Book,
        MediumInfo = new Medium { Id = 2,
          MediaType = ItemType.Book, Name = "Book" }
    };
    var bluRay = new MediaItem
    {
        Id = 3,
        Name = "The Mummy",
        MediaType = ItemType.Video,
        MediumInfo = new Medium { Id = 3,
          MediaType = ItemType.Video, Name = "Blu Ray" }
```

```
        };
        _items = new List<MediaItem>
        {
            cd,
            book,
            bluRay
        };
    }
```

You will need to add the using statements to MainWindow for the MyMediaCollection. Model and MyMediaCollection.Enums namespaces.

2. Define _items IList and isLoaded bool as private class members. We will later change the collection of items to an ObservableCollection. ObservableCollection is a special collection that notifies data-bound items on the UI when items have been added or removed from the collection. For now, an IList will suit our needs. The code can be seen in the following snippet:

```
    private IList<MediaItem> _items { get; set; }
    private bool _isLoaded;
```

3. Next, add a line of code to the MainWindow constructor, after the call to Initialize Component, to call the new PopulateData method. Any code added to a Window or UserControl constructor must be added after this initialization code. This is where all the XAML code in MainWindow.xaml is initialized. If you attempt to reference any of those elements before the call to InitializeComponent, it will result in an error. The constructor should now look like this:

```
    public MainWindow()
    {
        this.InitializeComponent();
        PopulateData();
    }
```

We will return to this file to add some data-binding logic after creating some UI components in the XAML file. Let's go and do that now.

Building the initial UI

Earlier in the chapter, we added a single TextBlock to the MainWindow.xaml file with the Text property set to Media. We are going to add a ListView control beneath the existing TextBlock. A ListView control is a powerful and flexible control to display a list of items in a vertical list. It is like the **WinForms** ListBox control in basic list functionality (item selection, multi-selection, and automatic scroll bars), but each list item can be templated to display in just about any way imaginable.

> **Note**
>
> For more information about the `ListView` class, documentation with sample code and markup is available on Microsoft Learn: `https://learn.microsoft.com/windows/windows-app-sdk/api/winrt/microsoft.ui.xaml.controls.listview`.

1. First, add some markup to create two rows inside the top-level `Grid` control. `RowDefinitions` should be added before the existing `TextBlock` element. `TextBlock` will remain in the first row, and we'll add the `ListView` control to the second row. Create `RowDefinitions` as illustrated in the following code snippet:

```
<Grid.RowDefinitions>
    <RowDefinition Height="Auto"/>
    <RowDefinition Height="*"/>
</Grid.RowDefinitions>
```

As you can see, we're automatically sizing the first `RowDefinition` to the size of the `TextBlock` and allocating the remaining space inside the `Grid` to the `ListView` control's `RowDefinition` by using `"*"`. If you assign more than one row with `"*"`, those rows will split the remaining available space equally. This is the default value for the `Height` attribute. It would be sized the same if `"*"` were omitted, but most XAML developers explicitly include it for completeness and improved readability.

> **Note**
>
> For more information about row sizing, see the following Microsoft Learn documentation: `https://learn.microsoft.com/windows/windows-app-sdk/api/winrt/microsoft.ui.xaml.controls.rowdefinition.height`.

2. Next, add a `ListView` control to the `Grid`, setting `Grid.Row` equal to 1 (row numbering is 0-based, meaning the first row is row 0), and name it `ItemList`. It is not necessary to name your XAML elements. This is only required if you either want to reference them by `ElementName` in XAML data binding or as a variable in the code-behind file. Naming a control causes a variable to be created in the `InitializeComponent` call, and to optimize performance, you should only name your controls if you need to reference them elsewhere. The markup can be seen in the following snippet:

```
<ListView Grid.Row="1" x:Name="ItemList"
    Background="LightGoldenrodYellow"/>
```

By setting the background color to `LightGoldenrodYellow`, we can see the `ListView` in the application's main window before we populate any data. Depending on whether you are using a *Light* or *Dark* Windows theme, you can choose a color that works best for you. Run the app, and it should look something like this:

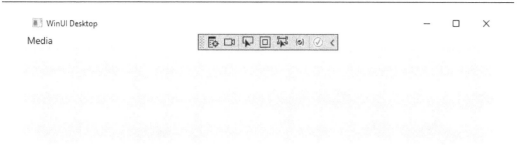

Figure 2.9 – A ListView added to the UI

Let's return to the code-behind file to start wiring up the data binding.

> **Note**
>
> If you are new to data binding concepts in XAML programming, Microsoft Learn has a great overview of data binding for Windows App SDK developers at the following web page: `https://learn.microsoft.com/windows/apps/develop/data-binding/`.

Completing the data-binding initialization

Return to the `MainWindow.xaml.cs` file and add a line of code before the `PopulateData()` method call, as follows:

```
ItemList.Loaded += ItemList_Loaded;
```

After typing +=, Visual Studio **IntelliSense** will prompt you to press *Tab* to automatically create the `ItemList_Loaded` event handler, as illustrated in the following screenshot:

```
2 references
public MainWindow()
{
    this.InitializeComponent();
    ItemList.Loaded +=
    PopulateData();         ItemList_Loaded;   (Press TAB to insert)
}
```

Figure 2.10 – Inserting the ItemList_Loaded event handler

Alternatively, if you type the entire line and press *Ctrl +*, you'll be prompted to create the new method.

To keep the `MainWindow` constructor simple and keep our data-loading code together, move the `PopulateData` call to the `ItemList_Loaded` method. Then, add the two other lines of code to the new event handler, as follows:

```
private void ItemList_Loaded(object sender,
  Microsoft.UI.Xaml.RoutedEventArgs e)
{
    var listView = (ListView)sender;
    PopulateData();
    listView.ItemsSource = _items;
}
```

This code is called after the `ItemsList` control has completed loading in the UI. We're getting the instance of the control from the `sender` parameter and setting the `ItemsSource` of the list to the `_items` collection that was loaded in `PopulateData()`. Now, we have data in the list, but things don't look quite right, as can be seen from the following screenshot:

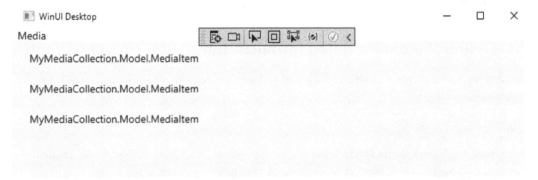

Figure 2.11 – A ListView with three rows of data

The `ListView` is displaying three rows for our three sample data items, but it's displaying the data type for each item instead of the data. That's because we haven't told the `ListView` which properties it should display for the items in the collection. By default, the list will display whatever is returned by an object's `ToString()` method. If `ToString()` is not overridden, the data type name of the class is returned.

Creating the DataTemplate and binding the UI

Let's return to `MainWindow.xaml` and tell the `ListView` which data we want to display for each item in the list. Try making this change with the application still running. Thanks to Visual Studio's **XAML Hot Reload** feature, you should see the UI reload without having to restart the debugging session.

Customizing the appearance of each ListView item is accomplished by defining a DataTemplate inside ListView.ItemTemplate. A DataTemplate can contain any WinUI controls we need to define the layout of each list item. Let's keep it simple and add a Grid containing two columns. Each column will contain a TextBlock. The ListView should now look like this:

```
<ListView Grid.Row="1"
          x:Name="ItemList"
          Background="LightGoldenrodYellow">
    <ListView.ItemTemplate>
        <DataTemplate x:DataType="model:MediaItem">
            <Grid>
                <Grid.ColumnDefinitions>
                    <ColumnDefinition Width="100"/>
                    <ColumnDefinition Width="*"/>
                </Grid.ColumnDefinitions>
                <TextBlock Text="{x:Bind
                    Path=MediumInfo.Name}"/>
                <TextBlock Grid.Column="1"
                    Text="{x:Bind Path=Name}"/>
            </Grid>
        </DataTemplate>
    </ListView.ItemTemplate>
</ListView>
```

We are beginning to create some more complex XAML and need to keep formatting in mind to optimize its readability.

> **Note**
>
> To quickly reformat your XAML, you can use the *Ctrl + K | D* keyboard shortcut. There is also an extension on the **Visual Studio Marketplace** called **XAML Styler**. You can search for it in Visual Studio's **Manage Extensions** dialog or get more information on the Marketplace here: https://marketplace.visualstudio.com/items?itemName=TeamXavalon.XAMLStyler2022.

To enable each TextBlock to bind to the properties of MediaItem, we must set an x:DataType property on the DataTemplate. To resolve MediaItem, a namespace declaration needs to be added to the Window definition, like this:

```
xmlns:model="using:MyMediaCollection.Model"
```

A shortcut to add this `using` statement is to place your cursor in `x:DataType` and press *Ctrl +*. Visual Studio will suggest adding the missing namespace to the file. We now have access to objects in the `MyMediaCollection.Model` namespace by using the `model` prefix, and `x:DataType="model:MediaItem"` will resolve `MediaItem` when we build and run the app.

Each `TextBlock` has its `Text` property bound to a property of `MediaItem`, using the `x:Bind` **markup extension**.

> **Note**
>
> Using `x:Bind` instead of the `Binding` markup extension to bind data to the UI has the benefit of compile-time validation and increased performance. The previously noted data-binding overview on Microsoft Learn covers the differences in depth. I prefer to use `x:Bind` where possible. One important difference between `Binding` and `x:Bind` you should note is that while `Binding` defaults to `OneWay` mode, `x:Bind` defaults to `OneTime`. This change to the default binding behavior was made for performance considerations. `OneWay` binding requires more code behind the scenes to wire up the change detection needed for monitoring changes to the source value. You can still explicitly update your `x:Bind` usages to be `OneWay` or `TwoWay`. For more information about `x:Bind`, see this Microsoft Learn article: `https://learn.microsoft.com/windows/uwp/xaml-platform/x-bind-markup-extension`.
>
> For more information on markup extensions in XAML, you can read this .NET article: `https://learn.microsoft.com/dotnet/desktop/xaml-services/markup-extensions-overview`.

Now, when you run the application, you can see the `MediumType` name and the item name for each item in the `ListView`, as illustrated in the following screenshot:

Figure 2.12 – The ListView with two columns of sample data

That's some pretty good progress! Before we expand on the functionality, let's talk a little about how WinUI, the Windows App SDK, and .NET fit together in terms of the app development process.

Understanding WinUI and Windows App SDK

Let's review the WinUI controls available to use in our project and see how they can help us build the **My Media Collection** application. The `Microsoft.WindowsAppSDK` package we saw in **Solution Explorer** earlier in the chapter contains these controls and much more.

To view the contents of this package, open the **Object Browser** window from Visual Studio's **View** menu. The controls will be listed here under several namespaces inside the **Microsoft.WinUI** tree node, as illustrated in the following screenshot:

Figure 2.13 – WinUI controls in Object Browser

The majority of WinUI controls we will be using can be found inside the **Microsoft.UI.Xaml.Controls** namespace under **Microsoft.WinUI**, along with other related classes and interfaces.

So far, we have used in our application the `Grid`, `TextBlock`, and `ListView` controls. Open the **Object Browser** window from the **View** menu. Then, find the `ListView` class, expand **Microsoft. UI.Xaml.Controls.ListView** | **Base Types**, and select the `ListViewBase` class. This base class contains the methods, properties, and events available to the `ListView`. The members of `ListViewBase` will display in the right pane. Take some time to review these members and see whether you recognize any of them from your use of the control so far.

Clear `ListView` from your search, scroll down in the left pane of **Object Browser**, and find the `TextBlock` control. Select it and, in the right pane, find and select the **Text** property. The bottom-right pane displays details of the property, as illustrated in the following screenshot:

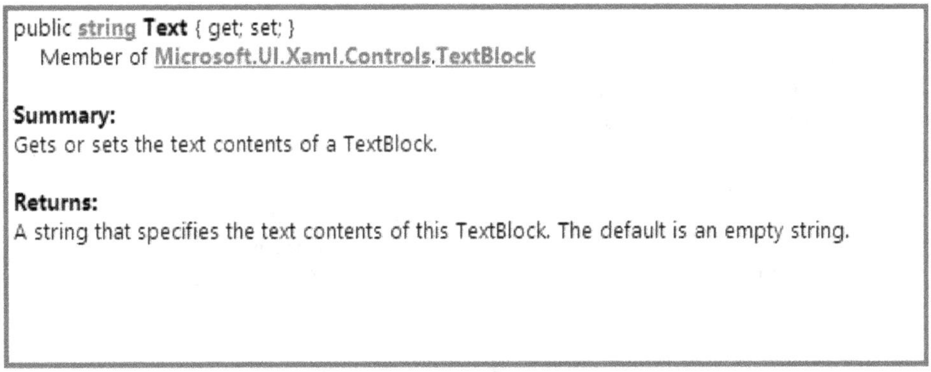

```
public string Text { get; set; }
    Member of Microsoft.UI.Xaml.Controls.TextBlock


Summary:
Gets or sets the text contents of a TextBlock.


Returns:
A string that specifies the text contents of this TextBlock. The default is an empty string.
```

Figure 2.14 – Details of the TextBlock.Text property in Object Browser

The **Object Browser** window can be a valuable resource when familiarizing yourself with a new library or project. All referenced projects, NuGet packages, and other references will appear here.

The controls and other components you have reviewed here make up the UI layer of Windows App SDK applications. The underlying application framework for the Windows App SDK is .NET.

Understanding the .NET app model

You may have heard that the underlying app model for WinUI apps can be Win32 for C++ apps or .NET for desktop apps. So, what exactly is the **.NET app model**?

The .NET app model in WinUI apps describes how applications are packaged and deployed. It also defines the following behaviors and capabilities:

- Data storage
- State management

- Lifecycle events (**Startup** and **Shutdown**)
- Multitasking
- Resource management
- Inter-app communication

WinUI 3 is one component of the Windows App SDK, the UI layer. Although the WinUI controls are decoupled from the Windows SDK, the underlying .NET app platform is still dependent on it when using the Windows App SDK. Selecting a target and minimum Windows version is one of the side effects of this dependency.

Now that you have a better understanding of WinUI controls and how they relate to the Windows App SDK and the .NET app platform, let's use a few more of them in our application.

Working with WinUI controls, properties, and events

It's time to enhance the UI of the application. Currently, the main page only consists of a `Media` label over a `ListView`, with columns for the media type and the name of the media item. The following are the enhancements we will add in this section:

- A header row for the `ListView`
- A `ComboBox` to filter the rows based on the media type
- A `Button` to add a new item to the collection

We will start by enhancing the `ListView` for our media collection.

Adding a ListView header

Before we create the header, let's change the background color of the `ListView`. The Aqua color worked well to highlight the control, but it would be distracting when the application is used by our customers. We will discuss WinUI theme brushes and look at **Fluent Design** concepts later in *Chapter 7, Fluent Design System for Windows Applications*. For now, just remove `Background="Aqua"` from the `ListView` definition in the `MainWindow.xaml` file.

Creating the header row for the media collection is relatively simple. To define the rows for each item, we created a `ListView.ItemTemplate` block containing a `DataTemplate`. To create the header, we do the same inside a `ListView.HeaderTemplate` block.

Just as with the item rows, the header row will consist of a `Grid` with two columns, with the same `Width` definitions. We again want to use two `TextBlock` controls inside the `Grid`, but to add some separation between the header and the items, we will add `Border` controls. Let's look at the markup for the header and then discuss the differences in more detail. Take some time to review the following markup:

```
<ListView.HeaderTemplate>
    <DataTemplate>
        <Grid>
            <Grid.ColumnDefinitions>
                <ColumnDefinition Width="100"/>
                <ColumnDefinition Width="*"/>
            </Grid.ColumnDefinitions>
            <Border BorderBrush="BlueViolet"
                    BorderThickness="0,0,0,1">
                <TextBlock Text="Medium"
                           Margin="5,0,0,0"
                           FontWeight="Bold"/>
            </Border>
            <Border Grid.Column="1"
                    BorderBrush="BlueViolet"
                    BorderThickness="0,0,0,1">
                <TextBlock Text="Title"
                           Margin="5,0,0,0"
                           FontWeight="Bold"/>
            </Border>
        </Grid>
    </DataTemplate>
</ListView.HeaderTemplate>
```

As you can see, each `TextBlock` is nested inside a `Border` element. This will wrap the text in a border with a `BlueViolet` color. However, by setting `BorderThickness="0,0,0,1"`, the border color will only appear on the bottom of the header row items. Here is how that appears in the application:

Figure 2.15 – The ListView with a header row added

> **Note**
> The same bottom border could be achieved by nesting the entire `Grid` inside a `Border` instead of putting one around each header item. However, by doing it this way, we have more control over the appearance of each column's border style. When we implement sorting later, the border's color can be modified to highlight the column on which sorting has been applied.

You probably also noticed that the header row text stands out from the rows in the grid. The `FontWeight="Bold"` property set inside each `TextBlock` in the `HeaderTemplate` helps to highlight the header row.

Creating the ComboBox filter

One of the requirements for the application is to allow users to filter several of the collection items' properties. Let's start simple, by adding a filter only on the medium (**Book**, **Music**, or **Movie**). The list also needs an **All** option, which will be the default selection when users open the application:

1. First, add some XAML to `MainWindow` to add a filter to the right of the `Media` label. Replace `Media TextBlock` with the following markup:

    ```
    <Grid>
        <Grid.ColumnDefinitions>
            <ColumnDefinition Width="*"/>
            <ColumnDefinition Width="Auto"/>
        </Grid.ColumnDefinitions>
        <TextBlock Text="Media Collection"
                   Margin="4"
                   FontWeight="Bold"
                   VerticalAlignment="Center"/>
        <StackPanel Grid.Column="1"
                    Orientation="Horizontal"
                    HorizontalAlignment="Right">
            <TextBlock Text="Media Type:" Margin="4"
                    FontWeight="Bold"
                    VerticalAlignment="Center"/>
            <ComboBox x:Name="ItemFilter"
                    MinWidth="120" Margin="0,2,6,4"/>
        </StackPanel>
    </Grid>
    ```

    The single `TextBlock` label has been replaced with a two-column `Grid`. The first column contains the `TextBlock`, with a few modifications. First, the `Text` property has been updated to `"Media Collection"`. `FontWeight` has been changed to `"Bold"` and some margin has been added. Finally, the element is vertically centered.

The second column contains a new `StackPanel` (a container control that stacks its contents horizontally or vertically). The default orientation is `Vertical`. In our case, we want a horizontal stack, which is why the `Orientation` property has been set.

`StackPanel` contains a `TextBlock` label and a `ComboBox` for the filter selection. The `ComboBox` filter has been given an `x:Name` so we can reference it from the C# code-behind file when initializing its contents. We have also configured a `MinWidth` value of `120`. If the contents of the `ComboBox` filter require more than 120 **pixels (px)**, it can grow larger, but its width cannot be less than the value set here.

> **Note**
>
> The pixels being referenced in XAML are effective pixels. To read more about responsive layouts and sizing with XAML, see this Microsoft Learn article: `https://learn.microsoft.com/windows/apps/design/layout/layouts-with-xaml`.

1. In the `MainWindow.xaml.cs` file, add a new variable to hold the list of mediums, as follows:

    ```
    private IList<string> _mediums { get; set; }
    ```

    This collection can be an `IList` rather than `ObservableCollection` because we don't expect its contents to change while the application is running.

2. Inside the `PopulateData()` method, add some code at the end of the method to populate the `_mediums` list, as follows:

    ```
    _mediums = new List<string>
    {
        "All",
        nameof(ItemType.Book),
        nameof(ItemType.Music),
        nameof(ItemType.Video)
    };
    ```

    We're adding an item to the collection for each of the possible values in our `ItemType` enum, plus the default `"All"` value.

3. The `ComboBox` filter will be bound to the collection after it has loaded, so add a `Loaded` event handler in the `MainWindow` constructor, as we did for the `ItemList` earlier, like this:

    ```
    ItemFilter.Loaded += ItemFilter_Loaded;
    ```

4. The `ItemFilter_Loaded` event handler will look much like the `ItemList_Loaded` handler. Use the following code:

    ```
    private void ItemFilter_Loaded(object sender,
      Microsoft.UI.Xaml.RoutedEventArgs e)
    ```

```
    {
        var filterCombo = (ComboBox)sender;
        PopulateData();
        filterCombo.ItemsSource = _mediums;
        filterCombo.SelectedIndex = 0;
    }
```

The code casts the sender to the `ComboBox` data type and sets its `ItemSource` to the list we populated in the previous step. Finally, an additional step is needed to default the `ComboBox` filter to default to the `"All"` item. This is accomplished by setting `SelectedIndex` equal to 0.

Let's run the application and see how it looks now. You can see the result in the following screenshot:

Figure 2.16 – Media Collection with the Media Type filter added

Pretty sharp! If you click the **Media Type** filter, you can see the four values available for selection, as illustrated here:

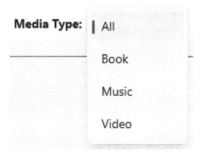

Figure 2.17 – Media Type values

Notice how the dropdown of ComboBox has picked up the Windows style with some transparency without having to add any additional code or markup. Select one of the other values in the list and see what happens. Nothing! That's because we haven't added any code to do the filtering when the selection changes on the filter. We can add a little bit of extra code to fix that, as follows:

1. First, create a new _allItems collection to store a list of all available media items, regardless of the current filter, like this:

    ```
    private IList<MediaItem> _allItems { get; set; }
    ```

2. Next, in the PopulateData() method, after populating the _items collection, add the same items to _allItems, like this:

    ```
    _allItems = new List<MediaItem>
    {
        cd,
        book,
        bluRay
    };
    ```

3. Now, we need to do some filtering when the filter selection changes. We want to handle the SelectionChanged event on the ComboBox control, but we don't want to hook it up until after the entire page has loaded. This will prevent the event from being handled while the ComboBox filter is initially being populated.

4. At the end of the implementation of ItemFilter_Loaded, add an event handler for the SelectionChanged event on the ComboBox control:

    ```
    ItemFilter.SelectionChanged +=
        ItemFilter_SelectionChanged;
    ```

5. In the new ItemFilter_SelectionChanged event handler, we will iterate through the _allItems list and determine which of the items to include in the filtered list, based on their MediaType property, as follows:

    ```
    private void ItemFilter_SelectionChanged(
      object sender,Microsoft.UI.Xaml.Controls.
        SelectionChangedEventArgs e)
    {
            var updatedItems =
              (from item in _allItems
            where
              string.IsNullOrWhiteSpace(ItemFilter.
                SelectedValue.ToString()) ||

              ItemFilter.SelectedValue.ToString() ==
    ```

```
            "All" ||

        ItemFilter.SelectedValue.ToString() ==
            item.MediaType.ToString()
     select item).ToList();
   ItemList.ItemsSource = updatedItems;
}
```

If the filter value is empty or **All** is selected, we want to include the item, regardless of its `MediaType`. Otherwise, we check whether the `MediaType` matches the selection in `ItemFilter ComboBox`. When there is a match, we add it to the `updatedItems` list. Then, we set `updatedItems` as `ItemsSource` on the `ListView`.

> **Note**
>
> A filter should never be empty unless there is an error while initializing the data. This condition is only a safeguard for unforeseen scenarios.

Now, run the app again and select **Book** in the filter, as illustrated in the following screenshot:

Figure 2.18 – Media Collection filtered to display only books

That takes care of the filter implementation for the time being. Let's finish up this part of the UI design with a `Button`.

Adding a new item button

We are not quite ready to start working with multiple windows or navigation yet. You should have some understanding of the **MVVM** pattern before we put too much logic into the app. This will minimize our code refactoring in later chapters. However, we can add a `Button` to the current page and add some code to ensure everything is hooked up correctly.

Open the `MainWindow.xaml` file and add a third `RowDefinition` to the top-level `Grid` on the `Window`, as follows:

```
<Grid.RowDefinitions>
    <RowDefinition Height="Auto"/>
    <RowDefinition Height="*"/>
    <RowDefinition Height="Auto"/>
</Grid.RowDefinitions>
```

The new row will have a height of `Auto` so that it sizes itself to fit the `Button`. We still want the `ListView` to take up most of the screen.

Now, after the closing tag of the `ListView` control, add the new `Button`, as follows:

```
<Button x:Name="AddButton" Content="Add Item"
    HorizontalAlignment="Right" Grid.Row="2" Margin="8"/>
```

As discussed in the previous chapter, the `Button` control does not have a `Text` property. Instead, if you only want a `Button` control to contain text, you assign it to the `Content` property. We are also assigning the `Button` control to the third row of the `Grid`, setting the margin, and aligning it to the right side of the `Grid`.

Let's see how the app looks now, as follows:

Figure 2.19 – My Media Collection with an Add Item button

The button doesn't do anything yet. Because we're not yet ready to add an additional window to the application to add items, let's open a message popup to inform the user that this function is not available.

In MainWindow.xaml, wire up a new event handler inside AddButton. You can also remove the x:Name attribute. We're able to remove the name because we do not need to reference it in the code-behind file. The code is shown in the following snippet:

```
<Button Content="Add Item"
    HorizontalAlignment="Right"
      Grid.Row="2" Margin="8" Click="AddButton_Click"/>
```

You can create the event handler by placing the cursor on the name of the handler, AddButton_Click, and pressing *F12*. This will create the handler and navigate to it in the MainWindow.xaml.cs file. Inside the AddButton_Click event handler, we will create a new ContentDialog with the message we want to display to the user.

> **Note**
>
> The call to dialog.ShowAsync() must be awaited, so remember to add the async directive to the event handler, as shown next.

The async directive is highlighted in the following code snippet for the new event handler:

```
private async void AddButton_Click(object sender,
   RoutedEventArgs e)
{
    var dialog = new ContentDialog
        {
            Title = "My Media Collection",
            Content = "Adding items to the collection is
                not yet supported.",
            CloseButtonText = "OK",
            XamlRoot = Content.XamlRoot
        };
    await dialog.ShowAsync();
}
```

Now, run the application again and click the **Add Item** button, as illustrated in the following screenshot:

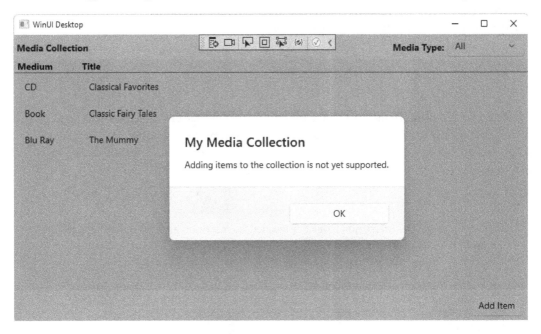

Figure 2.20 – Displaying a ContentDialog popup

That's all there is to adding a functional `Button` to a WinUI page. As we have discussed, some of this code will change and be moved to a `ViewModel` in the next chapter, but you should now have a good idea of how to work with some basic `Button` properties and events.

Summary

We have made some great initial progress on the **My Media Collection** application in this chapter. Along the way, you have learned how to use several common WinUI controls. You have also learned how to change the appearance, layout, and behavior of WinUI controls by using different layout controls and updating control properties in XAML. Finally, you saw how to leverage data binding and events to add and update data displayed to the user.

Next, we will learn how to decouple some of the logic we have been writing in the code-behind files to build testable and maintainable applications.

Questions

1. How do you add or remove features to or from Visual Studio?

2. What is the lowest minimum version of Windows that must be targeted when creating a new WinUI 3 project?

3. Where can you add XAML resources that can be shared by components in a whole application?

4. What is the default name of the first window loaded in a new WinUI app?

5. Which XAML container control allows you to define rows and columns to lay out its contents?

6. Which XAML container control stacks its contents horizontally or vertically?

7. What is the name of the message box that WinUI apps can use to display simple messages to users?

8. Challenge: What type of layout panel in WinUI allows its contents to be positioned absolutely?

3

MVVM for Maintainability and Testability

When building XAML-based applications, one of the most important design patterns to learn is the MVVM pattern. MVVM provides a clear separation of concerns between the XAML markup in the view and the C# code in the View Model using data binding. With this separation comes ease of maintenance and testability. The View Model classes can be tested without taking a dependency on the underlying **User Interface** (**UI**) platform. For large teams, another benefit of this separation is that changing the XAML enables UI designers to work on the UI independently of developers who specialize in writing the business logic and the backend of the application.

In this chapter, you will learn about the following concepts:

- Fundamentals of the MVVM design pattern

- Popular MVVM frameworks

- Implementing MVVM in WinUI applications

- Handling View Model changes in the view

- Event handling in MVVM

- Streamline View Model implementations with the MVVM Toolkit

By the end of the chapter, you will understand the basics of the MVVM design pattern, have some familiarity with some popular MVVM frameworks available to developers, and know how to implement MVVM in a WinUI application. We will wrap up by getting hands-on with the open source **MVVM Toolkit**.

Technical requirements

To follow along with the examples in this chapter, please refer to the *Technical requirements* section of *Chapter 2, Configuring the Development Environment and Creating the Project*.

You will find the code files of this chapter here: `https://github.com/PacktPublishing/Learn-WinUI-3-Second-Edition/tree/main/Chapter03`

Understanding MVVM

MVVM was introduced by Microsoft in 2005 and gained popularity with developers following the launch of **Windows Presentation Foundation** (**WPF**) and **Silverlight** because it lends itself so well to building applications with XAML. It is like the **Presentation Model** pattern, which was created by Martin Fowler – one of the most influential proponents of design patterns.

The MVVM pattern consists of the following three layers:

- **Model**: The Model layer contains the application's business logic and should perform all the data access operations. The View Model communicates with the Model to retrieve and save the application's data.

- **View**: The View layer is only responsible for the presentation of data in the application. The layout or structure is defined here, along with style definitions. This is the layer responsible for interacting with the user and receiving input events and data. The View is aware of the View Model only through data-binding expressions.

- **ViewModel**: The View Model (or ViewModel) layer is responsible for maintaining the state of data for the View. It has a set of properties that provide data to the View through data binding and a set of commands invoked by the View in response to user input events. View Model classes have no knowledge of their corresponding Views.

MVVM – the big picture

Let's look at how the components of MVVM fit into the overall architecture of an application implementing the pattern, depicted in the following diagram:

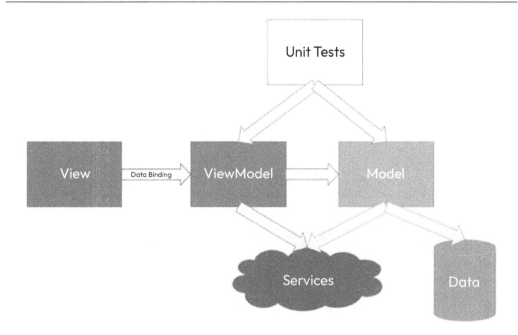

Figure 3.1 – The MVVM pattern in use

In *Figure 3.1*, you can see a representation of the MVVM pattern along with other parts of the application: services, data, and unit tests. The arrows in the diagram represent dependencies, not the data flow. You can imagine that data would need to move both ways along most of these pathways to create a functional application.

As with many design patterns, the MVVM pattern is meant to be a guide for developers to create reliable, maintainable applications. However, not all developers implement the pattern in the same way. The differences usually lie in the implementation of the model. Some developers will create a domain model in the **Domain-Driven Design** (**DDD**) style. This makes sense for large applications with complex business logic. For simpler applications, the model may only be a simple data access layer, residing either on the client or behind a service layer. In some of these cases, the **Services** cloud in the preceding diagram would move between the View Model and Model layers.

The point of MVVM is to help guide you in building the best app for your users. As you gain experience with MVVM and WinUI, you will find the right implementation for your applications. A good way to get started is to find some frameworks that make it easier to work with MVVM.

MVVM libraries for WinUI

When working with MVVM in WinUI applications, you must create a little infrastructure code to facilitate data binding between Views and View Models. You can either write this yourself or choose a framework that abstracts this plumbing code away from your application. Although we will start by writing our own plumbing code for the application in the next section, let's review some popular MVVM frameworks for WinUI.

The MVVM Toolkit

We will discuss the **Windows Community Toolkit (WCT)** and **.NET Community Toolkit** in more detail in *Chapter 9, Enhancing Applications with the Windows Community Toolkit*, but one of the libraries included in this open source toolkit is the **MVVM Toolkit**. The toolkit supports any .NET application platform, including UWP, WinUI 3, .NET MAUI, Uno Platform, WPF, and others. You can get the `CommunityToolkit.Mvvm` **NuGet package** through the **NuGet Package Manager** in Visual Studio or view its details on the NuGet website, at `https://www.nuget.org/packages/CommunityToolkit.Mvvm/`.

The library includes base classes to support `INotifyPropertyChanged`, `IMessenger`, and `ICommand`. It also includes other messaging and **Inversion of Control** (**IoC**) helper classes. In addition, the latest versions of the MVVM Toolkit use **Roslyn source generators** to reduce the amount of boilerplate code developers need to write.

> **Note**
>
> If you are unfamiliar with Roslyn, it is the code name of the **.NET Compiler Platform**. It was first **released to manufacturing** (**RTM**) with Visual Studio 2015, and it is the current compiler for the C# and VB.NET languages. Roslyn's extensibility, via the .NET Compiler Platform SDK, allows developers to create things such as custom source generators and source code analyzers for Visual Studio. For more information about the platform, you can check out the documentation on Microsoft Learn: `https://learn.microsoft.com/dotnet/csharp/roslyn-sdk/`.

Later in the chapter, after you have learned how to implement your own MVVM base class, we will leverage the MVVM Toolkit in our sample application.

The Prism Library

Prism started out as a library created and maintained by Microsoft. It was part of the **Patterns & Practices** guidance, reference architectures, and libraries that Microsoft's developer division used to maintain.

> **Note**
>
> The remaining *Patterns & Practices* projects still maintained by Microsoft are available on GitHub here: `https://github.com/mspnp`.

Microsoft decided to open source the Prism Library and transferred ownership to the community. The project is hosted on GitHub and can be found on the web at `https://prismlibrary.com/`. Prism has packages available for WPF, Xamarin, UWP, and WinUI projects.

Prism is much more than an MVVM framework. It also includes **application programming interfaces (APIs)** that help developers implement **dependency injection (DI)**, commands, and `EventAggregator` for loosely coupled application messaging. Prism can be added to a project through NuGet. There is also an installer available on the Prism site to add a Visual Studio project and item templates.

MVVMCross

MVVMCross is an MVVM framework that was first created for Xamarin developers. It now has NuGet packages available for Xamarin, .NET MAUI, WPF, UWP, and WinUI. As with Prism, MVVMCross does much more than facilitate data binding in WinUI applications. It has helpers for the following:

- Data binding
- Navigation
- Logging and tracing
- DI and IoC
- Unit testing

There are some additional libraries, but most are specific to .NET MAUI applications. The MVVMCross package can also be added to your project via NuGet. For more information about MVVMCross use with WinUI, check out their site: `https://www.mvvmcross.com/`.

Choosing a framework for WinUI applications

Using a third-party framework for building production XAML applications is a great choice. These provide built-in support for things such as logging and DI. For the WinUI application in this book, we will use the MVVM Toolkit for data binding at the end of this chapter. However, first, we will implement the MVVM pattern from scratch. This will help you understand the underlying mechanisms of data binding, DI, and other core concepts relating to MVVM.

Before jumping into the code, you should have some background on exactly how data binding works in WinUI.

Understanding data binding in WinUI

In the previous chapter, you saw some simple examples of data binding, using both the `Binding` and `x:Bind` markup extensions. Let's dissect some of the components that allow the View to receive updates when the View Model data changes.

What are markup extensions?

An in-depth discussion of markup extensions is beyond the scope of this introductory book. In brief, they are a class that executes some logic to return a value to the XAML parser. You can identify their use in XAML by looking for some markup inside curly braces. Take this example of `Binding` in the `Text` property of a `TextBlock`:

```
<TextBlock Text="{Binding Path=Name, Mode=TwoWay}"/>
```

From this, you can derive that there is a markup extension class named `Binding` and that two of its properties are `Path` and `Mode`. This markup extension takes these properties, resolves a value, and returns it to the XAML parser for display in the application's View.

Some XAML markup languages allow developers to write their own custom markup extensions. WPF and .NET MAUI have custom markup extensions, but WinUI does not. If you're curious about the implementation of a markup extension, Microsoft Learn has documentation on how to create one for .NET MAUI: `https://learn.microsoft.com/dotnet/maui/xaml/markup-extensions/create`.

Now, let's learn more about the `Binding` markup extension in WinUI.

Binding markup extension

As you briefly saw, the `Binding` markup extension maps data from the binding source, the View Model in MVVM, and provides it to a binding target in the View. These are all the properties of the `Binding` markup extension:

- `Path`: The path to the value in the data-binding source. For our application, this will be the property name on the View Model.

- `Converter`: If the data type of the source property does not match the data type of the control's property in the View, a `Converter` property is used to define the mapping between the two data types.

- `ConverterLanguage`: If a `Converter` property is specified, a `ConverterLanguage` property can optionally be set to support internationalization.

- `ConverterParameter`: If a `Converter` property takes a parameter, use the `ConverterParameter` property to provide it. It's not common to use a `Converter`

`Parameter` property, and it is typically a `string` value. If you need to provide multiple values to a `Converter`, you can concatenate them and then parse them inside the method.

- `ElementName`: This parameter is used when binding to an attribute of another element in the View.

- `FallBackValue`: If the data binding fails for any reason, you can specify a `FallBackValue` property to display in the View.

- `Mode`: This defines whether the data binding is `OneTime` (sets the value only when the XAML is first parsed), `OneWay` (fetches the value from the View Model when changes are detected), or `TwoWay` (the value flows both ways between the View and View Model). The default `Mode` setting for `Binding` varies depending on the control and property being bound. It is important to check the documentation if you are unsure of the default `Mode`.

- `RelativeSource`: This is used to define a data-binding source that is relative to the current control. This is usually used with control templates that get their data through a parent element.

- `Source`: Specifies the data-binding source. This is usually defined at a top-level control level in WinUI as the View Model. However, it is possible for child controls to set a different `Source`, overriding the `Source` inherited from their ancestor. The `Source` value defined at any level in the View will be inherited by all child elements unless a new `Source` is set.

- `TargetNullValue`: Specifies a default value to display if the data-binding source is resolved but has a `null` value.

- `UpdateSourceTrigger`: Specifies the frequency with which to update `TwoWay` binding sources. The options are `PropertyChanged`, `Explicit`, and `LostFocus`. The default frequency for most properties is `PropertyChanged`.

`Path` is the default property and is assumed when no property name is given for a parameter. For example, the earlier `TextBlock` example could also be written as follows:

```
<TextBlock Text="{Binding Name, Mode=TwoWay}"/>
```

Here, `Name` is assumed to be the value provided for the `Path` parameter. Providing two parameters without specifying parameter names will result in a XAML parser error.

The `Binding` markup extension is found in every XAML language. The other option for data binding, `x:Bind`, is not. It is only an option with UWP and WinUI.

x:Bind markup extension

`x:Bind` is an alternative markup extension for WinUI. It is faster and uses less memory than `Binding` and has better debugging support. It achieves this performance gain by generating code at compile time to be used during binding at runtime. By contrast, the `Binding` markup extension is executed by the XAML parser at runtime, which incurs additional overhead. Compile-time bindings also result in incorrect data binding expressions being caught when compiling, rather than generating data binding failures at runtime.

Another important distinction between `Binding` and `x:Bind` is that `Binding` requires a `Data Context` to be set. Data is bound to properties of objects within the `DataContext`. When using `x:Bind`, you are binding directly to properties on the current `Window` or `UserControl`. You can also bind events directly to event handlers in the code-behind for the Window with `x:Bind`.

While most of the properties of `x:Bind` are the same as those in `Binding`, let's highlight those that differ, as follows:

- `ElementName`: Not available in `x:Bind`. You must use `Binding` to data-bind to other XAML element attributes. If your application must bind to other elements, `x:Bind` and `Binding` can be used in the same View.

- `Mode`: The only difference here is that the default `Mode` for `x:Bind` is usually `OneTime`, not `OneWay`.

- `RelativeSource`: Not available in `x:Bind`.

- `Source`: Not available in `x:Bind`. Instead, you will typically define a `ViewModel` property in the code-behind file of each View with a data type of the corresponding View Model class. You could also create a domain-specific name for the property, such as `MediaItems` for our application.

- `BindBack`: This property is unique to `x:Bind`. It allows a custom function to be called in `TwoWay` binding when reverse data binding is invoked. This is not commonly used, and we will not use it in our application.

`x:Bind` is a powerful and complex markup extension. For more information about it, you can read this page on Microsoft Learn: `https://learn.microsoft.com/windows/uwp/xaml-platform/x-bind-markup-extension`.

Next, let's discuss `INotifyPropertyChanged`, the interface that enables changes in data-bound properties in the ViewModel to be reflected in the view.

Updating View data with INotifyPropertyChanged

So, how does the View get notified when data changes in the ViewModel? That magic lies within the `Microsoft.UI.Xaml.Data.INotifyPropertyChanged` interface. This interface consists of a single member, as shown here:

```
public interface INotifyPropertyChanged
{
    event PropertyChangedEventHandler PropertyChanged;
}
```

Every ViewModel class must implement this interface and raise the `PropertyChanged` event to update the View. Indicate which property is changed by passing its name in the `PropertyChangedEventArgs` parameter. To refresh all properties, pass `null` or `string.Empty` as the property name, but be aware of the potential performance implications this can have on large views.

Updating collection data with INotifyCollectionChanged

`INotifyPropertyChanged` works great for most properties, but it will not update the View if items from a collection have been added or removed. This is where the `Microsoft.UI.Xaml.Interop.INotifyCollectionChanged` interface is used. Again, this interface only has a single member, as shown here:

```
public interface INotifyCollectionChanged
{
    event NotifyCollectionChangedEventHandler
        CollectionChanged;
}
```

None of the collections or collection interfaces commonly used in .NET (`List<T>`, `IEnumerable<T>`, and so on) implement this interface. You can create your own collection derived from an existing list type and implement `INotifiedCollectionChanged` yourself, but it's much easier to use the `ObservableCollection<T>` list type that is already available to WinUI developers. This is a collection that will update the View when items are added or removed, or when the contents are completely refreshed.

The `Items` property of an `ObservableCollection<T>` is read-only, thus it cannot be directly set. You can add items by passing a `List<T>` or `IEnumerable<T>` to the constructor when creating `ObservableCollection<T>` or by using its `Add` or `Insert` methods (there is no `AddRange` method to add multiple items). You can update individual values in the collection by assigning a new item to the current index. You can remove items with the `Remove`, `RemoveAt`, `ClearItems`, or `Clear` methods.

In the next section, when we implement the MVVM pattern for ourselves, you will see these concepts in practice.

Implementing MVVM in WinUI applications

It's time to start converting our project to use MVVM. To gain a thorough understanding of the MVVM pattern, we will start by building our own MVVM infrastructure. For simple applications, it doesn't require more than a single base class:

1. Start by adding a **ViewModels** folder to the project. If you are using the code from GitHub, you can either continue with your project from the previous chapter or use the **Start** project in the folder for this chapter.

2. Next, add a new class to the **ViewModels** folder and name it `BindableBase`. This will be the base class for all our View Model classes in the project. It will be responsible for notifying the corresponding views of any property changes. This is accomplished by implementing the `INotifyPropertyChanged` interface. Let's review the `BindableBase` class code, as follows:

```
public class BindableBase : INotifyPropertyChanged
{
    public event PropertyChangedEventHandler
      PropertyChanged;
    protected void OnPropertyChanged(
      [CallerMemberName] string propertyName = null)
    {
        PropertyChanged?.Invoke(this, new Property
          ChangedEventArgs(propertyName));
    }
    protected bool SetProperty<T>(ref T originalValue,
      T newValue, [CallerMemberName] string
        propertyName = null)
    {
        if (Equals(originalValue, newValue))
        {
            return false;
        }
        originalValue = newValue;
        OnPropertyChanged(propertyName);
        return true;
    }
}
```

By using this as the base class of our View Models, they will have two new methods available to use, as follows:

- `OnPropertyChanged`: Use this to trigger a `PropertyChanged` event to notify the View of changes in the data

- `SetProperty`: This method is used to set the value of a property if the value has been changed and will then call `OnPropertyChanged`

> **Note**
>
> Be sure you have these two using directives at the top of the `BindableBase` class file:
>
> `using System.ComponentModel;`
>
> `using System.Runtime.CompilerServices;`

Now that we have a base class, let's add our first View Model to the project. Right-click the **ViewModels** folder and add a new class named `MainViewModel`. This View Model is going to replace most of the code in the **MainWindow.xaml.cs** code-behind file for our `MainWindow`. The following code is part of the revised class. Please refer to `MainViewModel.txt` in the GitHub repository for the chapter (`https://github.com/PacktPublishing/Learn-WinUI-3-Second-Edition/tree/main/Chapter03/Complete/MyMediaCollection/ViewModels`) for the current version of the complete class:

```
public class MainViewModel : BindableBase
{
    private string selectedMedium;
    private ObservableCollection<MediaItem> items;
    private ObservableCollection<MediaItem> allItems;
    private IList<string> mediums;
    public MainViewModel()
    {
        PopulateData();
    }
    ...
    public IList<string> Mediums
    {
        get
        {
            return mediums;
        }
        set
        {
            SetProperty(ref mediums, value);
        }
    }
    ...
}
```

You may have noticed that the code has been updated, using the new `BindableBase.SetProperty` method inside each property's `Set` block. This ensures that the UI will be notified when the property value has been changed:

1. Now, we'll need to make the `MainViewModel` class available to the `MainWindow` view. Because there will be a single instance of this View Model used throughout the lifetime of the app, we will add a static read-only property to the `App.xaml.cs` file to make it available to the application, as follows:

    ```
    public static MainViewModel ViewModel { get; } = new
    MainViewModel();
    ```

2. We can now strip out all the code from **MainWindow.xaml.cs** that we copied to the MainViewModel class. In addition, add a property to make App.ViewModel available to MainWindow for data binding, as follows:

```
public sealed partial class MainWindow : Window
{
    public MainWindow()
    {
        this.InitializeComponent();
        Loaded += MainPage_Loaded;
    }
    public MainViewModel ViewModel => App.ViewModel;
    private async void AddButton_Click(object sender,
      Microsoft.UI.Xaml.RoutedEventArgs e)
    {
        var dialog = new MessageDialog("Adding items
          to the collection is not yet available.",
            "My Media Collection");
        await dialog.ShowAsync();
    }
}
```

The only other code we need to keep in the code-behind file right now is for the **Add** button, which we will update in the next section.

Finally, it's time to update the **MainWindow.xaml** file to bind to the data of the MainViewModel. There are only two changes required to handle the new data source, detailed next.

3. First, update ComboBox to remove the x:Name property and add x:Bind data binding for the ItemsSource and SelectedItem properties. The SelectedItem binding needs to be set to TwoWay. This will ensure that the data in MainViewModel is updated when the user changes SelectedMedium in the UI. The code can be seen in the following snippet:

```
<ComboBox ItemsSource="{x:Bind ViewModel.Mediums}"
    SelectedItem="{x:Bind ViewModel.SelectedMedium,
        Mode=TwoWay}" HorizontalAlignment="Right"
        MinWidth="120" Margin="0,2,6,4"/>
```

4. Now, update ListView to remove the x:Name property and add an ItemsSource x:Bind data binding, as follows:

```
<ListView Grid.Row="1" ItemsSource="{x:Bind
    ViewModel.Items}">
```

The assigned names for these controls are no longer needed because we are not referencing them anywhere in the code.

> **Note**
>
> Assigning names to XAML elements allocates additional resources. It is recommended to only name elements when the elements must be referenced directly from code-behind files or by other View elements' data binding via `ElementName`.

5. Now, run the application and try changing the `Medium` filter with the `ComboBox`. It should behave exactly as it did before, but now we have decoupled the View Model data from the UI, making it easier to test or potentially reuse.

Next, we will address the button `Click` event that we still have in the **MainWindow.xaml.cs** file.

Working with events and commands

It's time to update the project to move the event handling code to `MainViewModel`. By the end of this section, you will have removed all the code that was added to the **MainWindow.xaml.cs** file, except for the `ViewModel` property. This will be great for the separation of concerns, as well as for the maintainability and testability of the project.

We could use the same process of wiring up events with the **Add** button's `Click` event and connect it to a method on the `MainViewModel` class. There are two problems with this approach:

- The View and View Model layers become more tightly coupled, reducing maintainability
- UI concerns are injected into the view model, reducing the testability of the class

Let's take another route. The MVVM pattern has the concept of **Commands** to handle events. Instead of adding a handler to the event of our view element, we will bind that event to a property on the view model. The `Command` properties all expect a type of `System.Windows.Input.ICommand`.

Implementing ICommand

To use commands in the project, we'll start by creating an implementation of `ICommand`.

> **Note**
>
> Another advantage of using an MVVM framework such as Prism or the MVVM Toolkit is that they provide implementations of `ICommand`.

Add a new class to the `ViewModel` folder in the project and name it `RelayCommand`. This class will implement the `ICommand` interface. The `RelayCommand` class will look like this:

```
public class RelayCommand : ICommand
{
```

```
        private readonly Action action;
        private readonly Func<bool> canExecute;
        public RelayCommand(Action action)
            : this(action, null)
        {
        }
        public RelayCommand(Action action, Func<bool>
          canExecute)
        {
            if (action == null)
                throw new ArgumentNullException
                   (nameof(action));
            this.action = action;
            this.canExecute = canExecute;
        }
        public bool CanExecute(object parameter) => canExecute
          == null || canExecute();
        public void Execute(object parameter) => action();
        public event EventHandler CanExecuteChanged;
        public void RaiseCanExecuteChanged() =>
          CanExecuteChanged?.Invoke(this, EventArgs.Empty);
}
```

`RelayCommand` has two constructors that both take an `Action` that will be invoked when the command is executed. One of the constructors also takes a `Func<bool>`. This will allow us to enable or disable UI actions based on the return value of `CanExecute`. We will use this to enable a **Delete** button only when a media item is selected in the `ListView`.

Using commands in the View Model

Now, it's time to update `MainViewModel` to handle commands from the **Add** and **Delete** buttons. In the next chapter, we will enhance the add operation so it can add or edit items. So, let's name the command and method accordingly:

1. First, add two new private variables to the `MainViewModel` class:

    ```
    private MediaItem selectedMediaItem;
    private int additionalItemCount = 1;
    ```

    The `additionalItemCount` variable is a temporary variable that we will use to track how many new items we have added to the list. The counter will help to generate unique IDs and names for each new media item. `selectedMediaItem` is a backing variable for the new `SelectedMediaItem` property.

2. Add the `SelectedMediaItem` property next:

```
public MediaItem SelectedMediaItem
{
    get => selectedMediaItem;
    set
    {
        SetProperty(ref selectedMediaItem, value);
        ((RelayCommand)DeleteCommand)
            .RaiseCanExecuteChanged();
    }
}
```

In addition to calling `SetProperty` to notify the UI that `SelectedMediaItem` has changed, we also need to call `RaiseCanExecuteChanged` on a new `DeleteCommand`.

3. Next, let's add `DeleteCommand` and `AddEditCommand` along with their corresponding actions:

```
public ICommand AddEditCommand { get; set; }
public void AddOrEditItem()
{
    // Note this is temporary until
    // we use a real data source for items.
    const int startingItemCount = 3;
    var newItem = new MediaItem
    {
        Id = startingItemCount + additionalItemCount,
        Location = LocationType.InCollection,
        MediaType = ItemType.Music,
        MediumInfo = new Medium { Id = 1, MediaType =
            ItemType.Music, Name = "CD" },
        Name = $"CD {additionalItemCount}"
    };
    allItems.Add(newItem);
    Items.Add(newItem);
    additionalItemCount++;
}
public ICommand DeleteCommand { get; set; }
private void DeleteItem()
{
    allItems.Remove(SelectedMediaItem);
    Items.Remove(SelectedMediaItem);
}
private bool CanDeleteItem() => selectedMediaItem !=
    null;
```

There is an `ICommand` property for each UI operation (`AddEditCommand` and `Delete Command`) and new methods for each command to execute (`AddOrEditItem` and `DeleteItem`). There is also a `CanDeleteItem` method that returns a `bool` value to indicate whether a media item has been selected by the user.

4. At the end of the `MainViewModel` constructor, add two lines of code to initialize the commands, connecting them to the corresponding methods:

```
DeleteCommand = new RelayCommand(DeleteItem,
  CanDeleteItem);
// No CanExecute param is needed for this command
// because you can always add or edit items.
AddEditCommand = new RelayCommand(AddOrEditItem);
```

The preceding code is part of the revised `MainViewModel` class. Please refer to `MainViewModel2.txt` in the GitHub repository for the chapter (`https://github.com/PacktPublishing/Learn-WinUI-3-Second-Edition/tree/main/Chapter03/Complete/MyMediaCollection/ViewModels`) for the current version of the complete class.

Our View Model has been updated to use commands. Next, we will update the view to bind to them.

Updating the View

Our view model is ready to go. It's now safe to remove all the event handling code from the `MainWindow` code. It should look like this when you're finished:

```
public sealed partial class MainWindow : Window
{
    public MainWindow()
    {
        this.InitializeComponent();
    }
    public MainViewModel ViewModel => App.ViewModel;
}
```

The **MainWindow.xaml** file will need a few updates to get the **Add Item** and **Delete Item** buttons fully functional with the temporary test data. Perform the following steps to accomplish this:

1. Update the `ListView` to bind the `SelectedItem` property to `SelectedMediaItem` in the view model:

```
<ListView Grid.Row="1" ItemsSource="{x:Bind
  ViewModel.Items}" SelectedItem="{x:Bind
    ViewModel.SelectedMediaItem, Mode=TwoWay}">
```

`TwoWay` data binding is required to allow the UI to update the view model.

2. Next, move the **Add Item** button inside the first column of a new two-column `Grid`. Then, create a **Delete Item** button in the second column. Remove the `Click` event handler and set the properties of the grid and two buttons to match the following snippet:

```
<StackPanel Grid.Row="2"
            HorizontalAlignment="Right"
            Orientation="Horizontal">
    <Button Command="{x:Bind
       ViewModel.AddEditCommand}"
            Content="Add Item"
            Margin="8,8,0,8"/>
    <Button Command="{x:Bind ViewModel.DeleteCommand}"
            Content="Delete Item"
            Margin="8"/>
</StackPanel>
```

Each button's `Command` property will be bound to the new `ICommand` properties in the view model. The `Command` property of a button is invoked when it's clicked by the user.

3. We're now done updating the project to use MVVM. Run the application to see how it works.

4. When it first loads, the **Delete Item** button will be disabled. Select an item in the list and notice that the button is automatically enabled. If you click **Delete Item**, the selected item is removed from the list and the button is disabled again.

5. Finally, click **Add Item** a few times to see how new items are created and added to the list. Each new item has a unique name using the counter we created in the view model, as illustrated in the following screenshot:

Figure 3.2 – My Media Collection after adding and removing a few items

`MainWindow` now has a view model that is completely decoupled from any UI concerns. This will allow you to maximize the unit test coverage on the project.

Before we wrap up, let's see how we can reduce the amount of code in our project by using an MVVM framework such as the MVVM Toolkit.

Leveraging the MVVM Toolkit

We briefly introduced the MVVM Toolkit earlier in the chapter. In this section, we will update the `MainViewModel` to see how we can remove the need for a `BindableBase` class and reduce the amount of code in the view model itself:

1. Start by right-clicking on the solution file in **Solution Explorer** and select **Manage NuGet Packages for Solution**.

2. In the NuGet window, select the **Browse** tab and search for `CommunityToolkit.Mvvm`.

3. Select the **CommunityToolkit.Mvvm** package in the results and install the latest stable version (8.2.0 or later).

4. Close the NuGet window and open the `MainViewModel` class. The first thing we need to do to use the MVVM Toolkit's source generators is update `MainViewModel` to be a partial class and have it inherit from `CommunityToolkit.Mvvm.ComponentModel.ObservableObject` instead of our own `BindableBase` class:

    ```
    public partial class MainViewModel : ObservableObject
    ```

> **Note**
>
> To learn more about how the MVVM Toolkit uses **.NET source generators** to generate public properties and commands, check out the documentation on Microsoft Learn: `https://learn.microsoft.com/dotnet/communitytoolkit/mvvm/generators/overview`. If you are unfamiliar with .NET source generators, you can also read about them on Microsoft Learn in the .NET documentation: `https://learn.microsoft.com/dotnet/csharp/roslyn-sdk/source-generators-overview`.

5. Next, each simple property that only calls `SetProperty` in its setter will be removed, and the backing variable will be updated to have an `ObservableProperty` attribute. Remove the `Mediums` and `Items` properties and the private `mediums` and `items` fields should now look like this:

    ```
    [ObservableProperty]
    private IList<string> mediums;
    [ObservableProperty]
    private ObservableCollection<MediaItem> items;
    ```

    We have two public properties remaining in the class. Let's start with `SelectedMedium`. We will remove `SelectedMediaItem` after updating the commands.

6. The setter for `SelectedMedium` has some custom logic after the call to `SetProperty`. Create a new partial method named `OnSelectedMediumChanged` to contain that code:

```
partial void OnSelectedMediumChanged(string value)
{
    Items.Clear();
    foreach (var item in allItems)
    {
        if (string.IsNullOrWhiteSpace(value) ||
            value == "All" ||
            value == item.MediaType.ToString())
        {
            Items.Add(item);
        }
    }
}
```

Notice that we also updated the uses of `selectedMedium` to `value`. The `value` parameter contains the new `selectedMedium` value. You may have also noticed some green squiggles in Visual Studio inside the `PopulateData` method, indicating that you should be using the generated properties instead of using the private `ObservableProperty` members directly. You can update all of these uses by capitalizing the first letter of each variable.

7. Next, we will update the two commands. Add the `RelayCommand` attribute to the `AddOr EditItem` and `DeleteItem` methods and rename them to `AddEdit` and `Delete` to ensure that the generated commands have the same names that our old commands had.

8. Remove the two commands and the code to initialize them in the `MainViewModel` constructor. The code for the constructor and the signatures for the two command methods should now look like this:

```
public MainViewModel()
{
    PopulateData();
}
[RelayCommand]
public void AddEdit()
{
...
}
[RelayCommand(CanExecute = nameof(CanDeleteItem))]
public void Delete()
{
...
}
```

```
private bool CanDeleteItem() => SelectedMediaItem !=
  null;
```

The attribute for `DeleteItem` also indicates that `CanDeleteItem` should be used for checking whether the command can be invoked.

9.   Finally, let's replace the `SelectedMediaItem` property with a source-generated property from the MVVM Toolkit. The existing public property tells the `DeleteCommand` that `CanExecute` should be checked. Remove that property and update the private `selectedMediaItem` variable to add two attributes:

```
[ObservableProperty]
[NotifyCanExecuteChangedFor(nameof(DeleteCommand))]
private MediaItem selectedMediaItem;
```

In addition to the `ObservableProperty` attribute, we've added a `NotifyCanExecuteChangedFor` attribute, providing the name of the `DeleteCommand` generated `ICommand` property. The generated property, which is invisible to us, would be equivalent to this:

```
public MediaItem SelectedMediaItem
{
    get => selectedMediaItem;
    set
    {
        if (SetProperty(ref selectedMediaItem, value))
        {
            DeleteCommand.NotifyCanExecuteChanged();
        }
    }
}
```

That's all you need to do. There are no changes needed in the view, and the application works exactly as it did before. All we've done is remove quite a bit of code from `MainViewModel`.

We will continue to use the MVVM Toolkit throughout the remaining chapters. Now, let's review what we've learned in this chapter.

Summary

We've made quite a bit of progress with the application in this chapter. While it's not yet connected to a live data source, we have methods in place to add and remove items from the media collection in memory. In addition, the project has been refactored to use the **MVVM** pattern, moving all the existing view logic from the `MainWindow` code-behind file to a new `MainViewModel` class. The new `MainViewModel` class has no dependencies on the UI. Finally, we saw how integrating the

MVVM Toolkit into the project can reduce the boilerplate code in our view models. These good software design habits will serve us well in the chapters ahead as we build more functionality onto the project.

In the next chapter, we will continue learning how to use the MVVM pattern to write robust, maintainable WinUI applications. We will cover some more advanced MVVM topics and learn some techniques for window management in a WinUI project.

Questions

1. What does MVVM stand for?
2. Which layer typically defines the business entities in the MVVM pattern?
3. Name one of the popular MVVM frameworks discussed in the chapter.
4. Which interface must every View Model class implement in an MVVM application?
5. Which special collection type in .NET notifies the UI of changes to the collection, via data binding?
6. Which control property of `ComboBox` and `ListView` is used to get or set the currently selected item in the control?
7. Which interface is implemented to create commands for event binding?

4

Advanced MVVM Concepts

After learning the basics of the MVVM pattern and its implementation in WinUI, it's now time to build on that knowledge base to handle some more advanced techniques. Now, you will learn how to keep components loosely coupled and testable when adding new dependencies to the project.

Few modern applications have only a single page or window. There are MVVM techniques that can be leveraged to navigate between pages from a `ViewModel` command without being coupled to the UI layer.

In this chapter, you will learn about the following concepts:

- Understanding the basics of **Dependency Injection (DI)**

- Leveraging DI to expose `ViewModel` classes to WinUI views

- Using MVVM and `x:Bind` to handle additional UI events with event handlers in the ViewModel

- Navigating between pages with MVVM and DI

By the end of this chapter, you will have a deeper understanding of the MVVM pattern and will know how to decouple your view models from any external dependencies.

Technical requirements

To follow along with the examples in this chapter, please reference the *Technical requirements* section in *Chapter 2, Configuring the Development Environment and Creating the Project*.

You will find the code files for this chapter here: `https://github.com/PacktPublishing/Learn-WinUI-3-Second-Edition/tree/main/Chapter04`.

Understanding the basics of DI

Before starting down the path of using DI in our project, we should take some time to understand what DI is and why it is fundamental for building modern applications. You will often see DI referenced with another related concept, **Inversion of Control (IoC)**. Let's discuss these two concepts by doing the following:

- Clarify the relationship between them
- Prepare you to use DI properly in this chapter

DI is used by modern developers to inject dependent objects into a class rather than creating instances of the objects inside the class. There are several ways to inject those objects:

- **Method injection**: Objects are passed as parameters to a method in the class
- **Property injection**: Objects are set through properties
- **Constructor injection**: Objects are passed as constructor parameters

The most common method of DI is constructor injection. In this chapter, we will be using both property injection and constructor injection. Method injection will not be used because it is not common to use methods to set a single object's value in .NET projects. Most developers use properties for this purpose.

IoC is the concept that a class should not be responsible for (or have knowledge of) the creation of its dependencies. You're inverting control over object creation. This sounds a bit like DI, doesn't it? Well, DI is one method of achieving this IoC in your code. There are other ways to implement IoC, including the following:

- **Delegate**: This holds a reference to a method that can be used to create and return an object
- **Event**: Like a delegate, this is typically used in association with user input or other outside actions
- **Service Locator Pattern**: This is used to inject the implementation of a service at runtime

When you separate the responsibilities of object creation and use, it facilitates code reuse and increases testability.

The classes that will be taking advantage of DI in this chapter are views and ViewModels. So, if we will not be creating instances of objects in those classes, where will they be created? Aren't we just moving the tight coupling somewhere else? In a way, that is true, but the coupling will be minimized by centralizing it to one part of the project, the App.xaml.cs file. If you remember from the previous chapter, the App class is where we handle application-wide actions and data.

We are going to use a **DI container** in the App class to manage the application's dependencies. A DI container is responsible for creating and maintaining the lifetime of the objects it manages. The object's lifetime in the container is usually either *per instance* (each object request returns a new instance of the object) or a *singleton* (every object request returns the same instance of the object). The container is configured in the App class, and it makes instances available to other classes in the application.

In .NET 6 and later, DI is now a part of .NET itself. We will leverage the **host builder** configuration in .NET to register our application's dependencies and resolve them in the classes where they are needed.

There are a number of other DI implementations that can be leveraged from MVVM frameworks. If you would like to explore some of them, here are their respective links:

- **Unity**: This DI implementation supports all types of .NET applications and has a full-featured IOC container (`http://unitycontainer.org/articles/introduction.html`)

- **DryIoc**: This small, lightweight IOC container supports .NET Standard 2.0 and .NET 4.5 and later applications (`https://github.com/dadhi/DryIoc`)

- **Prism**: This MVVM framework does not support WinUI 3, but developers can still leverage the DI capabilities (`https://prismlibrary.com/docs/dependency-injection/index.html`)

These concepts will be easier to understand as we implement the code in our application. Now, it's time to see DI and DI containers in practice.

Using DI with ViewModel classes

Most of the popular MVVM frameworks today include a DI container to manage dependencies. Because .NET now includes its own DI container, we will use that one. The .NET team has incorporated the DI container that used to be bundled with **ASP.NET Core**. It's both lightweight and easy to use. Luckily, this container is now available to all types of .NET projects via a **NuGet** package:

1. Open the project from the previous chapter or use the project in the `Start` folder in the GitHub repository for this chapter. In the `MyMediaCollection` project, open **NuGet Package Manager** and search for `Microsoft.Extensions.Hosting`:

Figure 4.1 – Microsoft's DI NuGet package

2. Select the package and install the latest stable version. After the installation completes, close the **NuGet Package Manager** tab and open `App.xaml.cs`. We will make a few changes here to start using the DI container.

   The DI container implements DI through interfaces called `IHostBuilder` and `IServiceCollection`. As the names imply, they are intended to create a collection of services for the application through a shared host. However, we can add any type of class to the container. Its use is not restricted to services. `IServiceCollection` builds the container, implementing the `IServiceProvider` interface. In the following steps, you will add support for DI to the application.

3. The first thing you should do is add a `public` property to the App class that makes the host container available to the project:

    ```
    public static IHost HostContainer { get; private set;
    }
    ```

    Here, `get` is public, but the property has a `private set` accessor. This restricts the creation of the container to the App class. Don't forget to add the required `using` statements to the code:

    ```
    using Microsoft.Extensions.DependencyInjection;
    using Microsoft.Extensions.Hosting;
    ```

4. The next step is to create a new method that initializes the container, sets it to the `public` property, and adds our first dependency:

    ```
    private void RegisterComponents()
    {
        HostContainer = Host.CreateDefaultBuilder()
            .ConfigureServices(services =>
        {
            services.AddTransient<MainViewModel>();
        }).Build();
    }
    ```

    In the new `RegisterComponents` method, we are creating `HostContainer` and its service collection, registering `MainViewModel` as a **transient** (one instance per container request) object, and using the `Build` method to create and return the DI container. Although it's not strictly required, when adding multiple types to the container, it's a good practice to add dependent objects to the service collection first. We'll be adding more items to the container soon.

5. Finally, you will call `RegisterComponents` before creating the instance of `MainWindow` in the `App.OnLaunched` event handler:

    ```
    protected override void
    OnLaunched(LaunchActivatedEventArgs args)
    {
        RegisterComponents();
        m_window = new MainWindow();
        m_window.Activate();
    }
    ```

That's all the code needed to create and expose the DI container to the application. Now that we are delegating the creation of `MainViewModel` to the container, you can remove the property that exposes a static instance of `MainViewModel` from the App class.

Using the ViewModel controlled by the container is simple. Go ahead and open `MainWindow.xaml.cs` and update the `ViewModel` property to remove the initialization. Then, set the value of the `ViewModel` property using `HostContainer.Services.GetService` from the App class before the call to `InitializeComponent`:

```
public MainWindow()
{
    ViewModel = App.HostContainer.Services
      .GetService<MainViewModel>();
    this.InitializeComponent();
}
public MainViewModel ViewModel;
```

If you build and run the application now, it will work just as it did before. However, now our `MainViewModel` instance will be registered in the App class and managed by the container. As new models, view models, services, and other dependencies are added to the project, they can be added to the `HostContainer` in the `RegisterComponents` method.

We will be adding page navigation to the app later in this chapter. First, let's discuss the **event-to-command** pattern.

Leveraging x:Bind with events

In the previous chapter, we bound `ViewModel` commands to the `Command` properties of the **Add Item** and **Delete Item** buttons. This works great and keeps the ViewModel decoupled from the UI, but what happens if you need to handle an event that isn't exposed through a `Command` property? For this scenario, you have two options:

- Use a custom behavior such as `EventToCommandBehavior` in the .NET MAUI Community Toolkit. This allows you to wire up a command in the ViewModel to any event.

- Use `x:Bind` in the view to bind directly to an event handler on the view model.

In this application, we will use `x:Bind`. This option will provide compile-time type checking and added performance. If you want to learn more about the .NET MAUI Community Toolkit, you can read the documentation on Microsoft Learn: `https://learn.microsoft.com/dotnet/communitytoolkit/maui/behaviors/event-to-command-behavior`.

We want to provide users of the **My Media Collection** application with the option to double-click (or double-tap) a row on the list to view or edit its details. The new **Item Details** window will be added in the next section. Until then, double-clicking an item will invoke the same code as the **Add Item** button, as this will become the **Add/Edit Item** button later:

1. Start by adding an `ItemRowDoubleTapped` event handler to the `MainViewModel` class that calls the existing `AddEdit` method:

    ```
    public void ListViewDoubleTapped(object sender,
    DoubleTappedRoutedEventArgs args)
    {
        AddEdit();
    }
    ```

2. Next, bind the `ListView.DoubleTapped` event to the ViewModel:

    ```
    <ListView Grid.Row="1" ItemsSource="{x:Bind
        ViewModel.Items}"
        SelectedItem="{x:Bind
        ViewModel.SelectedMediaItem,
        Mode=TwoWay}"
        DoubleTapped="{x:Bind ViewModel
        .ListViewDoubleTapped}">
    ```

3. Finally, to ensure that the double-clicked row is also selected, modify the `Grid` inside `ListView.ItemTemplate` to set the `IsHitTestVisible` property to `False`:

    ```
    <ListView.ItemTemplate>
        <DataTemplate x:DataType="model:MediaItem">
            <Grid IsHitTestVisible="False">
                ...
            </Grid>
        </DataTemplate>
    </ListView.ItemTemplate>
    ```

Now when you run the application, you can either click the **Add Item** button or double-click a row in the list to add new items. In the next section, you will update the **Add Item** button to be an **Add/Edit Item** button.

Page navigation with MVVM and DI

Until this point, the application has consisted of only a single window. Now it's time to implement page navigation by adding a host `Frame` and two `Page` objects so we can handle adding new items or editing existing items. The new `Page` will be accessible from the **Add/Edit Item** button or by double-clicking on an item in the list.

Migrating MainWindow to MainPage

If you're familiar with UWP app development, you should already understand page navigation. In UWP, the application consists of only a single window. At the root of the window, there is a `Frame` object, which hosts pages and handles the navigation between them. To achieve the same result in a desktop WinUI 3 app, we will create a new `MainPage`, move all the XAML content from `MainWindow` into `MainPage`, and update the `App` class to create a `Frame` as the new content of `MainWindow`. Then we can display the same contents by navigating to `MainPage`. Let's get started:

1. First, add a new folder to the project named `Views`.

2. Right-click the **Views** folder and select **Add | New Item**.

3. On the **Add New Item** dialog, select **WinUI** on the left and choose the **Blank Page (WinUI 3)** item template. Name the page `MainPage` and click **Create**.

4. Open `MainWindow.xaml` and cut the entire XAML contents of the `Window`.

5. Open `MainPage.xaml` and paste the XAML from `MainWindow`, replacing the empty `Grid` control.

6. You will also need to cut and paste the `xmlns` declaration for `model` from `MainWindow` to `MainPage`:

   ```
   xmlns:model="using:MyMediaCollection.Model"
   ```

7. In `MainWindow.xaml.cs`, remove the `ViewModel` variable and the constructor code that fetches it from the `HostContainer`. Put this same code into `MainPage.xaml.cs`:

   ```
   public MainPage()
   {
       ViewModel = App.HostContainer.Services.GetService
         <MainViewModel>();
       this.InitializeComponent();
   }
   public MainViewModel ViewModel;
   ```

8. Next, open `App.xaml.cs` and add some code inside `OnLaunched` to create a `rootFrame`, add it to the `MainWindow`, and navigate to `MainPage` before activating the window:

   ```
   protected override void OnLaunched
     (LauchActivatedEventArgs args)
   {
       m_window = new MainWindow();
       var rootFrame = new Frame();
       RegisterComponents();
       rootFrame.NavigationFailed +=
         RootFrame_NavigationFailed;
   ```

```
        rootFrame.Navigate(typeof(MainPage), args);
        m_window.Content = rootFrame;
        m_window.Activate();
    }
    private void RootFrame_NavigationFailed(object sender,
      NavigationFailedEventArgs e)
    {
        throw new Exception($"Error loading page
          {e.SourcePageType.FullName}");
    }
```

We've also added an event handler to handle navigation failures for the `Frame`.

9. Make sure to add the necessary `using` statements to the file:

```
using System;
using Microsoft.UI.Xaml;
using Microsoft.UI.Xaml.Controls;
using Microsoft.UI.Xaml.Navigation;
using MyMediaCollection.Views;
```

If you run the app now, it should look and behave just as it did before, but now the controls are nested within a `Page` and a `Frame` on the `Window`. Let's add a second page and get ready to start navigating between our list and detail pages.

Adding ItemDetailsPage

The full `ItemDetailsPage.xaml` code can be found on GitHub (`https://github.com/ PacktPublishing/Learn-WinUI-3-Second-Edition/blob/main/Chapter04/ Complete/MyMediaCollection/Views/ItemDetailsPage.xaml`). You can follow along with the steps in this section or review the final code on GitHub.

> **Note**
>
> The project will not compile successfully until we have added the new ViewModel to the project and added it to the DI container for consumption by the view. Before we add the ViewModel, we need to create some services to enable navigation and data persistence between views.

We will be showing **Item Details** in the same host window, and our content will reside within a new Page control. The `Page` will be set as the content and navigated to by the `Frame` we created. For more information about page navigation with WinUI, you can read this Microsoft Learn article: `https:// learn.microsoft.com/windows/apps/design/basics/navigate-between- two-pages?tabs=wasdk`.

To add `ItemDetailsPage`, follow these steps:

1. Right-click the **Views** folder in **Solution Explorer** and select **Add | New Item**.

2. On the new item dialog, select **Blank Page (WinUI 3)** and name the page `ItemDetailsPage`.

3. There are going to be several input controls with some common attributes on the page. Start by adding three styles to a `Page.Resources` section just before the top-level `Grid` control:

```xml
<Page.Resources>
    <Style x:Key="AttributeTitleStyle"
      TargetType="TextBlock">
        <Setter Property="HorizontalAlignment"
          Value="Right"/>
        <Setter Property="VerticalAlignment"
          Value="Center"/>
    </Style>
    <Style x:Key="AttributeValueStyle"
        TargetType="TextBox">
        <Setter Property="HorizontalAlignment"
          Value="Stretch"/>
        <Setter Property="Margin" Value="8"/>
    </Style>
    <Style x:Key="AttributeComboxValueStyle"
        TargetType="ComboBox">
        <Setter Property="HorizontalAlignment"
          Value="Stretch"/>
        <Setter Property="Margin" Value="8"/>
    </Style>
</Page.Resources>
```

In the next step, we can assign `AttributeTitleStyle` to each `TextBlock`, `AttributeValueStyle` to each `TextBox`, and `AttributeComboValueStyle` to each `ComboBox`. If you need to add any other attributes to input labels later, you will only update `AttributeTitleStyle` and the attributes will automatically be applied to every `TextBlock` using that style.

4. The top-level `Grid` will contain three child `Grid` controls to partition the view into three areas—a header, the input controls, and the **Save** and **Cancel** buttons at the bottom. The input area will be given the bulk of the available space, so define `Grid.RowDefinitions` like this:

```xml
<Grid.RowDefinitions>
    <RowDefinition Height="Auto"/>
    <RowDefinition Height="*"/>
    <RowDefinition Height="Auto"/>
</Grid.RowDefinitions>
```

5. The header area will contain only a `TextBlock`. You are welcome to design this area however you like:

```
<TextBlock Text="Item Details" FontSize="18"
Margin="8"/>
```

6. The input area contains a `Grid` with four `RowDefinitions` and two `ColumnDefinitions` for the labels and input controls for the four fields that users can currently edit:

```
<Grid Grid.Row="1">
    <Grid.RowDefinitions>
        <RowDefinition Height="Auto"/>
        <RowDefinition Height="Auto"/>
        <RowDefinition Height="Auto"/>
        <RowDefinition Height="Auto"/>
    </Grid.RowDefinitions>
    <Grid.ColumnDefinitions>
        <ColumnDefinition Width="200"/>
        <ColumnDefinition Width="*"/>
    </Grid.ColumnDefinitions>
    <TextBlock Text="Name:" Style="{StaticResource
      AttributeTitleStyle}"/>
    <TextBox Grid.Column="1"
        Style="{StaticResource AttributeValueStyle}"
        Text="{x:Bind ViewModel.ItemName, Mode=TwoWay,
UpdateSourceTrigger=PropertyChanged}"/>
    <TextBlock Text="Media Type:" Grid.Row="1"
        Style="{StaticResource AttributeTitleStyle}"/>
    <ComboBox Grid.Row="1" Grid.Column="1"
        Style="{StaticResource AttributeCombox
          ValueStyle}"
        ItemsSource="{x:Bind ViewModel.ItemTypes}"
        SelectedValue="{x:Bind ViewModel
          .SelectedItemType, Mode=TwoWay}"/>
    <TextBlock Text="Medium:" Grid.Row="2"
        Style="{StaticResource AttributeTitleStyle}"/>
    <ComboBox Grid.Row="2" Grid.Column="1"
        Style="{StaticResource
          AttributeComboxValueStyle}"
        ItemsSource="{x:Bind ViewModel.Mediums}"
        SelectedValue="{x:Bind ViewModel
          .SelectedMedium, Mode=TwoWay}"/>
    <TextBlock Text="Location:" Grid.Row="3"
        Style="{StaticResource AttributeTitleStyle}"/>
```

```
<ComboBox Grid.Row="3" Grid.Column="1"
    Style="{StaticResource
      AttributeComboxValueStyle}"
    ItemsSource="{x:Bind ViewModel.LocationTypes}"
    SelectedValue="{x:Bind ViewModel
      .SelectedLocation,Mode=TwoWay}"/>
</Grid>
```

7. The item's Name is a free-text entry field, while the others are ComboBox controls to allow the user to pick values from lists bound to ItemsSource. The final child element of the top-level Grid is a right-aligned horizontal StackPanel containing the **Save** and **Cancel** buttons:

```
<StackPanel Orientation="Horizontal"
      Grid.Row="2" HorizontalAlignment="Right">
    <Button Content="Save" Margin="8,8,0,8"
      Command="{x:Bind ViewModel.SaveCommand}"/>
    <Button Content="Cancel" Margin="8"
      Command="{x:Bind ViewModel.CancelCommand}"/>
</StackPanel>
```

The next stage is to add interfaces and services, so let's work on this next.

Adding new interfaces and services

Now that we have more than a single page to manage in the application, we need some services to centralize the page management and abstract the details from the ViewModel code. Start by creating Services and Interfaces folders in the project. Each service will implement an interface. This interface will be used for DI and later, if you were to add unit tests to a test project.

Creating a navigation service

The first service we need is a **navigation service**. Start by defining the INavigationService interface in the Interfaces folder. The interface defines methods to get the current page name, navigate to a specific page, or navigate back to the previous page:

```
public interface INavigationService
{
string CurrentPage { get; }
void NavigateTo(string page);
void NavigateTo(string page, object parameter);
void GoBack();
}
```

Now, create a `NavigationService` class in the `Services` folder. In the class definition, make sure that `NavigationService` implements the `INavigationService` interface. The full class can be viewed on GitHub (`https://github.com/PacktPublishing/Learn-WinUI-3-Second-Edition/blob/master/Chapter04/Complete/MyMediaCollection/Services/NavigationService.cs`). Let's discuss a few highlights.

The purpose of a navigation service in MVVM is to store a collection of available pages in the application so that when its `NavigateTo` method is called, the service can find a page that matches the requested `Name` or `Type` and navigate to it.

The collection of pages will be stored in a `ConcurrentDictionary<T>` collection. The `ConcurrentDictionary<T>` functions like the standard `Dictionary<T>`, but it can automatically add locks to prevent changes to the dictionary simultaneously across multiple threads:

```
private readonly IDictionary<string, Type> _pages = new
ConcurrentDictionary<string, Type>();
```

The `Configure` method will be called when you create `NavigationService` before adding it to the DI container. This method is not a part of the `INavigationService` interface and will not be available to classes that consume the service from the container. There is a check here to ensure views are only added to the service once. We check the dictionary to determine whether any pages of the same data type exist. If this condition is `true`, then the page has already been registered:

```
public void Configure(string page, Type type)
{
    if (_pages.Values.Any(v => v == type))
    {
        throw new ArgumentException($"The {type.Name} view
            has already been registered under another
                name.");
    }
    _pages[page] = type;
}
```

These are the implementations of the three navigation methods in the service. The two `NavigateTo` methods navigate to a specific page, with the second providing the ability to pass a parameter to the page. The third is `GoBack`, which does what you would think: it navigates to the previous page in the application. They wrap the `Frame` navigation calls to abstract the UI implementation from the view models that will be consuming this service:

```
public void NavigateTo(string page)
{
    NavigateTo(page, null);
}
public void NavigateTo(string page, object parameter)
```

```
{
    if (!_pages.ContainsKey(page))
    {
        throw new ArgumentException($"Unable to find a page
            registered with the name {page}.");
    }
    AppFrame.Navigate(_pages[page], parameter);
}
public void GoBack()
{
    if (AppFrame?.CanGoBack == true)
    {
        AppFrame.GoBack();
    }
}
}
```

We're ready to start using `NavigationService`, but first, let's create a data service for the application.

> **Note**
>
> You can jump ahead to implementing the services in the next section if you like. The `DataService` and `IDataService` code is available in the completed solution on GitHub: `https://github.com/PacktPublishing/Learn-WinUI-3-Second-Edition/tree/master/Chapter04/Complete/MyMediaCollection`.

Creating a data service

The data on `MainPage` of **My Media Collection** currently consists of a few sample records created and stored in `MainViewModel`. This isn't going to work very well across multiple pages. By using a data service, view models will not need to know how the data is created or stored.

For now, the data will still be sample records that are not saved between sessions. Later, we can update the data service to save and load data from a database without any changes to the view models that use the data.

The first step is to add an interface named `IDataService` to the `Interfaces` folder:

```
public interface IDataService
{
    IList<MediaItem> GetItems();
    MediaItem GetItem(int id);
    int AddItem(MediaItem item);
    void UpdateItem(MediaItem item);
    IList<ItemType> GetItemTypes();
```

```
        Medium GetMedium(string name);
        IList<Medium> GetMediums();
        IList<Medium> GetMediums(ItemType itemType);
        IList<LocationType> GetLocationTypes();
        int SelectedItemId { get; set; }
    }
```

These methods should look familiar to you from previous chapters, but let's briefly review the purpose of each:

- `GetItems`: Returns all the available media items

- `GetItem`: Finds a media item with the provided `id`

- `AddItem`: Adds a new media item to the collection

- `UpdateItem`: Updates a media item in the collection

- `GetItemTypes`: Gets the list of media item types

- `GetMedium`: Gets a `Medium` with the provided name

- `GetMediums`: These two methods either get all available mediums or any available for the provided `ItemType`

- `GetLocationTypes`: Gets all the available media locations

- `SelectedItemId`: Persists the ID of the selected item on `MainPage`

Now, create the `DataService` class in the `Services` folder. Make sure that `DataService` implements `IDataService` in the class definition.

Again, we will only review parts of the code. You can review the entire implementation on GitHub (`https://github.com/PacktPublishing/Learn-WinUI-3-Second-Edition/blob/master/Chapter04/Complete/MyMediaCollection/Services/DataService.cs`). The data in `DataService` will be persisted in four lists and the `SelectedItemId` property:

```
private IList<MediaItem> _items;
private IList<ItemType> _itemTypes;
private IList<Medium> _mediums;
private IList<LocationType> _locationTypes;
public int SelectedItemId { get; set; }
```

Copy the `PopulateItems` method from `MainViewModel` and modify it to use `List<T>` collections and add the `Location` property assignment to each item.

Start by creating the three MediaItem objects:

```
var cd = new MediaItem
{
    Id = 1,
    Name = "Classical Favorites",
    MediaType = ItemType.Music,
    MediumInfo = _mediums.FirstOrDefault(m => m.Name ==
      "CD"),
    Location = LocationType.InCollection
};
var book = new MediaItem
{
    Id = 2,
    Name = "Classic Fairy Tales",
    MediaType = ItemType.Book,
    MediumInfo = _mediums.FirstOrDefault(m => m.Name ==
      "Hardcover"),
    Location = LocationType.InCollection
};
var bluRay = new MediaItem
{
    Id = 3,
    Name = "The Mummy",
    MediaType = ItemType.Video,
    MediumInfo = _mediums.FirstOrDefault(m => m.Name ==
      "Blu Ray"),
    Location = LocationType.InCollection
};
```

Then, initialize the _items list and add the three MediaItem objects you just created:

```
_items = new List<MediaItem>
{
    cd,
    book,
    bluRay
};
```

There are three other methods to pre-populate the sample data: PopulateMediums, Populate ItemTypes, and PopulateLocationTypes. All of these are called from the Data Service constructor. These methods will be updated later to use an **SQLite** data store for data persistence.

Most of the `Get` method implementations are very straightforward. The `GetMediums(ItemType itemType)` method uses **Language Integrated Query (LINQ)** to find all `Medium` objects for the selected `ItemType`:

```
public IList<Medium> GetMediums(ItemType itemType)
{
    return _mediums
        .Where(m => m.MediaType == itemType)
        .ToList();
}
```

> **Note**
>
> If you are not familiar with LINQ expressions, Microsoft has some good documentation on the topic: https://learn.microsoft.com/dotnet/csharp/programming-guide/concepts/linq/.

The `AddItem` and `UpdateItems` methods are also simple. They add to and update the `_items` collection:

```
public int AddItem(MediaItem item)
{
    item.Id = _items.Max(i => i.Id) + 1;
    _items.Add(item);
    return item.Id;
}
public void UpdateItem(MediaItem item)
{
    var idx = -1;
    var matchedItem = (from x in _items
                       let ind = idx++
                       where x.Id == item.Id
                       select ind).FirstOrDefault();
    if (idx == -1)
    {
        throw new Exception("Unable to update item. Item
            not found in collection.");
    }
    _items[idx] = item;
}
```

The `AddItem` method has some basic logic to find the highest `Id` and increment it by 1 to use at the new item's `Id`. `Id` is also returned to the calling method in case the caller needs the information.

The services are all created. It is time to set them up when the application launches and consume them in the view models.

Increasing maintainability by consuming services

Before using the services in view models, open the `RegisterServices` method in `App.xaml.cs` and add the following code to register the new services in the DI container and register a new `ItemDetailsViewModel` (yet to be created). We're also adding a parameter to the method to pass along to the constructor of the `NavigationService`. This will provide access to the `Frame` for page navigation:

```
private IServiceProvider RegisterServices(Frame rootFrame)
{
var navigationService = new NavigationService(rootFrame);
navigationService.Configure(nameof(MainPage),
typeof(MainPage));
navigationService.Configure(nameof(ItemDetailsPage),
typeof(ItemDetailsPage));
HostContainer = Host.CreateDefaultBuilder()
    .ConfigureServices(services =>
    {
        services.AddSingleton<INavigationService>
            (navigationService);
        services.AddSingleton<IDataService, DataService>();
        services.AddTransient<MainViewModel>();
        services.AddTransient<ItemDetailsViewModel>();
    }).Build();
}
```

Both `INavigationService` and `IDataService` are registered as **singletons**. This means that there will be only a single instance of each stored in the container. Any state held in these services is shared across all classes that consume them.

You will notice that when we're registering `INavigationService`, we are passing the instance we already created to the constructor. This is a feature of Microsoft's DI container and most other DI containers. It allows for initialization and configuration of instances before they're added to the container.

We need to make a few changes to `MainViewModel` to consume `IDataService` and `INavigationService`, update the `PopulateData` method, and navigate to `ItemDetailsPage` when `AddEdit()` is invoked:

1. Start by adding properties to `MainViewModel` for `INavigationService` and `IDataService`:

    ```
    private INavigationService _navigationService;
    private IDataService _dataService;
    ```

Don't forget to add a using statement for MyMediaCollection.Interfaces.

2.   Next, update the constructor to receive and store the services:

```
public MainViewModel(INavigationService
navigationService, IDataService dataService)
{
    _navigationService = navigationService;
    _dataService = dataService;
    PopulateData();
}
```

Wait, we've added two parameters to the constructor but haven't changed the code that adds them to the DI container. How does that work? Well, the container is smart enough to pass them because both of those interfaces are also registered. Pretty cool!

3.   Next, update PopulateData to get the data the view model needs from _dataService:

```
public void PopulateData()
{
    items.Clear();
    foreach(var item in _dataService.GetItems())
    {
        items.Add(item);
    }
    allItems = new
    ObservableCollection<MediaItem>(Items);
    mediums = new ObservableCollection<string>
    {
        AllMediums
    };
    foreach(var itemType in _dataService
        .GetItemTypes())
    {
        mediums.Add(itemType.ToString());
    }
    selectedMedium = Mediums[0];
}
```

You need to add the AllMediums string constant with a value of "All" to the mediums collection because it's not part of the persisted data. It's only needed for the UI filter. Be sure to add this constant definition to MainViewModel.

4. Finally, when the hidden AddEditCommand calls the AddEdit method, instead of adding hardcoded items to the collection, you will pass selectedItemId as a parameter when navigating to ItemDetailsPage:

```
private void AddEdit()
{
    var selectedItemId = -1;
    if (SelectedMediaItem != null)
    {
        selectedItemId = SelectedMediaItem.Id;
    }
    _navigationService.NavigateTo("ItemDetailsPage",
      selectedItemId);
}
```

That's it for MainViewModel. Now let's work on the ItemDetailsPage.

Handling parameters in ItemDetailsPage

To accept a parameter passed from another page during navigation, you must override the OnNavigatedTo method in ItemDetailsPage.xaml.cs. The NavigationEventArgs parameter contains a property named Parameter. In our case, we passed an int containing the selected item's Id. Cast this Parameter property to int and pass it to a method on the ViewModel named InitializeItemDetailData, which will be created in the next section:

```
protected override void OnNavigatedTo(NavigationEventArgs
e)
{
    base.OnNavigatedTo(e);
    var itemId = (int)e.Parameter;
    if (itemId > 0)
    {
        ViewModel.InitializeItemDetailData(itemId);
    }
}
```

In the next section, we'll add the final piece of the puzzle, the ItemDetailsViewModel class.

Creating the ItemDetailsViewModel class

To add or edit items in the application, you will need a view model to bind to ItemDetails Page. Right-click the ViewModels folder in **Solution Explorer** and add a new class named ItemDetailsViewModel.

The class will inherit from ObservableObject like MainViewModel. The full class can be found on GitHub at https://github.com/PacktPublishing/Learn-WinUI-3-Second-Edition/blob/master/Chapter04/Complete/MyMediaCollection/ViewModels/ItemDetailsViewModel.cs. Let's review some of the important members of the class.

The constructor receives the two services from the container and calls PopulateLists to populate ComboBox data from the data service:

```
public ItemDetailsViewModel(INavigationService
  navigationService, IDataService dataService)
{
    _navigationService = navigationService;
    _dataService = dataService;
    PopulateLists();
}
```

A public method named InitializeItemDetailData will accept the itemId parameter passed by ItemDetailsPage.OnNavigatedTo. It will call methods to populate the lists and initializes an IsDirty flag to enable or disable the SaveCommand:

```
public void InitializeItemDetailData(int itemId)
{
    _selectedItemId = itemId;
    PopulateExistingItem(_dataService);
    IsDirty = false;
}
```

The PopulateExistingItem method will add existing item data if the page is in edit mode, and PopulateLists, called from the constructor, fills the drop-down data to be bound to the view:

```
private void PopulateExistingItem(IDataService dataService)
{
    if (_selectedItemId > 0)
    {
        var item = _dataService.GetItem(_selectedItemId);
        Mediums.Clear();
        foreach (string medium in dataService.GetMediums
          (item.MediaType).Select(m => m.Name))
            Mediums.Add(medium);
        _itemId = item.Id;
        ItemName = item.Name;
        SelectedMedium = item.MediumInfo.Name;
        SelectedLocation = item.Location.ToString();
        SelectedItemType = item.MediaType.ToString();
    }
}
```

```
    }
    private void PopulateLists()
    {
        ItemTypes.Clear();
        foreach (string iType in Enum.GetNames
          (typeof(ItemType)))
            ItemTypes.Add(iType);
        LocationTypes.Clear();
        foreach (string lType in Enum.GetNames
          (typeof(LocationType)))
            LocationTypes.Add(lType);
        Mediums = new TestObservableCollection<string>();
    }
```

Most of this view model's properties are straightforward, but `SelectedItemType` has some logic to repopulate the list of `Mediums` based on the `ItemType` selected. For instance, if you are adding a book to the collection, there's no need to see the DVD or CD mediums in the selection list. We'll handle this custom logic in `OnSelectedItemTypeChanged`:

```
    partial void OnSelectedItemTypeChanged(string value)
    {
        IsDirty = true;
        Mediums.Clear();
        if (!string.IsNullOrWhiteSpace(value))
        {
            foreach (string med in _dataService.GetMediums
              ((ItemType)Enum.Parse(typeof(ItemType),
                SelectedItemType)).Select(m => m.Name))
                Mediums.Add(med);
        }
    }
```

Lastly, let's look at the code that `SaveCommand` and `CancelCommand` will invoke to save and navigate back to `MainPage`:

```
    private void Save()
    {
        MediaItem item;
        if (_itemId > 0)
        {
            item = _dataService.GetItem(_itemId);
            item.Name = ItemName;
            item.Location = (LocationType)Enum.Parse
              (typeof(LocationType), SelectedLocation);
```

```
            item.MediaType = (ItemType)Enum.Parse(typeof
              (ItemType), SelectedItemType);
            item.MediumInfo = _dataService.GetMedium
              (SelectedMedium);
            _dataService.UpdateItem(item);
        }
        else
        {
            item = new MediaItem
            {
                Name = ItemName,
                Location = (LocationType)Enum.Parse
                  (typeof(LocationType), SelectedLocation),
                MediaType = (ItemType)Enum.Parse(typeof
                  (ItemType), SelectedItemType),
                MediumInfo = _dataService.GetMedium
                  (SelectedMedium)
            };
            _dataService.AddItem(item);
        }
        _navigationService.GoBack();
    }
    private void Cancel()
    {
        _navigationService.GoBack();
    }
```

The other change needed before you run the application to test the new page is to consume
`ItemDetailsViewModel` from `ItemDetailsPage.xaml.cs`:

```
public ItemDetailsPage()
{
    ViewModel = App.HostContainer.Services.GetService
      <ItemDetailsViewModel>();
    this.InitializeComponent();
}
public ItemDetailsViewModel ViewModel;
```

Now, run the app and try to add or edit an item—you should see the new page. If you are editing, you
should also see the existing item data in the controls:

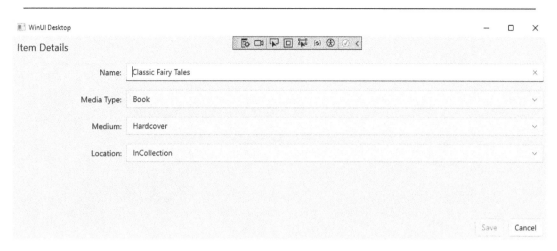

Figure 4.2 – The Item Details page with edited data populated

Great! Now when you save, you should see any added records or edited data appear on `MainPage`. Things are really starting to take shape in our project. Let's review what we have learned about WinUI and MVVM in this chapter.

Summary

You have learned quite a bit about MVVM and WinUI page navigation in this chapter. You have learned how to create and consume services in your application, and you have leveraged DI and DI containers to keep your view models and services loosely coupled. Understanding and using DI is key to building testable, maintainable code. At this point, you should have enough knowledge to create a robust, testable WinUI application.

In the next chapter, you will learn about more of the available controls and libraries in WinUI 3.

Questions

1. How do DI and IoC relate?

2. How do you navigate to the previous page in a WinUI application?

3. What object do we use to manage dependencies?

4. With Microsoft's DI container, what method can you call to get an object instance?

5. What is the name of the framework that queries objects in memory?

6. What event argument property can you access to get a parameter passed to another `Page`?

7. Which dictionary type is safe to use across threads?

5

Exploring WinUI Controls

WinUI 3 and the Windows App SDK offer many controls and APIs for developers building desktop applications for Windows. The WinUI controls include some controls not previously available to Windows developers, as well as updated controls that were already available in WinUI 2.x and **UWP**. Using these new and updated controls with WinUI 3 enables their use in older versions of Windows that did not previously support this full suite of components. Developers can also leverage Windows App SDK APIs to get direct access to Windows features.

In this chapter, we will cover the following topics:

- Learning more about the controls that are available in WinUI 3

- Exploring the **WinUI 3 Gallery** app for Windows to learn about the WinUI controls and design guidance

- How other Windows App SDK APIs provide Windows developers access to features such as power management and notifications

- How to implement `SplitButton` and `TeachingTip` controls in your own apps

By the end of this chapter, you will have a greater understanding of the controls and libraries in WinUI 3. You will also feel comfortable using the WinUI 3 Gallery app for Windows to explore the controls and find samples that demonstrate how to use them.

Technical requirements

To follow along with the examples in this chapter, please reference the *Technical requirements* section of *Chapter 2, Configuring the Development Environment and Creating the Project*.

The source code for this chapter is available on GitHub here: `https://github.com/PacktPublishing/Learn-WinUI-3-Second-Edition/tree/master/Chapter05`.

Understanding what WinUI offers developers

In *Chapter 1, Introduction to WinUI*, you learned some background information about the origins of WinUI and UWP. That chapter also covered some of the controls available in the various releases of WinUI. Now, it's time to explore a few of these in more detail. Let's start by looking at a list of controls available to developers in WinUI 3:

Animated icon	Hyperlink button	Scroll viewer
Animated visual player	Images and image	Semantic zoom
Auto-suggest box	brushes	Shapes
Breadcrumb bar	Info bar	Slider
Button	List view	Split button
Calendar date picker	Media playback	Split view
Calendar view	Menu bar	Swipe control
Checkbox	Menu flyout	Tab view
Color picker	Navigation view	Teaching tip
Combo box	Number box	Text block
Command bar	Parallax view	Text box
Command bar flyout	Password box	Time picker
Content dialog	Person picture	Toggle switch
Context menu	Pips pager	Toggle button
Date picker	Progress bar	Toggle split button
Drop down button	Progress ring	Tooltips
Expander	Radio button	Tree view
Flip view	Rating control	Two-pane view
Flyout	Repeat button	Web view
Grid view	Rich edit box	
Hyperlink	Rich text block	

Figure 5.1 – List of WinUI 3 controls

This is quite an extensive list of controls available to developers in the Windows App SDK.

> **Tip**
>
> For an up-to-date list of the available controls, you can check this page on *Microsoft Learn*: https://learn.microsoft.com/windows/apps/design/controls/#alphabetical-index.

If you have developed Windows applications before, most of these control names probably look familiar to you. In the sections ahead, we'll get an overview of some controls that you may not have seen before.

Animated visual player (Lottie)

The `AnimatedVisualPlayer` control, shown in *Figure 5.2*, is a WinUI control that can display **Lottie animations**. Lottie is an open source library that can parse and display animations on Windows, the web, iOS, and Android. These animations are created by designers in tools such as **Adobe After Effects** and exported in JSON format. You can learn more about Lottie animations at the official website, `http://airbnb.io/lottie/#/`:

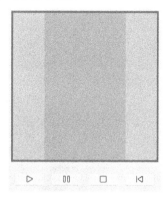

Figure 5.2 – The AnimatedVisualPlayer control

Navigation View

`NavigationView` provides a user-friendly page navigation system. Use it to give users quick access to all your application's top-level pages. `NavigationView` can be configured to appear as a menu at the top of the application, with each page's link appearing like a tab across the top of the page:

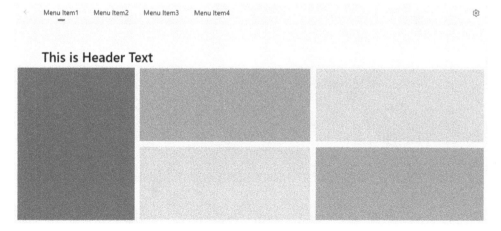

Figure 5.3 – NavigationView configured at the top of a page

`NavigationView` can also be configured to appear on the left-hand side of the page. This is a view that should be familiar to Windows and Android users. This menu format is commonly known as a **hamburger menu**. This is how the view appears when the menu is in a collapsed state:

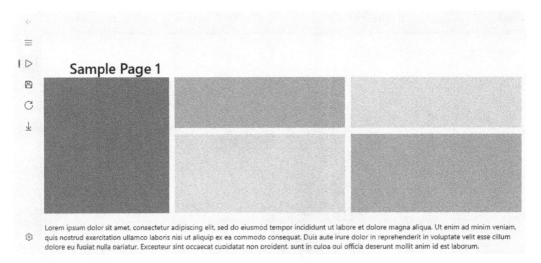

Figure 5.4 – A collapsed left NavigationView control

In either configuration, `NavigationView` can hide or show a back arrow to navigate to the previous page and has a **Settings** menu item to show the application's settings page. If your application does not have a settings page, this item should be hidden. When the left menu is expanded by clicking the *hamburger* icon below the back arrow, the menu text is displayed, along with the respective icons:

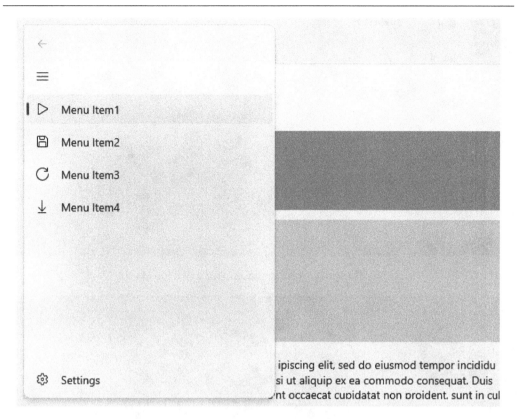

Figure 5.5 – The expanded left NavigationView control

Everything on the menu is configurable. You can group pages with the **Actions** section. You can hide or show the search box, the **More Info** link, and, as we previously mentioned, the **Settings** item. If your application navigates multiple top-level pages, you should absolutely consider using NavigationView.

Parallax view

Parallax scrolling is a design concept that links scrolling a list or web page to scrolling a background image or other animations. A great example of a website with parallax scrolling is *History of the Web* (https://webflow.com/ix2). The ParallaxView control brings this concept to your WinUI applications. You link ParallaxView to ListView and a background image, and it will provide a parallax effect when ListView is scrolled. There are settings to control the relationship between scrolling the list and the amount the image scrolls. This effect has a great impact on users when it is not overused:

Figure 5.6 – The ParallaxView control scrolled to the top of a list

Figure 5.7 – The ParallaxView control scrolled partially through a list

Rating control

Everyone is familiar with rating controls. You see them on shopping websites, streaming apps, and online surveys. The WinUI `RatingControl` control allows users to rate items in your application from 1 to 5 stars:

Output:
3

Figure 5.8 – RatingControl displaying the user's rating

The control can also allow you to clear a rating by swiping left on the control and can show a placeholder value before the user has provided their own rating. Applications frequently use the placeholder value as a means of showing users the average rating given by other users.

Now that we have discussed a few of the controls that were added with WinUI, let's explore a Windows application that makes it easy to explore them on your own.

Exploring the WinUI 3 Gallery app for Windows

Because there are so many powerful and configurable WinUI controls available, the WinUI team at Microsoft decided to create an application that allows Windows developers to explore and even try the controls. **WinUI 3 Gallery** is a great tool to get familiar with the controls, decide which ones are a good fit for your application, and get some sample code and design guidance.

> **Note**
>
> There is also a **WinUI 2 Gallery** app for UWP developers. The two apps used to be a single app called **XAML Controls Gallery**.

To install the WinUI 3 Gallery app, you can visit its Microsoft Store page on the web (`https://apps.microsoft.com/store/detail/winui-3-gallery/9P3JFPWWDZRC`) or launch the Microsoft Store app for Windows and search for `WinUI 3 Gallery`. The Gallery app itself is open source. You can browse the code to learn more about it on GitHub: `https://github.com/microsoft/WinUI-Gallery`.

Once it's been installed, launch the application:

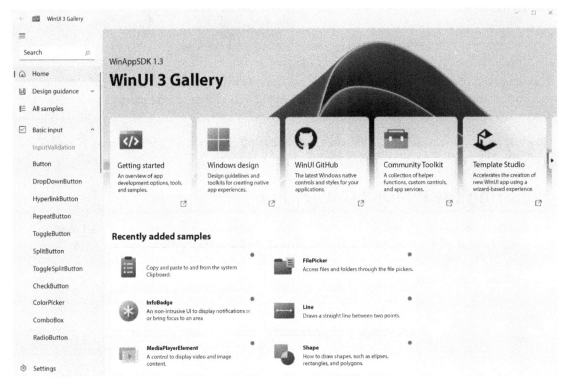

Figure 5.9 – The WinUI 3 Gallery application

In the **Recently added samples** and **Recently updated samples** sections of the application's main page, you can quickly see which controls and samples have been recently added or updated. The application uses a navigation system that should look familiar. The app uses a `NavigationView` control, and the left-hand menu allows for quickly browsing or searching the various controls in the gallery.

> **Note**
>
> If you search for the controls shown in the previous section, you may notice that the screenshots provided for the controls in this chapter were taken from the WinUI 3 Gallery application.

Learning about the ScrollViewer control

Suppose you were considering adding scrolling capability to a region of a page in your application. In the gallery application, you can click **Scrolling** on the left navigation menu and then click on the **ScrollViewer** card on the **Scrolling** page. That will bring you to the details page for the WinUI `ScrollViewer` control:

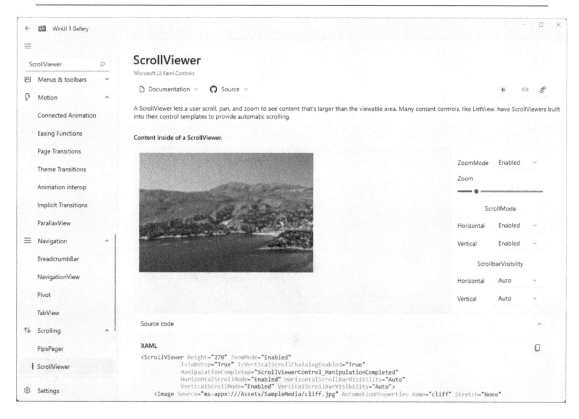

Figure 5.10 – The ScrollViewer control detail page in XAML Controls Gallery

The control details page includes several sections. The header area provides a brief description of the control and its purpose. The right pane provides useful links to online documentation, other related controls in the gallery, and a link to provide feedback on the current gallery page.

The middle area of the page itself contains three sections: a rendered control, a functional control, and a properties panel. Using the properties panel, you can update some of the properties of `ScrollViewer` and see the rendered control immediately update. In the bottom center, you will find a panel containing the source code for the rendered control. The source control pane is very handy for copying the code to use as a starting point in your own project.

The gallery application's design also responds well to being resized. If you drag the right-hand side of the window to make it as narrow as possible, you will see the left and right panels collapse, and the center area will realign to a single vertical column:

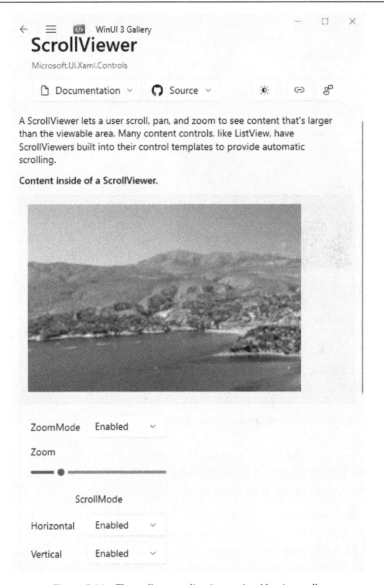

Figure 5.11 – The gallery application resized horizontally

You can imagine this view would fit well on a **Microsoft Surface Go laptop** or other small PC.

Take some time to explore the controls in the gallery. Some of the code samples can be quite lengthy. Try changing some control properties and notice how the XAML code updates to reflect the new property values. This is a great way to learn XAML and familiarize yourself with the WinUI controls.

Now, let's take a tour of the new features of WinUI 3.

Reviewing what's new in WinUI 3 and the Windows App SDK

Although WinUI 3 is a major release, the number of new features, as compared to WinUI 2.x, is not extensive. That may be surprising to many people, but simply creating WinUI 3 and the Windows App SDK as a standalone release was quite an undertaking. We'll look at the most significant features in the following subsections.

Backward compatibility

To make WinUI applications compatible with more versions of Windows (it works with Windows 10, version 1809 and later), the WinUI team had to extract the UWP controls from the Windows SDK and move them to the new `Microsoft.UI.*` libraries in the Windows App SDK. The result of this work not only creates compatibility with more versions of Windows but also enables developers to consume WinUI, regardless of whether they are using .NET or Win32 as the underlying platform. C# developers can build .NET apps with WinUI for Desktop projects, and C++ developers can consume WinUI on the Win32 platform.

Fluent UI and modern look and feel

Developers who maintain **Windows Presentation Form** (**WPF**), WinForms, and **Microsoft Foundation Class** (**MFC**) applications aren't easily able to achieve the modern look and feel of Windows with **Fluent UI** the way you can in WinUI. We will be covering Fluent UI in depth in *Chapter 7, Fluent Design System for Windows Applications*.

Visual Studio tooling

Visual Studio can now add WinUI project templates without installing a separate extension from the Visual Studio Marketplace. As discussed in the opening chapter, WinUI support can be added along with the **.NET Desktop Development** workload for Visual Studio. Starting a new project with WinUI in Visual Studio is literally as easy as going to **File** | **New Project**.

The WebView2 control

One new control available to developers in WinUI 3 is `WebView2`. This new version of `WebView` is built on the Chromium-based Microsoft Edge web browser. If you need to embed some web content into your app, `WebView2` is the control you should use to ensure maximum compatibility with modern web standards.

Here is a screenshot of **WebView2** running in the **WinUI 3 Gallery** app:

Figure 5.12 – WebView2 running in the WinUI 3 Gallery application

Web content can be loaded into the control from the web or local network, from files in local storage, or from files embedded into the application's binaries. Here are some examples of loading into WebView2 from each type of source:

```
<!-- Load a website. -->
<WebView2 x:Name="WebView_Web"
  Source="https://www.packtpub.com"/>
<!— Load web files from local storage. -->
<WebView2 x:Name="WebView_Local" Source="ms-appdata:
  ///local/site/index.html"/>
<!— Load web files embedded from the app package. -->
<WebView2 x:Name="WebView_Embedded" Source="ms-appx-
  web:///web/index.html"/>
```

If you have an existing application written for the web, then the WebView2 control is a great way to integrate it into your new WinUI client application.

Let's shift gears for a moment and talk about some features of the Windows App SDK outside of the WinUI 3 controls.

What's new in the Windows App SDK

You know by now that WinUI 3 is a part of the Windows App SDK. The Windows App SDK has its own versions, while WinUI 3 will always be known as WinUI 3. The latest stable release of the Windows App SDK at the time of this writing is version 1.4. In this section, we will review some of the Windows App SDK features that are outside the controls in WinUI. For a complete list of the current Windows App SDK features, you can review this page on *Microsoft Learn*: `https://learn.microsoft.com/windows/apps/windows-app-sdk/#windows-app-sdk-features`.

Power management

Your app can subscribe and respond to power management events as part of the Windows App SDK's app lifecycle API. Some of the events exposed by the `PowerManager` class in the SDK include the following:

- `BatteryStatusChanged`: Raised when the status of the battery in the system has changed. Use the `BatteryStatus` property to get the current status.

- `DisplayStatusChanged`: Raised when the status of the display where the app is running changes. Use the `DisplayStatus` property to get the current status.

- `EffectivePowerModeChanged`: Raised when the effective power mode of the system has changed. These can also be referred to as power plans, such as battery saver and high performance. Use the `EffectivePowerMode` property to get the current mode.

- `SystemSuspendStatusChanged`: Raised when the system is suspended or resumes. In UWP, these types of events were part of the built-in lifecycle in the `App` class. Use the `SystemSuspendStatus` property to get the current status.

- `UserPresenceStatusChanged`: Raised when the system detects a change in the user's presence. Use the `UserPresenceStatus` property to get the current status.

A full list of `PowerManager` events and properties can be viewed on *Microsoft Learn*: `https://learn.microsoft.com/windows/windows-app-sdk/api/winrt/microsoft.windows.system.power.powermanager`.

Responding to changes in these events can help your app be intelligent in how and when it performs resource-intensive actions. You may have some background processing that should only be performed when a system is plugged in or its battery capacity is above a certain percentage. You could also choose to suspend screen animations or dashboard updates when a user's screen is dimmed or turned off in order to conserve power.

Next, let's discuss the windowing capabilities in the Windows App SDK.

Window management

The Windows App SDK has some limited window management capabilities that can be leveraged by using the AppWindow class. By using some of the interop APIs, your app can get the HWND and WindowId values for the current window. In Win32 development, a **window handle** (or **HWND**) uniquely identifies a window object in the operating system. WindowId can then be used to get a reference to the current AppWindow object:

```
var appWindow = Microsoft.UI.Windowing.AppWindow
  .GetFromWindowId(windowId)
```

Most of the properties on AppWindow are read-only. You can get information such as its size, position, visibility, and the WindowId value of its owner. One writable property of AppWindow is Title. Setting Title allows you to change the text in the title bar of the current window.

Push notifications and app notifications

Push notifications can be used to either interact with the app without notifying the user or display a toast notification in Windows. The latter is considered an **app notification** and is most familiar to users. The other raw notifications that trigger within the app are used for things such as waking the app from an inactive state or for data syncing purposes.

The Windows App SDK supports both types of notifications. The APIs for these are in the Microsoft.Windows.PushNotifications and Microsoft.Windows.AppNotifications namespaces. Exploring notifications is beyond the scope of this chapter, but you can explore some quick starts on *Microsoft Learn* from the *Push notifications overview* page: https://learn.microsoft.com/windows/apps/windows-app-sdk/notifications/push-notifications/. We will add notifications to our project in *Chapter 8, Adding Windows Notifications to WinUI Applications*.

Now that we've learned about some of the new features in WinUI and the Windows App SDK, let's get back to our project and add a couple of new controls to it.

Adding some new controls to the project

In this section, we are going to use two controls that are only available to Windows applications with WinUI. We are going to change the **Save** button to SplitButton to allow users to save and return to a list of items, or save and continue adding another item to the item details page. Then, we will add a TeachingTip control to inform users of the new saving capabilities. To follow along with these steps, you can use the starter project on GitHub (https://github.com/PacktPublishing/Learn-WinUI-3-Second-Edition/tree/master/Chapter05/Start). Let's start by updating the **Save** button.

Using the SplitButton control

Follow these steps:

1. First, in `ItemDetailsViewModel`, add a new `SaveItemAndContinue` method to be bound to the `Click` event of our new `SplitButton` control:

```
public void SaveItemAndContinue()
{
    Save();
    _itemId = 0;
    ItemName = string.Empty;
    SelectedMedium = null;
    SelectedLocation = null;
    SelectedItemType = null;
    IsDirty = false;
}
```

In the `SaveItemAndContinue` method, we are calling `Save` and then resetting all the item state data so that it's ready for a new item to be entered. The one problem here is that `Save` currently navigates back to the previous page. Let's fix that.

2. To remove the call from `Save` to return to the previous page, we need a new method for the **Save** button to use. Create a new method named `SaveItemAndReturn`:

```
public void SaveItemAndReturn()
{
    Save();
    _navigationService.GoBack();
}
```

Here, we are calling `Save` and then navigating back to the previous page. The call to `_navigationService.GoBack` can now be removed from `Save`.

3. We're currently using `x:Bind` to bind directly to the save methods instead of using `ICommand`. So, you can remove the `RelayCommand` attribute from `Save` and the `CanSaveItem` method from `ItemDetailsViewModel`. You will also need to remove the `NotifyCanExecuteChangedFor` attribute from the `isDirty` private member.

4. Finally, open `ItemDetailsPage` and update the **Save** button to be a `SplitButton` control:

```
<SplitButton x:Name="SaveButton"
             Content="Save and Return"
             Margin="8,8,0,8"
             Click="{x:Bind ViewModel
                .SaveItemAndReturn}"
```

```
                    IsEnabled="{x:Bind ViewModel.IsDirty,
                        Mode=OneWay}">
        <SplitButton.Flyout>
            <Flyout>
              <StackPanel>
                <Button Content="Save and Create New"
                        Click="{x:Bind ViewModel
                          .SaveItemAndContinue}"
                        IsEnabled="{x:Bind
                          ViewModel.IsDirty,
                            Model=OneWay}"
                        Background="Transparent"/>
                <Button Content="Save and Return"
                        Click="{x:Bind ViewModel
                          .SaveItemAndReturn}"
                        IsEnabled="{x:Bind
                          ViewModel.IsDirty, Mode=OneWay}"
                        Background="Transparent"/>
              </StackPanel>
            </Flyout>
        </SplitButton.Flyout>
      </SplitButton>
```

The content of SplitButton has been updated to Save and Return. We've also updated the binding to use the Click event to invoke the action and the IsEnabled property with IsDirty. A new child Flyout item is also added. Flyout contains a StackPanel control with Button controls for both the **Save and Return** and the new **Save and Create New** action, with the Click event invoking SaveItemAndContinue.

5.   That's it! Now, run the application and try out this new feature. Here's how the new button looks when you click the drop-down arrow:

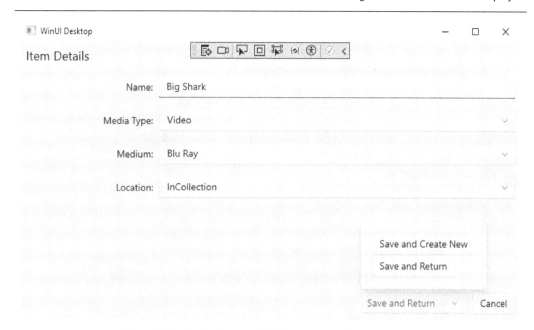

Figure 5.13 – Using the new SplitButton control to save items

Adding a TeachingTip control to the Save button

A `TeachingTip` control is a great way to educate users about features in your application. It is a small popup with header text and content text. You may have seen them in some of the Windows applications you use.

`TeachingTip` can either be linked to a control on the page or it can be placed directly on the page with an optional `PreferredPlacement` property, controlling where it appears on the page. It can be configured to be dismissed by the user with a **Close** button or automatically when the user starts interacting with the page.

To add a `TeachingTip` control for our `SplitButton` control, add it to the `Resources` control in `ItemDetailsPage`, like so:

```
<SplitButton x:Name="SaveButton" Content="Save and Return"
  Margin="8,8,0,8" Command="{x:Bind ViewModel.SaveCommand}">
    <SplitButton.Flyout>
        <Flyout>
            <Button Content="Save and Create New"
            Command="{x:Bind ViewModel
               .SaveAndContinueCommand}"
                Background="Transparent"/>
        </Flyout>
```

```
    </SplitButton.Flyout>
    <SplitButton.Resources>
        <TeachingTip x:Name="SavingTip"
                     Target="{x:Bind SaveButton}"
                     Title="Save and create new"
                     Subtitle="Use the dropdown button
                     option to save your item and create
                     another.">
        </TeachingTip>
    </SplitButton.Resources>
</SplitButton>
```

Inside the `TeachingTip` control, we're binding `Target` to `SaveButton` and setting `Title` and `Subtitle` to educate users about the new **Save and create new** feature.

There's an additional call needed in the `ItemDetailsPage` constructor to make the tip appear:

```
SavingTip.IsOpen = true;
```

If you run the application now, `TeachingTip` is going to appear every time the user opens `ItemDetailsPage`. This is going to quickly annoy our users. We can add a little bit of code to `ItemDetailsPage.xaml.cs` to save a user-level setting indicating that the current user has already seen this `TeachingTip` control. Then, the next time we load the page, we'll check this setting so that the app can skip the code that displays the tip.

We're going to leverage Windows local storage to save and load the user setting:

```
Windows.Storage.ApplicationDataContainer localSettings =
    Windows.Storage.ApplicationData.Current.LocalSettings;
// Load the user setting
string haveExplainedSaveSetting = localSettings.Values
    [nameof(SavingTip)] as string;
// If the user has not seen the save tip, display it
if (!bool.TryParse(haveExplainedSaveSetting, out bool
    result) || !result)
{
    SavingTip.IsOpen = true;
    // Save the teaching tip setting
    localSettings.Values[nameof(SavingTip)] = "true";
}
```

Now, the user will only see this tip the first time they load `ItemDetailsPage`.

Let's see our `TeachingTip` control in action. Run the application, select an item, and click **Add/Edit Item** to open `ItemDetailsPage`:

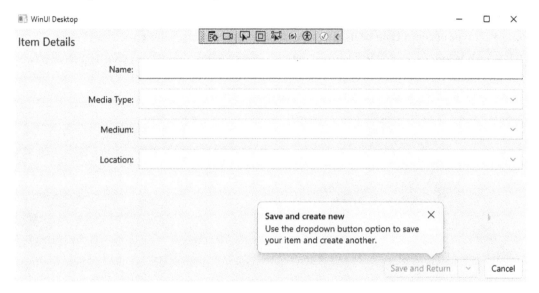

Figure 5.14 – Using the new TeachingTip control

Now, the application has a new feature and a great way to inform users of how to use it. Let's wrap up and discuss what we have learned in this chapter.

Summary

In this chapter, we explored many of the controls available in WinUI 3. We learned that the **WinUI 3 Gallery** application is a great tool for exploring the controls available to WinUI developers. We also explored some of the features in the Windows App SDK that are not part of WinUI. At the end, we learned about, and added, a couple of new WinUI controls to our application.

In the next chapter, we will learn more about services and will start persisting the data for our media items between sessions.

Questions

1. Which WinUI control can display Lottie animations?
2. Which WinUI control can display HTML content with the Chromium-based Microsoft Edge browser?
3. Can you create a WinUI 3 app with C++?

4. Which control would you use to educate users about a new feature?

5. Which application can you download from the Microsoft Store to learn about all the WinUI controls?

6. What type of control can be used to save and load user settings between sessions?

7. Which Windows App SDK feature would you use to notify users when your app has a new message to be viewed?

6

Leveraging Data and Services

Managing data is central to the operation of most applications. Learning how to load, maintain, and save that data is an important aspect of WinUI development. Two of the most important aspects of data management are **state management** and the **service locator pattern**. We will be covering these concepts and putting some of them to use in our application.

In this chapter, we will cover the following topics:

- Understanding the WinUI application lifecycle
- Learning to use **SQLite** to store application data
- Learning to use the **object-relational mapper (ORM) Dapper** to quickly map objects in a data service
- Continuing to explore the service locator pattern and implementing it with our data service

By the end of this chapter, you will have a working understanding of the WinUI application lifecycle and will know how to manage data and state in your projects.

Technical requirements

To follow along with the examples in this chapter, the following software is required:

- Windows 10 version 1803 (version 17134) or newer
- Visual Studio 2022 or newer, with the .NET desktop development workload configured for Windows App SDK development

The source code for this chapter is available on GitHub at `https://github.com/Packt Publishing/Learn-WinUI-3-Second-Edition/tree/master/Chapter06`.

Managing application state with app lifecycle events

Before working with data in any application, it is important to understand the application lifecycle for the target application platform. We have touched on these concepts briefly, but now, it's time to take a deeper dive into the Windows application lifecycle for **WinUI on Desktop** applications.

Exploring Windows application lifecycle events

WinUI on desktop applications has a slightly different set of lifecycle events than other desktop .NET applications. WPF and **Windows Forms (WinForms)** applications are either running or they're not. There are several events that occur while launching and shutting down WPF and WinForms applications:

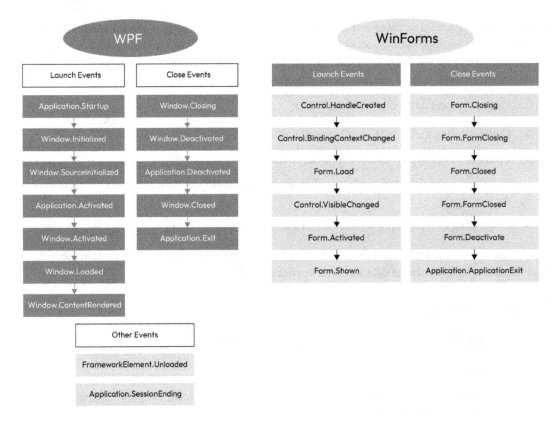

Figure 6.1 – WPF and WinForms application lifecycle events

> **Note**
>
> We won't go into the details here, as our primary focus is building WinUI 3 applications. However, for the two WPF events that fall outside of the launch and close, their sequences are as follows:
>
> 1. `FrameworkElement.Unloaded`: This event fires when an element is removed from the WPF visual tree. It does not fire during application shutdown.
>
> 2. `Application.SessionEnding`: This event fires when the current Windows user logs off or shuts down Windows. In the event handler, you can request that Windows cancels the process by setting the `SessionEndingCancelEventArgs.Cancel` property to `true`.

Lifecycle events of WinUI applications

Let's talk about the WinUI lifecycle. Lifecycle events give you a chance to initialize any data and state when your application starts execution, and this allows you to clean up or save the state when the application is closed. In UWP applications, you also had the ability to handle events when the application was suspended or resumed because of a user or operating system action. WinUI, like other .NET desktop applications, doesn't have this ability.

In the `Application` and `Window` classes, there are only a couple of events that can be handled. Every `Application` class overrides the `OnLaunched` method. This method will be invoked exactly once, when the application is launched either by a user or the operating system. We've already worked with the `OnLaunched` method in our sample application. It's where `MainWindow` is created and where we added a call to the method to configure our IOC container. In a new WinUI application, the `OnLaunched` method will look like this:

```
protected override void OnLaunched(Microsoft.UI.Xaml.
LaunchActivatedEventArgs args)
{
    m_window = new MainWindow();
    m_window.Activate();
}
```

The `Application` and `Window` classes only inherit from the .NET `Object` class, so there are no inherited events to leverage either. This is not the case with the `Page` class, which we will discuss shortly. First, we're going to discuss `Window`, which has a couple of events we can leverage when managing an app's lifecycle.

The `Window` class in WinUI does not have a `Loaded` event, which is used in a WPF `Window` class to indicate that the window and its contents are loaded and available for interaction. The `Window.Activated` event can be used in place of a `Loaded` event, but the `Activated` event fires every time the window receives focus. If this is your only option, you will need to add a flag to check whether it's the first time that `Activated` has fired.

The other lifecycle event in `Window` is the `Closed` event, which fires when the window has closed. If it is the last remaining window, usually `MainWindow`, the application will end after the window closes. This is where you should save any application data and state information.

This is the extent of the application lifecycle events provided out of the box by the `Application` and `Window` classes. However, you can tap into some other events provided by `FrameworkElement`, which is a base class of `Page` and all the other controls in WinUI.

Additional lifecycle events with FrameworkElement objects

Every control in WinUI inherits from `Control`, which inherits from `FrameworkElement`. Even the `Page` control, which we added to the **My Media Collection** app to provide navigation to an item details view, inherits from `Control`, through its inheritance from `UserControl`.

The `FrameworkElement` class provides three useful events that developers can leverage for the application lifecycle:

- `Loading`: This event occurs when the loading process has started. This event can be leveraged to start fetching and processing data from services or other sources. You could also start loading data sooner, in the constructor of the current `Window` or `Page`, or even in `Application.OnLoaded`.

- `Loaded`: The `Loaded` event is invoked when the current element and all its children are loaded and ready for interaction. Do not try to manipulate these elements before they are loaded, or the app will raise a runtime exception.

- `Unloaded`: This event is fired when the current element has been unloaded and removed from the **visual tree**. If you are handling this event for `Page`, you can use this to clean up resources or save any state for the page.

> **Note**
>
> We haven't discussed the WinUI visual tree up to this point. The concept of trees, physical and logical, in WinUI is the same as in other XAML frameworks. We will discuss the physical tree and logical tree in more detail when we discuss debugging WinUI applications in *Chapter 11, Debugging WinUI Apps with Visual Studio*. To learn more now, Microsoft Learn has a great WPF article about trees: `https://learn.microsoft.com/dotnet/desktop/wpf/advanced/trees-in-wpf`.

You can handle the `Loaded` event for any control in your current view, whether it's `Window` or `Page`, but always keep performance in mind. The `Loaded` event for the topmost `FrameworkElement` in the visual tree will not be fired until those of all its children have been completed. Network and filesystem operations can be expensive, so try to minimize and consolidate the calls to load the data needed to present your view whenever possible.

> **Note**
>
> For more information about handling lifecycle events, read the following Microsoft Learn page: `https://learn.microsoft.com/windows/apps/windows-app-sdk/applifecycle/applifecycle`.

Now that you have a solid understanding of WinUI's lifecycle, let's start working with some real data that will need to be persisted between user sessions.

Creating a SQLite data store

Until this point, the **My Media Collection** project has only worked with data stored inside in-memory collections. This means that every time the application is closed, all the user's data is lost. It has also meant calling a method to populate all the lists with hardcoded seed data each time the application is launched.

In the previous chapter, we took the first step in creating a maintainable data service for the application. By creating a data service class that implements `IDataService`, no changes will be required in the `ViewModel` classes when we start loading data from a database. This section will focus on creating a new `SqliteDataService` class so that we can use **SQLite** for data access. The starting code for this chapter can be found on GitHub at `https://github.com/PacktPublishing/Learn-WinUI-3-Second-Edition/tree/master/Chapter06/Start`.

What is SQLite?

SQLite (found at `https://sqlite.org/`) is a SQL-based database that is frequently used by mobile apps and simple desktop applications. It is a popular choice because it is small, fast, and self-contained in a single file. There are SQLite libraries available for virtually every platform. We will use Microsoft's **Microsoft.Data.Sqlite** ADO.NET provider for SQLite.

> **Note**
>
> For more information about Microsoft's SQLite provider, you can read `https://learn.microsoft.com/dotnet/standard/data/sqlite/`. To learn more about using SQLite with WinUI projects, check out this Microsoft Learn article: `https://learn.microsoft.com/windows/apps/develop/data-access/sqlite-data-access`.

Adding SQLite as a data service

Follow these steps:

1. Start by adding the **Microsoft.Data.Sqlite** NuGet package to the **MyMediaCollection** project by opening **Package Manager Console** from **View | Other Windows | Package Manager Console**

and running the following command. Also, make sure the **MyMediaCollection** project is selected in the **Package Manager Console** window's project dropdown before running this command:

```
Install-Package Microsoft.Data.Sqlite
```

Running this command is equivalent to finding and adding the package from the **NuGet Package Manager** window.

2.   When the process is complete, create a new class named `SqliteDataService` in the **Services** folder, and copy the contents of the `DataService` class into it as a starting point.

3.   Now, open **SqliteDataService.cs** and start by adding four `using` statements to the top of the file:

```
using Microsoft.Data.Sqlite;
using System.IO;
using System.Threading.Tasks;
using Windows.Storage;
```

The `System.IO` and `Windows.Storage` namespaces will be used when we initialize the SQLite database file, and we'll need the `System.Threading.Tasks` namespace imported to work with some `async` tasks.

4.   Next, add a new constant to the class to hold the database's filename:

```
private const string DbName = "mediaCollectionData.db";
```

5.   Now, let's create a private method to create or open the database file, create a `SqliteConnection` class for the database, open it, and return it to the caller. This method can be used throughout the class whenever a new database connection is needed. The database file will be created in the user's `LocalFolder`, which means the application's data will be saved with the user's local Windows profile data:

```
private async Task<SqliteConnection> GetOpenConnectionAsync()
{
    await ApplicationData.Current.LocalFolder.
CreateFileAsync(DbName, CreationCollisionOption.OpenIfExists).
AsTask().ConfigureAwait(false);
    string dbPath = Path.Combine(ApplicationData.Current.
LocalFolder.Path, DbName);
    var cn = new SqliteConnection($"Filename={dbPath}");
    cn.Open();
    return cn;
}
```

Note that we have declared this method as `async` and that it uses the `await` keyword when opening or creating the file. It is a good practice to use async/await when using external resources such as files, network connections, or databases to keep your application responsive.

> **Note**
>
> To find out more about async/await with C# and .NET, Microsoft Learn has a great article to get you started: `https://learn.microsoft.com/dotnet/csharp/asynchronous-programming/`.

6. Next, create two methods that will create the `MediaItems` and `Mediums` tables in the database. These will be called each time the app launches, but the SQL code only creates the tables if they do not exist. The `SqliteCommand` object accepts the `tableCommand` query string and `SqliteConnection`. It has several methods it can use to execute the command, depending on whether any data is expected to be returned by the query. In our case, no return values are expected, so `ExecuteNonQueryAsync` is the best of the async options for these two methods:

```
private async Task CreateMediumTableAsync(SqliteConnection db)
{
    string tableCommand = @"CREATE TABLE IF NOT
        EXISTS Mediums (Id INTEGER PRIMARY KEY AUTOINCREMENT NOT
NULL,
        Name NVARCHAR(30) NOT NULL,
        MediumType INTEGER NOT NULL)";
    using var createTable = new SqliteCommand(tableCommand, db);
    await createTable.ExecuteNonQueryAsync();
}
private async Task CreateMediaItemTableAsync(SqliteConnection
db)
{
    string tableCommand = @"CREATE TABLE IF NOT
        EXISTS MediaItems (Id INTEGER PRIMARY KEY AUTOINCREMENT,
        Name NVARCHAR(1000) NOT NULL,
        ItemType INTEGER NOT NULL,
        MediumId INTEGER NOT NULL,
        LocationType INTEGER,
        CONSTRAINT fk_mediums
        FOREIGN KEY(MediumId)
        REFERENCES Mediums(Id))";
    using var createTable = new SqliteCommand(tableCommand, db);
    await createTable.ExecuteNonQueryAsync();
}
```

7. Now, create a method for the `Mediums` table to insert a row into the table:

```
private async Task InsertMediumAsync(SqliteConnection db, Medium
medium)
```

```
{
    using var insertCommand = new SqliteCommand
    {
        Connection = db,
        CommandText = "INSERT INTO Mediums VALUES (NULL, @Name,
@MediumType);"
    };
    insertCommand.Parameters.AddWithValue("@Name", medium.Name);
    insertCommand.Parameters.AddWithValue("@MediumType", (int)
medium.MediaType);
    await insertCommand.ExecuteNonQueryAsync();
}
```

8. Now, we need another method that will read all the rows from the Mediums table:

```
private async Task<IList<Medium>>
GetAllMediumsAsync(SqliteConnection db)
{
    IList<Medium> mediums = new List<Medium>();
    using var selectCommand = new SqliteCommand("SELECT Id,
Name, MediumType FROM Mediums", db);
    using SqliteDataReader query = await selectCommand.
ExecuteReaderAsync();
    while (query.Read())
    {
        var medium = new Medium
        {
            Id = query.GetInt32(0),
            Name = query.GetString(1),
            MediaType = (ItemType)query.GetInt32(2)
        };
        mediums.Add(medium);
    }
    return mediums;
}
```

There's a bit of code needed for these two simple operations. The insert method needs to add parameters for each property to be saved in the table, and the select method uses a while loop to add each table's record to the collection. Let's see whether we can simplify this in the next section.

Before we implement the remaining methods for the **Create, Read, Update, Delete (CRUD)** operations, a new library must be added to the project to simplify the data access code we will write.

Leveraging a Micro ORM to simplify data access

As you saw in the previous section, writing data access code for even the simplest application can take some time.

ORMs, such as **Entity Framework Core** (**EF Core**), can greatly simplify and reduce the code required, but they can be overkill for a small app with just a handful of tables. In this chapter, we'll look at a **Micro ORM**. Micro ORMs are lightweight frameworks that handle mapping data between objects and data queries.

> **Note**
>
> EF Core is a popular ORM for .NET developers. If you want to learn more about how to use EF Core with your projects, you can view the Packt video *Entity Framework Core – a Full Tour* at `https://www.packtpub.com/product/entity-framework-core-a-full-tour-net-5-and-up-video/9781803242231`.

The framework we will be using for data access in our project, Dapper, is an open source .NET Micro ORM that was created by the developers at **Stack Overflow**. You can learn more about Dapper at `https://dapperlib.github.io/Dapper/` and get the package on NuGet: `https://www.nuget.org/packages/Dapper`.

Dapper is popular within the .NET community. While it doesn't offer some of the features of EF Core, such as model generation or entity change tracking, it does make it very easy to write a fast, slim data layer. When you add the `Dapper.Contrib` library (`https://www.nuget.org/packages/Dapper.Contrib`) into the mix, it is even easier to write the CRUD methods needed for your applications.

Adding Dapper to the project

Let's dive right into it:

1. Start by adding `Dapper` and `Dapper.Contrib` to the **MyMediaCollection** project. Open the **Package Manager Console** window again and add the two packages to your project:

   ```
   Install-Package Dapper
   Install-Package Dapper.Contrib
   ```

2. Now, revisit the `InsertMediaAsync` method. If we use the `QueryAsync` method provided by Dapper, we can reduce the code from our original method to this:

   ```
   private async Task InsertMediumAsync(SqliteConnection db, Medium medium)
   {
       var newIds = await db.QueryAsync<long>(
   ```

```
        $@"INSERT INTO Mediums
            ({nameof(medium.Name)}, MediumType)
            VALUES
            (@{nameof(medium.Name)}, @{nameof(medium.
    MediaType)});
        SELECT last_insert_rowid()", medium);
    medium.Id = (int)newIds.First();
}
```

The code we wrote to set the values of the query parameters is now gone. Dapper maps them for us from the medium object, which is passed into its QueryAsync method. You must ensure that the parameter names in the SQLite query match the property names on our object for Dapper's automatic mapping to work.

3. As a bonus, we can also get the generated ID back from the QueryAsync call by adding the following SQLite code, which will return it after the INSERT operation completes:

```
SELECT last_insert_rowid();
```

4. Next, update the code for GetAllMediumsAsync to use Dapper:

```
private async Task<IList<Medium>>
GetAllMediumsAsync(SqliteConnection db)
{
    var mediums =
        await db.QueryAsync<Medium>(@"SELECT Id,
                                            Name,
                                            MediumType AS
MediaType
                                       FROM Mediums");
    return mediums.ToList();
}
```

We've gone from 14 lines of code to only 2. Note, in the highlighted part of the query, how we use an alias of MediaType for the MediumType field. This is an easy way to map data to an object property that doesn't match the database field name, by simply renaming the field that's returned as part of the SQL select statement. Dapper has also helped us by directly returning a list of our Medium objects, instead of us having to use a while loop to iterate over the result set.

5. Next, create a query that will get all the media items to populate the main ListView control. This query is a little more complex because we join two tables, MediaItems and Mediums, on MediumId and return the data to be mapped to two corresponding objects, item and medium. These types are indicated by the first two generic types provided to the QueryAsync method. To perform this mapping, we give Dapper a lambda expression that directs it to set medium as the MediumInfo property of the item for each row that's returned from the query. The type of the returned object is defined by the third generic type provided to the

QueryAsync method. The remaining parameters will be mapped automatically by Dapper based on their property names:

```
private async Task<List<MediaItem>>
GetAllMediaItemsAsync(SqliteConnection db)
{
    var itemsResult = await db.QueryAsync<MediaItem, Medium,
MediaItem>
            (
                @"SELECT
                    [MediaItems].[Id],
                    [MediaItems].[Name],
                    [MediaItems].[ItemType] AS MediaType,
                    [MediaItems].[LocationType] AS Location,
                    [Mediums].[Id],
                    [Mediums].[Name],
                    [Mediums].[MediumType] AS MediaType
                FROM
                    [MediaItems]
                JOIN
                    [Mediums]
                ON
                    [Mediums].[Id] = [MediaItems].[MediumId]",
                (item, medium) =>
                {
                    item.MediumInfo = medium;
                    return item;
                }
            );
    return itemsResult.ToList();
}
```

6. Next, add the code to create the insert and update methods for our media items:

```
private async Task<int> InsertMediaItemAsync(SqliteConnection
db, MediaItem item)
{
    var newIds = await db.QueryAsync<long>(
        @"INSERT INTO MediaItems
            (Name, ItemType, MediumId, LocationType)
            VALUES
            (@Name, @MediaType, @MediumId, @Location);
        SELECT last_insert_rowid()", item);
    (int)newIds.First();
}
```

```
private async Task UpdateMediaItemAsync(SqliteConnection db,
MediaItem item)
{
    await db.QueryAsync(
        @"UPDATE MediaItems
          SET Name = @Name,
              ItemType = @MediaType,
              MediumId = @MediumId,
              LocationType = @Location
          WHERE Id = @Id;", item);
}
```

The code in `InsertMediaItemAsync` should look familiar. It's very similar to what we did when we inserted data into the `Mediums` table. The code to update a row in `MediaItems` is technically only one line now, thanks to Dapper.

7. There's one new read-only property that's been added to the `MediaItem` object in our model. This property allows Dapper to map `MediumId` to the `MediaItems` table:

```
public int MediumId => MediumInfo.Id;
```

8. Now, add the `Computed` attribute to the `MediaItem.MediumInfo` property. This tells Dapper to ignore the property when we attempt to insert or update rows in the database. We only need to have `MediumId` saved. Users are unable to make changes to the rows in the Mediums table:

```
[Computed]
public Medium MediumInfo { get; set; }
```

9. Finally, let's create a method that will delete items from the `MediaItems` table. This code is a little different, thanks to `Dapper.Contrib`. We don't need to write any parameterized SQL in the code because `Dapper.Contrib` has a `DeleteAsync` method that generates the code to delete from `MediaItems`, based on the `Id` property of the `MediaItem` class provided:

```
private async Task DeleteMediaItemAsync(SqliteConnection db, int
id)
{
    await db.DeleteAsync<MediaItem>(new MediaItem { Id = id });
}
```

To make this work, you must decorate the primary key properties of your model classes with Key attributes:

```
public class MediaItem
{
    [Key]
    public int Id { get; set; }
```

```
    ...
}
```

Make sure that every model class that uses one of the `Dapper.Contrib` attributes adds a `using` statement for `Dapper.Contrib.Extensions`.

Before we update all the public CRUD methods of the `SqliteDataService` class to call these private methods, we will complete the code that initializes the service when the application launches.

Updating the data service's initialization

Let's get started:

1. First, create a version of the `DataService.PopulateMediums` method in `Sqlite DataService`, make it `async`, and rename it `PopulateMediumsAsync`. Update this method so that it fetches the data from SQLite. The method will also create any required data if this is the first time the application has been launched for the current user:

```
private async Task PopulateMediumsAsync(SqliteConnection db)
{
    _mediums = await GetAllMediumsAsync(db);
    if (_mediums.Count == 0)
    {
        var cd = new Medium { Id = 1, MediaType = ItemType.
Music, Name = "CD" };
        var vinyl = new Medium { Id = 2, MediaType = ItemType.
Music, Name = "Vinyl" };
        var hardcover = new Medium { Id = 3, MediaType =
ItemType.Book, Name = "Hardcover" };
        var paperback = new Medium { Id = 4, MediaType =
ItemType.Book, Name = "Paperback" };
        var dvd = new Medium { Id = 5, MediaType = ItemType.
Video, Name = "DVD" };
        var bluRay = new Medium { Id = 6, MediaType = ItemType.
Video, Name = "Blu Ray" };
        var mediums = new List<Medium>
        {
            cd, vinyl, hardcover, paperback, dvd, bluRay
        };
        foreach (var medium in mediums)
        {
            await InsertMediumAsync(db, medium);
        }
        _mediums = await GetAllMediumsAsync(db);
    }
}
```

2. Second, remove `PopulateItems` from `SqliteDataService`, `DataService`, and `IDataService`. It will not be needed because we now persist all data between sessions. You can also remove the `_items` private variable.

3. Now, take the code from the `SqliteDataService` constructor, move it to a new public method named `InitializeDataAsync`, and update the code so that it uses the new private initialization methods. Don't forget to remove the call to populate the items collection. The `SqliteConnection` object should always be part of a `using` block to ensure that the connection is closed and the object is disposed of:

```
public async Task InitializeDataAsync()
{
    using (var db = await GetOpenConnectionAsync())
    {
        await CreateMediumTableAsync(db);
        await CreateMediaItemTableAsync(db);
        SelectedItemId = -1;
        PopulateItemTypes();
        await PopulateMediumsAsync(db);
        PopulateLocationTypes();
    }
}
```

4. This new initialization method will need to be added to `IDataService` to make it available to objects that resolve the service through our DI container. If you keep the original `DataService` class in your project, you will need to add an implementation of `InitializeDataAsync` so that the project will compile:

```
public interface IDataService
{
    Task InitializeDataAsync();
    ...
}
```

5. After changing the location of the code that initializes `SqliteDataService`, the `RegisterComponents` method in `App.xaml.cs` will need to be updated to use the new `SqliteDataService` and call `InitializeDataAsync`. While we're at it, rename the method to reflect its new async status:

```
private async Task RegisterComponentsAsync(Frame rootFrame)
{
    var navigationService = new NavigationService(rootFrame);
    navigationService.Configure(nameof(MainPage),
typeof(MainPage));
    navigationService.Configure(nameof(ItemDetailsPage),
typeof(ItemDetailsPage));
```

```
    var dataService = new SqliteDataService();
    await dataService.InitializeDataAsync();
    HostContainer = Host.CreateDefaultBuilder()
        .ConfigureServices(services =>
        {
            services.
    AddSingleton<INavigationService>(navigationService);
            services.AddSingleton<IDataService>(dataService);
            services.AddTransient<MainViewModel>();
            services.AddTransient<ItemDetailsViewModel>();
        }).Build();
}
```

Don't forget to update `OnLaunched` so that it's `async` and await the call to the renamed
`RegisterComponentsAsync`.

Now that the application initializes the data service when it launches, it's time to update the public
CRUD methods so they use the async private methods we created to fetch data from SQLite.

Retrieving data via services

Let's start retrieving and saving SQLite data with our service methods. It will only be necessary to update
the create, update, and delete operations. All the media items are stored in `List<MediaItem>` in
`DataService`, so the public methods used to retrieve items can remain as they were in the previous
chapter. Let's get started:

1. Start by updating the create, update, and delete methods for the media items in
    `SqliteDataService.cs`. Each of these will get an open connection to the database from
    `GetOpenConnectionAsync` and call its corresponding private method asynchronously:

    ```
    public async Task<int> AddItemAsync(MediaItem item)
    {
        using var db = await GetOpenConnectionAsync();
        return await InsertMediaItemAsync(db, item);
    }
    public async Task UpdateItemAsync(MediaItem item)
    {
        using var db = await GetOpenConnectionAsync();
        await UpdateMediaItemAsync(db, item);
    }
    public async Task DeleteItemAsync(MediaItem item)
    {
        using var db = await GetOpenConnectionAsync();
    ```

```
        await DeleteMediaItemAsync(db, item.Id);
    }
```

2. Update the public methods that fetch items to be async:

```
    public async Task<MediaItem> GetItemAsync(int id)
    {
        IList<MediaItem> mediaItems;
        using var db = await GetOpenConnectionAsync();
        mediaItems = await GetAllMediaItemsAsync(db);
        // Filter the list to get the item for our Id.
        return mediaItems.FirstOrDefault(i => i.Id == id);
    }
    public async Task<IList<MediaItem>> GetItemsAsync()
    {
        using var db = await GetOpenConnectionAsync();
        return await GetAllMediaItemsAsync(db);
    }
```

> **Note**
>
> If you need to do a lot of filtering when querying data, Entity Framework is a more robust ORM that can provide more extensive options. SQLite is best suited for simpler applications. Note that, in the preceding code, GetItemAsync queries all the items and then filters to the item that matches the provided ID by using a lambda expression.

3. The method names have been updated to include Async, all uses of the _items collection have been removed, and each method has been changed to return Task. So, update the IDataService interface members to reflect the same changes. Also, either remove DataService from the project or update its methods to also be async. It's best to try and anticipate that data access methods will need to be async when you set out, thus preventing breaking changes to your interfaces:

```
    Task<int> AddItemAsync(MediaItem item);
    Task UpdateItemAsync(MediaItem item);
    Task DeleteItemAsync(MediaItem item);
    Task<IList<MediaItem>> GetItemsAsync();
    Task<MediaItem> GetItemAsync(int id);
```

4. In `MainViewModel.cs`, the `Delete` method will be updated to use async/await with its data service call. Don't forget to rename it `DeleteAsync` to follow best practices when naming async methods. You will also need to add a `using` statement to the file for the `System.Threading.Tasks` namespace:

```
private async Task DeleteAsync()
{
    await _dataService.DeleteItemAsync(SelectedMediaItem);
    Items.Remove(SelectedMediaItem);
    allItems.Remove(SelectedMediaItem);
}
```

5. Update the `PopulateData` method so that it's named `PopulateDataAsync`, and use the async method of getting items:

```
public async Task PopulateDataAsync()
{
    items.Clear();
    foreach(var item in await _dataService.GetItemsAsync())
    {
        items.Add(item);
    }
    allItems = new ObservableCollection<MediaItem>(Items);
    mediums = new ObservableCollection<string>
    {
        AllMediums
    };
    foreach(var itemType in _dataService.GetItemTypes())
    {
        mediums.Add(itemType.ToString());
    }
    selectedMedium = Mediums[0];
}
```

6. Now, you will have to update the `MainViewModel` constructor to call to `PopulateDataAsync` at the end of the constructor:

```
public MainViewModel(INavigationService navigationService,
IDataService dataService)
{
    _navigationService = navigationService;
    _dataService = dataService;
    PopulateDataAsync();
}
```

7. Some similar changes will be needed in `ItemDetailsViewModel`. Update the `Save` method so that it's async and awaits the data service calls to `AddItemAsync`, `GetItemAsync`, and `UpdateItemAsync`. Don't forget to rename `Save` to `SaveAsync` and add a `using` statement for the `System.Threading.Tasks` namespace:

```csharp
private async Task SaveAsync()
{
    MediaItem item;
    if (_itemId > 0)
    {
        item = await _dataService.GetItemAsync(_itemId);
        item.Name = ItemName;
        item.Location = (LocationType)Enum.
Parse(typeof(LocationType), SelectedLocation);
        item.MediaType = (ItemType)Enum.Parse(typeof(ItemType),
SelectedItemType);
        item.MediumInfo = _dataService.
GetMedium(SelectedMedium);
        await _dataService.UpdateItemAsync(item);
    }
    else
    {
        item = new MediaItem
        {
            Name = ItemName,
            Location = (LocationType)Enum.
Parse(typeof(LocationType), SelectedLocation),
            MediaType = (ItemType)Enum.Parse(typeof(ItemType),
SelectedItemType),
            MediumInfo = _dataService.GetMedium(SelectedMedium)
        };
        await _dataService.AddItemAsync(item);
    }
}
```

8. Next, update the `SaveItemAndReturn` and `SaveAndContinue` methods so that they also use async/await:

```csharp
private async Task SaveItemAndReturnAsync()
{
    await SaveItemAsync();
    _navigationService.GoBack();
}
private async Task SaveItemAndContinueAsync()
{
```

```
await SaveItemAsync();
_dataService.SelectedItemId = 0;
_itemId = 0;
ItemName = "";
SelectedMedium = null;
SelectedLocation = null;
SelectedItemType = null;
IsDirty = false;
}
```

9. Finally, update `ItemDetailsViewModel.xaml` so that the save buttons use the async methods when they bind their `Click` methods:

```xml
<SplitButton x:Name="SaveButton"
             Content="Save and Return"
             Margin="8,8,0,8"
             Click="{x:Bind ViewModel.SaveItemAndReturnAsync}"
             IsEnabled="{x:Bind ViewModel.IsDirty,
Mode=OneWay}">
...
<Button Content="Save and Create New"
    Click="{x:Bind ViewModel.SaveItemAndContinueAsync}"
    IsEnabled="{x:Bind ViewModel.IsDirty, Mode=OneWay}"
    Background="Transparent"/>
<Button Content="Save and Return"
    Click="{x:Bind ViewModel.SaveItemAndReturnAsync}"
    IsEnabled="{x:Bind ViewModel.IsDirty, Mode=OneWay}"
    Background="Transparent"/>
```

> **Note**
>
> If you have any issues with the **Media Type** ComboBox not populating on the main page after adding or editing a media item, update Mode of its `ItemsSource` data binding to OneWay. The completed source code in GitHub has been updated to reflect this change.

That's it. Run the application and see how it works. Since we're no longer creating any dummy data for the media items list, the media collection in `ListView` will be empty when the app launches for the first time:

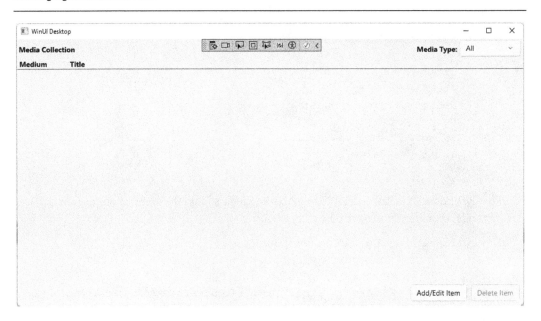

Figure 6.2 – Launching with a database for the first time

Try adding, updating, and removing some items. Then, close the application and run it again. You should see the same items on the list that were there when you closed it:

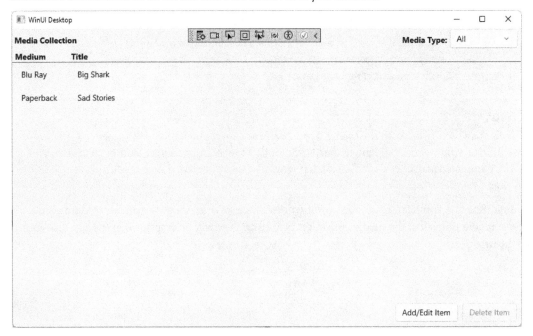

Figure 6.3 – Relaunching with saved data

Users can now retain their saved data. If you would like to browse your SQLite data outside your app, there are tools you can use to connect to a local db and inspect it. One of them is **DB Browser for SQLite**. Covering this tool is beyond the scope of this book, but you can explore it for yourself at `https://sqlitebrowser.org/`.

Let's wrap up and review what we've learned about working with data in a WinUI application.

Summary

We have covered a lot of important material in this chapter. You learned how to read and write data to a local SQLite database. Then, you learned how to simplify your data access code by leveraging Dapper, an ORM for .NET developers. Using an ORM will save you time creating boilerplate mapping code in your data access layers for WinUI projects (or any other .NET projects). All this data access code was made async to keep the UI responsive for the user.

In the next chapter, we will learn how to create a beautiful **Fluent UI** with Microsoft's Fluent UI design principles.

Questions

1. When will Windows put a WinUI 3 app into a suspended state?

2. When should you save the app state to ensure it is not lost if an application is closed?

3. What is the event you can handle on a `Page` class to perform some logic when every element on a page has finished loading?

4. What is a Micro ORM?

5. What is the name of the Dapper package that adds CRUD helpers such as `Delete` and `DeleteAsync`?

6. What is one of the powerful features of some more full-featured ORMs, such as Entity Framework?

7. What is the name of a tool that can be used to inspect data in a SQLite database?

Part 2: Extending WinUI and Modernizing Applications

In this part, you will build on what you have learned about WinUI application development and expand on it, with design concepts, platform options, and open source libraries. The Fluent design system that is native to WinUI controls provides Windows application users with a familiar look and feel. You will also learn how to integrate app notifications with the Windows App SDK. Then, you will explore the Windows Community Toolkit and .NET Community Toolkit, a set of open source packages that offer controls and helpers to WinUI developers. Finally, Template Studio will give WinUI developers a head-start with best practices when starting a new project.

This part has the following chapters:

- *Chapter 7, Fluent Design System for Windows Applications*
- *Chapter 8, Adding Windows Notifications to WinUI Applications*
- *Chapter 9, Enhancing Applications with the Windows Community Toolkits*
- *Chapter 10, Accelerating App Development with Template Studio*

7

Fluent Design System for Windows Applications

The **Fluent Design System** is a set of application design principles created by Microsoft and implemented across multiple desktop, mobile, and web platforms. The Fluent Design System for Windows is a set of controls, patterns, and styles for applications built for Windows. In fact, it is the implicit styling for all WinUI controls.

It is important to learn the tenets of Fluent Design and how to implement them in your WinUI applications. We will also explore the **Fluent XAML Theme Editor** application for Windows. This application assists developers in creating a theme for their applications, including color schemes and style elements such as borders and corners. Developers can then easily import the resources to implement the theme.

In this chapter, we will cover the following topics:

- Learning the concepts of Fluent Design
- How to find the latest information about Fluent Design
- Incorporating Fluent Design concepts into WinUI applications
- Using the Fluent XAML Theme Editor to customize and use a UI theme
- Exploring the **Acrylic** material and the Fluent Design System
- Using the **Mica** material in WinUI applications

By the end of this chapter, you will understand the Fluent Design System for Windows applications. You will also know how to incorporate these design standards into your WinUI applications.

Technical requirements

To follow along with the examples in this chapter, the following software is required:

- Windows 10 version 1803 (version 17134) or later
- Visual Studio 2022 or later with the .NET Desktop Development workload installed and configured for Windows App SDK development

The source code for this chapter is available on GitHub at this URL: `https://github.com/PacktPublishing/Learn-WinUI-3-Second-Edition/tree/master/Chapter07`.

What is the Fluent Design System?

The Fluent Design System is a cross-platform system that helps developers create beautiful, intuitive applications. The website for Fluent Design (`https://fluent1.microsoft.design/`) has dedicated pages with resources for developers on many platforms:

- Android
- iOS
- macOS
- Web
- Windows
- Cross-platform (React Native)

> **Note**
>
> Microsoft has started releasing their Fluent 2 design guidance at `https://fluent2.microsoft.design/`. You can think of Fluent 1 styles as Windows 10 style, whereas Fluent 2 style is similar to the look and feel of Windows 11. At the time of this writing, the Fluent 2 guidance has only been published for React web applications. Other platforms are not yet available.

Fluent Design aims to be simple and intuitive. While it maintains its design philosophy across platforms, it also adapts aspects of its design to feel native on every platform. In *Chapter 1, Introduction to WinUI*, we discussed the origins of some of the current Fluent Design concepts in the **Metro** design that was introduced with Windows Phone. While the look and feel of Microsoft's designs have evolved over the years, some of the principles remain. The three core principles of the Fluent Design System are the following:

- **Natural on every device**: Software should adapt to the device where it's running, whether it's a PC, tablet, game console, phone, or AR/VR device

- **Intuitive and powerful**: The UI anticipates users' actions and pulls them into the experience while using the app

- **Engaging and immersive**: The design pulls from real-world elements, using light, shadow, texture, and depth to create an immersive experience for the user

The driving philosophy behind the design is to adapt and feel natural. The device and the app should feel comfortable and anticipate the user's actions.

This is a very abstract and high-level explanation so far. Let's explore the specifics of Fluent Design for Windows in the next section.

Exploring Fluent Design for Windows

For Windows applications, Fluent Design covers several areas. When compared to other design systems, Fluent is more all-encompassing. Apple's **Human Interface Guidelines** (`https://developer.apple.com/design/human-interface-guidelines/`) have only been widely adopted on Apple's platforms: iOS, iPadOS, and macOS. Google's **Material Design** (`https://material.io/`) system has seen broader adoption but only has toolkits available for Android, Flutter, and the web.

Fluent Design is most often compared with Material Design as they share some concepts when it comes to shapes and texture, but Fluent Design uses transparency to much greater effect than Material Design. Fluent Design provides a rich toolset that you can use in WinUI and nearly any other development platform.

Let's explore some of these design aspects and how they apply to your WinUI applications.

Controls

A control equates to a single element of *user input* or *interaction*. We have already explored many of the controls available in WinUI in *Chapter 5, Exploring WinUI Controls*. This is what some of the common WinUI controls look like in light and dark modes in Windows 11:

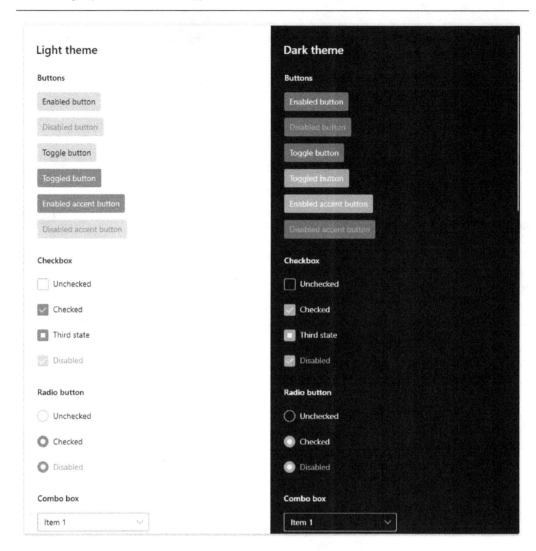

Figure 7.1 – Some common controls in light and dark modes

By default, the WinUI controls make use of Fluent styles. We will see how to override the default Fluent styles in our WinUI controls later in the chapter.

Patterns

Patterns are groups of related controls or a group of controls that becomes a single new element. This group could be added to a composite control for re-use. Some examples of patterns in WinUI include the following:

- **Search**: In its simplest form, a search pattern needs to have controls for accepting input, invoking the search, and displaying the search results. An additional element may be added for suggesting searches before any input is received. Assistants such as *Amazon Alexa* do this based on a user's calendar, contacts, news preferences, and so on. Adding an autosuggest list based on user input is a common feature of modern search controls. You could also integrate chat controls with **artificial intelligence** (**AI**) such as Microsoft's **Bot Framework** or OpenAI's **ChatGPT** to ask some follow-up questions based on the initial search parameters.

- **Forms**: Forms are a very common control pattern. They consist of groups of related labels, input controls, and command buttons that collect a related set of data elements. Some common forms with potential for re-use are user account creation forms and forms for collecting user feedback. Forms should follow the Fluent Design guidelines for spacing, flexible layout, and using typography for creating a hierarchy (Microsoft Learn example: `https://learn. microsoft.com/windows/apps/design/controls/forms`).

- **List/details**: The list/details control pattern is seen so frequently that we probably don't notice it most of the time. You may think our My Media Collection application follows this pattern (with the items list and a page to view and edit item details), but this pattern describes how to show these views on the same page. This is typically achieved with a `ListView` control and a `SplitView` control to separate the list from the selected item's details. Depending on the width of the page, the two views can either be stacked vertically or displayed side by side (Microsoft Learn example: `https://learn.microsoft.com/windows/apps/ design/controls/list-details`).

Each of these patterns encapsulates the elements of Fluent Design to create a composite control that can be reused across applications. You may have control patterns in your projects that could be added to a shared control library for ease of reuse. Shared libraries such as these can save time and ensure that good design practices are followed across teams.

Layout

The layout is important to ensure that an application adapts to any screen size or orientation. Flexibility is a key tenet of a well-designed layout. When a window or page is resized, the contents can adapt by repositioning controls, adding/removing items, changing the flow of items, replacing controls with others that better fit the current available space, or simply resizing items. This is typically handled in XAML with **Visual States**. You can define a different `VisualState` for each size threshold to which your page must adapt, possibly defined as **Narrow**, **Default**, **Wide**, and **ExtraWide**. Each `VisualState` updates control properties to adapt to the new layout. Microsoft Learn has a great example of this at `https://learn.microsoft.com/windows/apps/design/layout/layouts-with-xaml`. WinUI includes several different layout panels that can help developers create the right layout for their pages and respond to changes in size, orientation, and resolution.

Input

There are Fluent Design recommendations for responding to user input. There are guidelines for reacting to the traditional mouse and keyboard input that developers have been handling for decades. Modern applications can do things such as pan, zoom, rotate, or scroll based on mouse input. A keyboard may be a physical keyboard or an onscreen keyboard for mobile and touch users.

Input can come in other forms with today's hardware:

- Pen/stylus
- Touch
- Touchpad
- Gamepad/controller
- Remote control
- Surface Dial (see `https://learn.microsoft.com/windows/apps/design/input/windows-wheel-interactions`)
- AR/VR gestures
- Voice

User input can also be simulated with the input injection APIs. An example of where this might be useful is creating a **Show Me How** or **Guided Tour** feature in your app. Your code can execute some pre-defined steps, guiding the user through performing some action on the page. This API is beyond the scope of this book. To read about an example of using input injection to intercept mouse input and turn it into touch input, read this article on Microsoft Learn: `https://learn.microsoft.com/windows/apps/design/input/input-injection`.

Style

Style encompasses multiple aspects of Fluent Design:

- **Icons**: Good icons should be simple and convey the application's purpose.
- **Color**: The color choice is important. Allowing users to customize their colors is also a great way to make your app feel personal to them. WinUI makes it easy to adapt the user's light or dark theme choice and the Windows highlight color by using theme brushes.

- **Typography**: Microsoft recommends that Windows applications all use the Segoe UI font. Selecting the font size can help convey a hierarchy within the app, such as a book or document layout. To this end, Microsoft has defined a **type ramp** (available at `https://learn.microsoft.com/windows/apps/design/style/typography#type-ramp`). A type ramp defines the increase in font size for different styled elements on the screen, such as *Body*, *Title*, and *Subtitle*. There are static resources that can be leveraged in WinUI to select the right size for a control's intended use.

- **Spacing**: Spacing between and within controls is important for readability and usability. WinUI controls allow a Standard or Compact density to be selected. More information about sizing and Fluent densities can be found here: `https://learn.microsoft.com/windows/apps/design/style/spacing`.

- **Reveal focus**: Drawing attention to focusable elements is important for larger displays, such as an Xbox or Surface Hub. This is achieved through lighting effects with Fluent.

- **Acrylic**: This is a type of WinUI brush that creates texture with transparency. This texture gives a feeling of depth to the user interface. We will discuss Acrylic in more detail later in this chapter.

- **Mica**: This is a dynamic material like Acrylic, but unlike Acrylic it is opaque, not transparent. It creates the background of the app by incorporating elements of the current OS theme and desktop wallpaper. We will see how to incorporate Mica into your own WinUI applications later in the chapter.

- **Corner radius**: Fluent Design promotes the idea that rounded corners promote positive feelings in users. WinUI controls have a rounded corner radius consistent with Fluent Design recommendations.

- **Sound**: Sound can be an integral part of crafting an immersive experience in your apps. A subtle whooshing sound when panels slide open or closed and using just the right tone and volume in the sound of an alert can immerse the app's users.

- **Writing style**: Believe it or not, writing style is part of app design. Line-of-business applications should not have the same writing style as a casual consumer app or a puzzle game. Users will be pulled into the app experience if they don't notice the writing style at all because it fits what they expect for the application type.

These are just some of the aspects of style defined by Fluent Design. You can read more about them on Microsoft Learn: `https://learn.microsoft.com/windows/apps/design/style/`.

Many of the aspects of Fluent style are made available to our WinUI apps via XAML styles and other static resources. Next, we will look at how we can update our sample application to respond to changes in a user's Windows theme.

Incorporating Fluent Design in WinUI applications

It is time to incorporate a few of the Fluent Design principles into the **My Media Collection** application and polish the UI a little. Most of the WinUI controls are already designed to meet Fluent standards, but there were a few properties we modified without understanding Fluent Design.

Updating the title bar

Before we even get into the XAML to improve the styles, let's fix the application's title bar. Until now, the title bar always read **MyMediaCollection** without any spaces or indication of the current page:

1. First, to fix the spacing when the app is packaged and distributed, open `Package.appmanifest` from the **Solution Explorer** window. On the page that opens, update **Display name** to My Media Collection. If you like, you can also change **Description**.

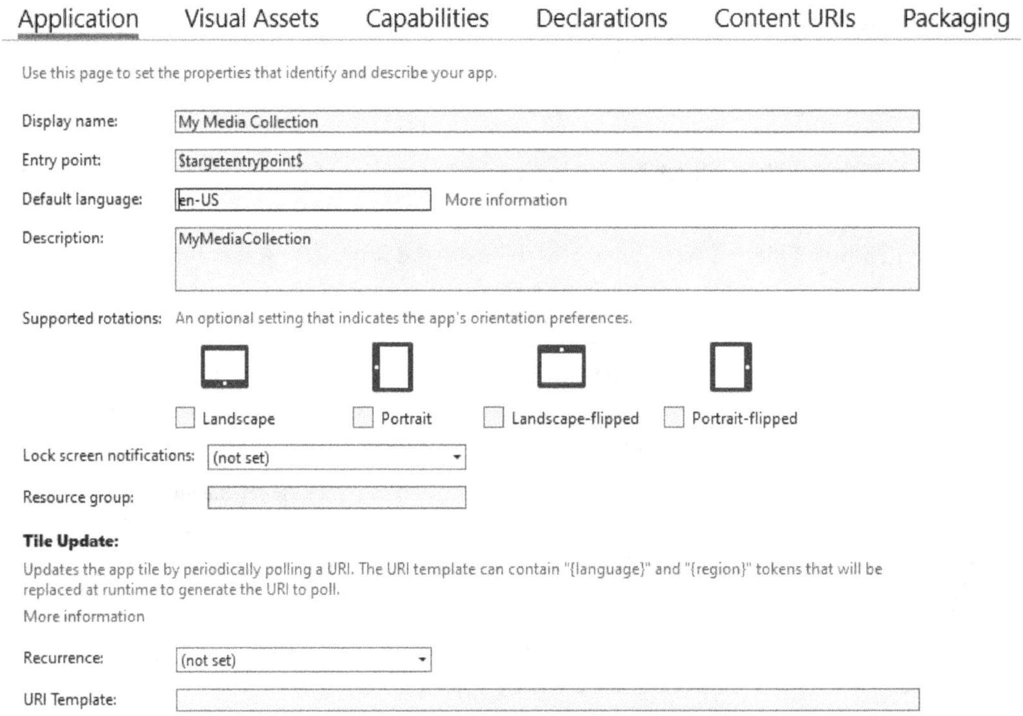

Application	Visual Assets	Capabilities	Declarations	Content URIs	Packaging

Use this page to set the properties that identify and describe your app.

Display name: My Media Collection

Entry point: $targetentrypoint$

Default language: en-US   More information

Description: MyMediaCollection

Supported rotations: An optional setting that indicates the app's orientation preferences.

☐ Landscape   ☐ Portrait   ☐ Landscape-flipped   ☐ Portrait-flipped

Lock screen notifications: (not set)

Resource group:

Tile Update:

Updates the app tile by periodically polling a URI. The URI template can contain "{language}" and "{region}" tokens that will be replaced at runtime to generate the URI to poll.

More information

Recurrence: (not set)

URI Template:

Figure 7.2 – Updating information in Package.appmanifest

Updating **Display name** will not change the application's title bar text in WinUI 3 as it does for UWP apps. We will have to handle that with the `AppWindow` class.

2. To update the text in the app's title bar, add the following code to `MainWindow.xaml.cs`:

```csharp
using Microsoft.UI;
using Microsoft.UI.Windowing;
using Microsoft.UI.Xaml;
using System;
using WinRT.Interop;

namespace MyMediaCollection
{
    public sealed partial class MainWindow : Window
    {
        private AppWindow _appWindow;
        private const string AppTitle = "My Media Collection";
        public MainWindow()
        {
            this.InitializeComponent();
            _appWindow = GetCurrentAppWindow();
            _appWindow.Title = AppTitle;
        }
        private AppWindow GetCurrentAppWindow()
        {
            IntPtr handle = WindowNative.GetWindowHandle(this);
            WindowId windowId = Win32Interop.
GetWindowIdFromWindow(handle);
            return AppWindow.GetFromWindowId(windowId);
        }
    }
}
```

3. Now, add an `internal` method named `SetPageTitle` so each page can append its title to the main window title:

```csharp
internal void SetPageTitle(string title)
{
    if (_appWindow == null)
    {
        _appWindow = GetCurrentWindow();
    }
    _appWindow.Title = $"{AppTitle} - {title}";
}
```

4. In order for each page to access `MainWindow`, expose an internal member in `App.xaml.cs`:

```csharp
internal Window Window => m_window;
```

5. Next, in `MainPage.xaml.cs`, add an event handler for the `Loaded` event of the page. In the event handler, add some code to append to the `Title` of the current window with the page title of Home. When we launch the application, the title bar should read **My Media Collection - Home**:

```
public MainPage()
{
    this.InitializeComponent();
    Loaded += MainPage_Loaded;
}
private void MainPage_Loaded(object sender, RoutedEventArgs e)
{
    var mainWindow = (Application.Current as App)?.Window as
MainWindow;
    if (mainWindow != null)
    {
        mainWindow.SetPageTitle("Home");
    }
}
```

6. Finally, make the same changes in `ItemDetailsView.xaml.cs`, but set the page title to `Item Details`.

Now, when you run the application, you should see the title bar text update as you navigate between the list of items and the item details. Let's make some changes to the styles of `MainPage` next.

Changing the style of MainPage

Currently, the main page of our application doesn't have many styles. We set the `FontWeight` of a few `TextBlock` controls to `Bold` to set them apart as important items, but this doesn't follow the Fluent Design guidelines for typography. There is also a purple border separating the `ListView` header from its items:

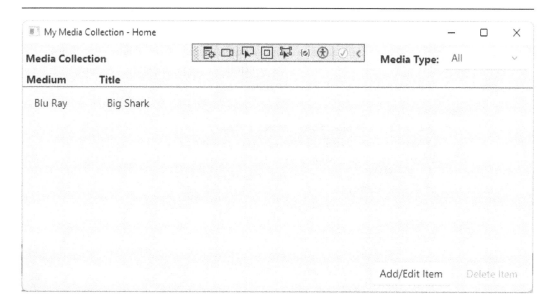

Figure 7.3 – The current main page of My Media Collection

Hard-coding colors is not a good practice. Even if you were using custom colors as product branding, you could centralize them in `Application.Resources`. Let's work our way through the `MainPage.xaml` file and make some improvements:

1. First, update the text of the first `TextBlock` from `Media Collection` to `Home`, matching the text in the window's title bar. Wrap it in a horizontally aligned `StackPanel` and add a preceding `SymbolIcon` control to display a **Home** symbol. Finally, remove the hardcoded font size and weight attributes and set the `Style` attribute to import the `SubheaderTextBlockStyle` `StaticResource`. Those changes should look like this:

```
<StackPanel Orientation="Horizontal">
    <SymbolIcon Symbol="Home" Margin="8"/>
    <TextBlock Text="Home"
               Style="{StaticResource SubheaderTextBlockStyle}"
               Margin="8"/>
</StackPanel>
```

2. We should also remove the `FontWeight` attribute from the **Media Type** label and use a Fluent style resource:

```
<TextBlock Text="Media Type:" Margin="4"
           Style="{StaticResource SubtitleTextBlockStyle}"
           VerticalAlignment="Bottom"/>
```

3. Next, change the surrounding `Grid` to a `StackPanel` and remove the `Grid.Column Definition` definitions. In addition to simplifying the layout, this will allow the **Home** symbol and text to appear above the rest of the controls on the page, reinforcing the hierarchy. The full block of code will look like this:

```
<StackPanel>
    <StackPanel Orientation="Horizontal">
        <SymbolIcon Symbol="Home" Margin="8"/>
        <TextBlock Text="Home"
                   Style="{StaticResource
SubheaderTextBlockStyle}"
                   Margin="8"/>
    </StackPanel>
    <StackPanel Orientation="Horizontal"
                HorizontalAlignment="Right">
        <TextBlock Text="Media Type:"
                   Margin="4"
                   Style="{StaticResource
SubtitleTextBlockStyle}"
                   VerticalAlignment="Bottom"/>
        <ComboBox ItemsSource="{x:Bind ViewModel.Mediums}"
                  SelectedItem="{x:Bind ViewModel.
SelectedMedium, Mode=TwoWay}"
                  MinWidth="120"
                  Margin="0,2,6,4"
                  VerticalAlignment="Bottom"/>
    </StackPanel>
</StackPanel>
```

4. Next, update the `HeaderTemplate` of the `ListView` to replace the purple `BorderBrush` attributes with `SystemAccentColor` from `ThemeResource`. This will make sure that the border's color picks up the user's preferred accent color from their selected Windows theme. Also, change each `TextBlock` to use a built-in `Style` instead of setting `FontWeight` and change the `Width` of the first column to be `120` to accommodate the larger title font:

```
<ListView.HeaderTemplate>
    <DataTemplate>
        <Grid Margin="4,0,4,0">
            <Grid.ColumnDefinitions>
                <ColumnDefinition Width="120"/>
                <ColumnDefinition Width="*"/>
            </Grid.ColumnDefinitions>
            <Border BorderBrush="{ThemeResource
SystemAccentColor}"
                    BorderThickness="0,0,0,1">
```

```xml
            <TextBlock Text="Medium"
                       Margin="4,0,0,0"
                       Style="{StaticResource
TitleTextBlockStyle}"/>
              </Border>
              <Border Grid.Column="1"
                      BorderBrush="{ThemeResource
SystemAccentColor}"
                      BorderThickness="0,0,0,1">
                <TextBlock Text="Title"
                           Margin="4,0,0,0"
                           Style="{StaticResource
TitleTextBlockStyle}"/>
              </Border>
          </Grid>
        </DataTemplate>
</ListView.HeaderTemplate>
```

Note that you will also need to change the first column Width to 120 in the ListView.
ItemTemplate.

5.   Finally, let's define the end of the list area by adding a border between the bottom of ListView and the command buttons. Do this by wrapping the buttons' StackPanel with a Border control, again using SystemAccentColor. Margin= "4,0" is shorthand that is equivalent to Margin= "4,0,4,0":

```xml
<Border Grid.Row="2"
        BorderBrush="{ThemeResource SystemAccentColor}"
        BorderThickness="0,1,0,0"
        Margin="4,0">
    <StackPanel Orientation="Horizontal"
                HorizontalAlignment="Right">
        <Button Command="{x:Bind ViewModel.AddEditCommand}"
                Content="Add/Edit Item" Margin="8,8,0,8"/>
        <Button Command="{x:Bind ViewModel.DeleteCommand}"
                Content="Delete Item"
                Grid.Column="1"
                Margin="8"/>
    </StackPanel>
</Border>
```

6.   Run the application and check out the restyled user interface. It looks much better. You can now easily see the hierarchy of data, however limited it may be in our simple application:

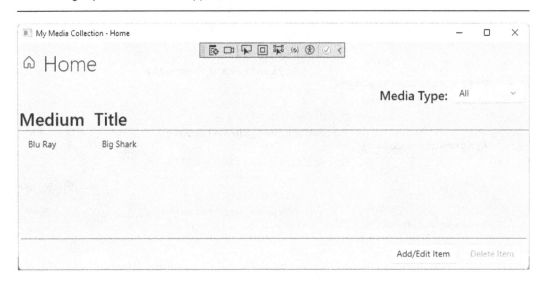

Figure 7.4 – The newly styled My Media Collection home page

Before moving on to the details page, let's see how the page looks if we select the dark mode in Windows. Open **Windows Settings**, go to **Personalization | Colors**, and select **Dark** from the **Choose your color** dropdown (if you normally use **Dark**, try changing it to **Light**):

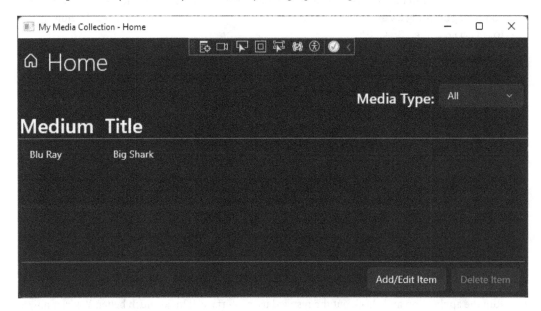

Figure 7.5 – My Media Collection running in dark mode

Everything on the page switches to dark mode without any code changes except for the title bar. To learn more about title bar customization, including changing colors or the icon, or even completely replacing it with a custom title bar, see this topic on Microsoft Learn: `https://learn.microsoft.com/windows/apps/develop/title-bar`.

If you have a good reason to keep your application in light or dark mode, you can update `Application.xaml` to add a single attribute to the `Application` element using this command:

```
RequestedTheme="Dark"
```

This will apply the `Dark` theme to the entire application. If you have a reason to only force this theme on part of the application, the `RequestedTheme` attribute can be applied to an individual `Page` or `Control`. Now, let's apply the same types of styles to the details page.

Changing the style of ItemDetailsPage

We want to update `ItemDetailsPage.xaml` to provide it with the same overall look and feel as the main page:

1. Open the file and start by updating `Item Details`. Give it the same `Subheader` `TextBlockStyle` that was used on Home and wrap it in a horizontally aligned `Stack Panel`. Precede `TextBlock` with a `SymbolIcon`, which uses the `Edit` symbol:

    ```
    <StackPanel Orientation="Horizontal">
        <SymbolIcon Symbol="Edit" Margin="8"/>
        <TextBlock Text="Item Details"
                   Style="{StaticResource SubheaderTextBlockStyle}"
                   Margin="8"/>
    </StackPanel>
    ```

2. Next, modify the `Grid` that follows the new `StackPanel` to have top and bottom borders. Also, modify the `Margin` to have 4 px on either side of `Grid`:

    ```
    <Grid Grid.Row="1"
          BorderBrush="{ThemeResource SystemAccentColor}"
          BorderThickness="0,1,0,1"
          Margin="4,0,4,8">
    ```

That's all we need to change on this page. Run the application again and navigate to the details page to see how it looks:

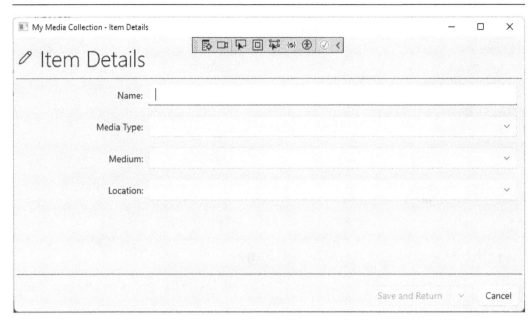

Figure 7.6 – The restyled Item Details page

This looks great. Now the styles of the two pages match, and the added border lines match the color of the highlighted active input field.

Let's now shift gears and review a tool that can help designers and developers when implementing Fluent Design.

Using the Fluent XAML Theme Editor

We've seen how easy it is to adopt the default color and theme resources from the user's Windows settings, but what if you or your company wants to create a custom theme for an application? Maybe that theme needs to be shared across a suite of applications. You could create a XAML file with `ResourceDictionary` in Visual Studio and code all the markup by hand for a new style. Visual Studio's **IntelliSense** will help in some regards. However, there is an easier way.

Microsoft has created an open source tool called the **Fluent XAML Theme Editor**. It is available on the Microsoft Store at `https://apps.microsoft.com/store/detail/9N2XD3Q8X57C`, and the source is available on GitHub at `https://github.com/Microsoft/fluent-xaml-theme-editor`. This application provides an easy-to-use visual designer to create a `ResourceDictionary` XAML file that you can drop into your projects.

> **Note**
> The Fluent XAML Theme Editor was created to adjust the styles for UWP controls, but these same styles will also work with WinUI 3 controls.

To install the application, open the **Microsoft Store** app, search for `fluent xaml` in the search field, and you will find **Fluent XAML Theme Editor** in the search results. Click it in the search results to view the product page:

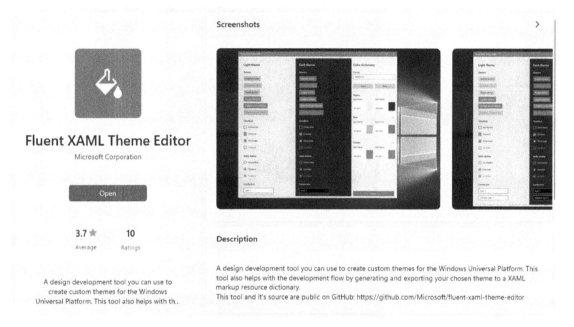

Figure 7.7 – The Fluent XAML Theme Editor page in the Microsoft Store

If you have already installed the app, there will be a **Launch** button. If it is not installed, you can click the **Install** button. When it completes its installation, you will find the app in your **Start** menu.

When you first launch the app, it will launch with the default styles for a UWP app, displayed in both light and dark themes. On the right-hand panel, you will find controls for changing the colors and shapes of UI elements. **Typography** is listed as **Coming Soon**, but it's been promising this for many years:

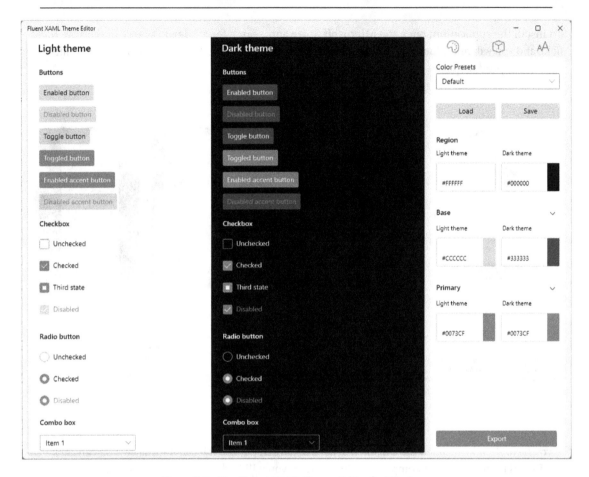

Figure 7.8 – The Fluent XAML Theme Editor for Windows

Colors

On the **Colors** tab, you can select one of the default profiles from the **Color Presets** dropdown. In addition to the default preset, there are **Lavender**, **Forest**, and **Nighttime** options. There are also options to load additional presets or to save your current color settings as a new preset. These color presets are saved in JSON format.

> **Note**
>
> Any colors you specify here will override the Windows system accent color that would otherwise be picked up by WinUI applications by default. Unless your application has a good reason to follow another theme, it's best to let WinUI use the user's chosen accent colors. Designing a custom theme should be undertaken by an experienced design team.

Clicking on any of the colors in the current preset will launch a color picker window, where you can adjust the current color:

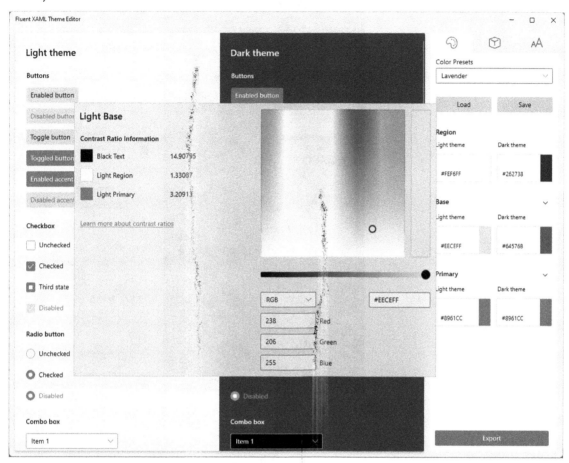

Figure 7.9 – Adjusting a preset color with a color picker

The **Region**, **Base**, and **Primary** colors can each be adjusted independently to change their light and dark theme appearance.

Shapes

The **Shapes** panel provides controls to adjust the **Corner Radius** of the **Controls** and the **Overlay**. This is also where you can adjust the default **Border Thickness** for the theme.

Shape presets, like colors, can also be saved and loaded. The app comes with two presets: **Default** and **No Rounding, Thicker Borders**. The difference is subtle but noticeable:

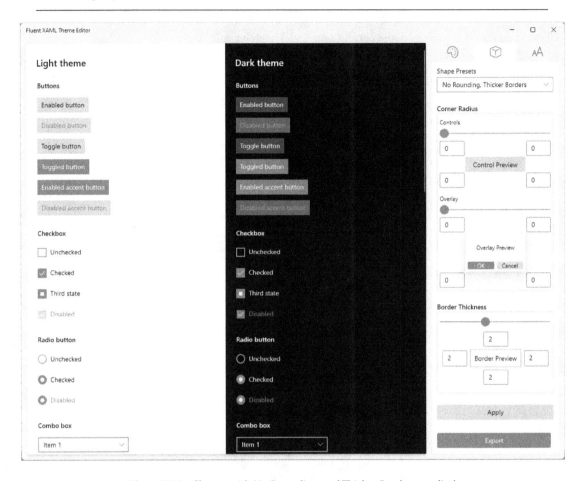

Figure 7.10 – Shapes with No Rounding and Thicker Borders applied

When you are done adjusting the color and shape settings, use the **Export** button to open a new window containing a `ResourceDictionary` with your theme data. You can copy the XAML and paste it into a `Resources` section in your project:

Figure 7.11 – Exporting a theme from the Fluent XAML Theme Editor

Next, let's explore the Acrylic material, which is part of the Fluent Design System that we touched on earlier in the chapter.

Acrylic material and the Fluent Design System

Acrylic is a WinUI brush that, when applied in your apps, provides a translucent texture. The texture works in both light and dark themes in Windows, and it is a great way to give users the feeling of depth when using your applications. The `AcrylicBrush` class is part of the `Microsoft.UI.Xaml.Media` namespace in the Windows App SDK, where `Brush`, `SolidColorBrush`, and `GradientBrush` are also found.

> **Note**
>
> The Acrylic material is also available to UWP applications that use WinUI 2.8.x.

If you want to explore the `AcrylicBrush` before deciding to use it in your own projects, you can try it in the WinUI 3 Gallery app:

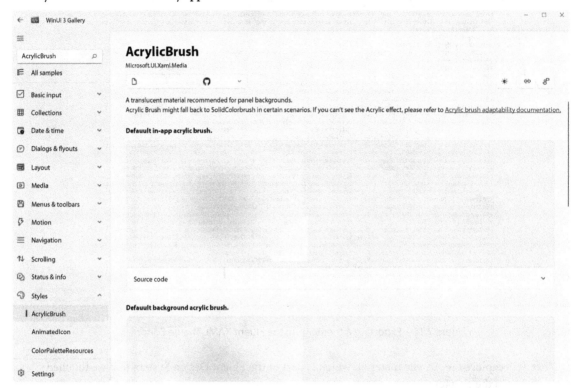

Figure 7.12 – Exploring AcrylicBrush in the WinUI 3 Gallery

On the gallery page, you can see the default styles of `AcrylicBrush` and how they'll appear in the Windows light and dark themes. Additionally, the gallery page provides controls to adjust the opacity and tint of the brush. You can also set a fallback solid color for the brush. The fallback color is used on systems without the resources to load an acrylic brush.

Depending on which brush is applied, the element will paint the acrylic brush based on background elements or in-app elements behind the current, overlapping element. The WinUI 3 Gallery has examples of how to apply either type of brush. This is an example of the in-app brush:

```
<Rectangle Fill="{ThemeResource AcrylicInAppFillColorDefaultBrush}"/>
```

This example shows how to apply a background acrylic brush:

```
<Rectangle Fill="{ThemeResource
AcrylicBackgroundFillColorDefaultBrush}"/>
```

When incorporated into your WinUI application, an acrylic brush gives users the feeling of texture and depth, which are two of the fundamental principles of Fluent Design. Another material you can choose to incorporate is Mica.

Use Mica in WinUI applications

Mica is another material that's available to WinUI applications. You can think of Mica as an Acrylic background brush without the transparency. It creates the brush style based on the current desktop background color in Windows. There are two variants of the Mica material: **Mica** and **Mica Alt**. Mica Alt creates the same kind of opaque background as Mica, but it has stronger tinting.

> **Note**
>
> Mica is only available in Windows 11 and later. If your app uses Mica and is installed on Windows 10, it will not apply the material.

If you use the WinUI 3 Gallery and open the System Backdrops (Mica/Acrylic) page, you can launch a WinUI window and cycle through the Mica, Mica Alt, and Acrylic materials applied to the window background:

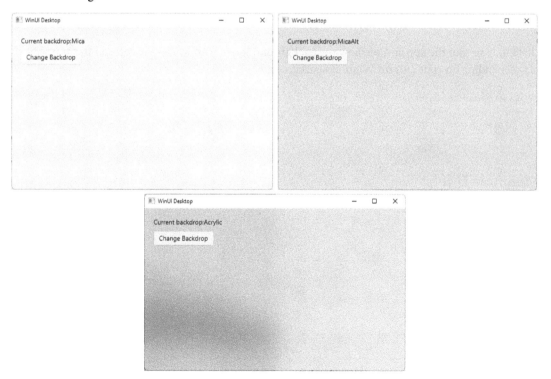

Figure 7.13 – Viewing the same window with Mica, Mica Alt, and Acrylic

The code to set the system backdrop for a window is more involved than just applying a brush to the `Fill` property of a `Rectangle` or another UI element. Let's try configuring Mica Alt in the My Media Collection app.

Incorporate Mica into My Media Collection

Bringing Mica into your own apps is easy with Windows App SDK 1.3 or later. Let's use the Mica Alt material in My Media Collection. It only takes a few steps:

1. First, check that your project is using Windows App SDK 1.3 or later. If it's not, you can use the **NuGet Package Manager** to upgrade it to the latest available version.

2. Next, open `MainPage.xaml` and `ItemDetailsPage.xaml` and remove the `Background` property for each `Page` element. If the `Page` elements (or any of their children) aren't transparent, you won't see the Mica backdrop.

3. Finally, open `MainWindow.xaml.cs` and add the following code to the constructor immediately after the call to `InitializeComponent`:

```
SystemBackdrop = new MicaBackdrop
{
    Kind = MicaKind.BaseAlt
};
```

That's it. Now run the app and see how the background looks with Mica. The color in the app will vary depending on your current Windows background:

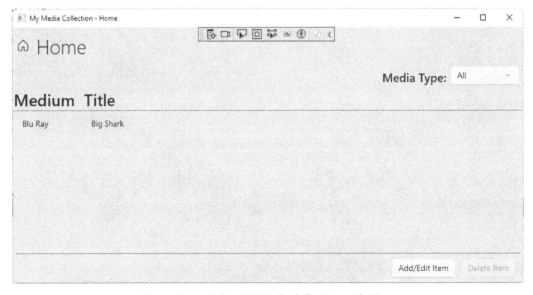

Figure 7.14 – Styling My Media Collection with Mica

Notice that the title bar does not pick up the Mica material, just as it ignores theme changes. If you would like to do this on your own, you can follow the Microsoft Learn instructions for extending your window contents into the title bar area: `https://learn.microsoft.com/windows/apps/develop/title-bar?tabs=wasdk#full-customization`. For this approach, you will need to create your own title bar control with any buttons and icons and update the title bar text there during page navigation.

Now, we will take a quick look at some additional Fluent Design tools geared toward designers.

Design resources and toolkits for Fluent Design

While a deep dive into user interface design is beyond the scope of this book, we will briefly review some of the Fluent Design toolkits available for popular design tools. Design resources and examples for several of these tools can be downloaded from Microsoft Learn at `https://learn.microsoft.com/windows/apps/design/downloads/`:

- **Figma**: This is a design and prototyping tool with free and paid options, depending on the team and project size. You can find out more about Figma on its website: `https://www.figma.com/`.

- **Sketch**: This is another popular tool for designing and prototyping applications individually or with teams. There is no free plan, but Sketch does have a free trial period. Sketch is available at `https://www.sketch.com/`.

- **Adobe XD**: XD is Adobe's design/prototype tool. Like Figma, Adobe XD has free and paid options for designing apps with their tool. Check out XD at `https://helpx.adobe.com/support/xd.html`.

- **Adobe Illustrator**: This is a powerful vector design tool from Adobe. There is a free trial available. Download and get started with Adobe Illustrator at `https://www.adobe.com/products/illustrator.html`.

- **Inkscape** (`https://inkscape.org/`) is a free vector image editor that can also work with **Adobe Illustrator (AI)** files.

- **Adobe Photoshop**: This is probably one of the best-known raster image editors. Adobe also has a free trial for Photoshop at `https://www.adobe.com/products/photoshop.html`.

The Fluent Design toolkit for Photoshop includes several PSD files. It is also possible to work with PSD files in free image editors such as **GIMP** (`https://www.gimp.org/`) or **Paint.NET** (`https://www.getpaint.net/`). Paint.NET requires an open source plugin, available at `https://www.psdplugin.com/`.

Summary

We have learned a lot about Fluent Design, design resources, and the tools available to WinUI developers in this chapter. You will be able to use these tools and techniques in your WinUI application design or recommend them to designers at your company. We also updated the My Media Collection app to be more compliant with Fluent Design recommendations and learned how to incorporate the Acrylic and Mica materials.

In the next chapter, we will examine how to add notifications to WinUI with the Windows App SDK notifications system.

Questions

1. Which platforms have Fluent Design implementations?

2. What is a control pattern?

3. Which font does Microsoft recommend using for Fluent Design?

4. Which aspect of style is specific to devices with large screens?

5. What are the names of the two spacing densities available in Fluent Design?

6. Which attribute can be set in `Application.xaml` to override a user's light/dark theme selection?

7. Which design tools have Fluent Design toolkits available?

8

Adding Windows Notifications to WinUI Applications

The Windows App SDK provides developers with the ability to implement **raw push notifications** and **app notifications** in their WinUI apps. It's important to understand the use case for each of these notification types. They have different implementations, and each has its own set of advantages and limitations. Push notifications can be surfaced to the user or received by the app to perform internal operations. App notifications, on the other hand, are used to communicate with the user. We'll cover examples of when you would want to use a particular notification type and add an app notification to the **My Media Collection** sample application.

In this chapter, we will cover the following topics:

- Understanding the different notification types in the Windows App SDK and the use case for each type

- Discovering how to leverage push notifications in a WinUI application

- Exploring how to use app notifications with WinUI

By the end of this chapter, you will understand the differences between push notifications and other app notifications exposed by the Windows App SDK. You will understand when to choose each notification type and how they are handled in a WinUI 3 project.

Technical requirements

To follow along with the examples in this chapter, the following software is required:

- Windows 10 version 1809 (build 17763) or newer

- Visual Studio 2022 or later with the .NET Desktop Development workload configured for Windows App SDK development

The source code for this chapter is available on GitHub at this URL: `https://github.com/PacktPublishing/Learn-WinUI-3-Second-Edition/tree/master/Chapter08`.

Overview of push notifications in the Windows App SDK

WinUI applications can leverage different types of notifications in the Windows App SDK. The notifications APIs were added in Windows App SDK 1.3 and can be either sent locally or through a cloud service, depending on the notification type. We most often associate notifications with the small, pop-up windows in the corner of the screen, called **toast notifications**, in Windows. However, a visual indicator isn't required for all notifications. They can also be used to signal your app to activate and perform an action or sync data from a remote service without relying on a timer in the app.

Raw push notifications

These internal notifications are known as **raw push notifications**. They require no user interaction and don't signal the user with a **toast notification**. Push notifications leverage the **Windows Push Notification Services** (**WNS**), which is part of the **Microsoft Store** services. To publish an application in the Store or leverage any of its services, a Store account is required, and your app must be registered in the Store's dashboard.

> **Note**
>
> We will discuss publishing apps to the Microsoft Store in *Chapter 14*, *Packaging and Deploying WinUI Applications*. We won't cover the Store registration process in this chapter, but you can skip ahead to review the process in *Chapter 14* if it's new to you.

Push notifications from WNS can be received directly by the app to signal the app to perform some action. In fact, your app doesn't need to be active to receive a notification. Windows will activate the app so it can process the notification and perform the requested action. Using notifications saves device resources and can reduce or eliminate the need for polling and timers.

Notifications from WNS may also notify the user. This is one type of app notification.

Cloud-based app notifications

App notifications involve notifying the user that some event has occurred or action is required. App notifications can be local or originate from the cloud. The cloud-based notifications, like raw notifications, leverage WNS.

The process for creating and sending these app notifications is similar to creating raw push notifications. The header and content types will distinguish the app notifications and signal Windows to display a visible, transient notification. Any notifications that haven't been dismissed or cleared by the user can be viewed in Windows settings in **Notification Center**.

> **Note**
>
> Certain types of self-contained apps or apps running with admin privileges may not be eligible to receive notifications. To view more information about these limitations, you can review this section of the push notifications documentation on Microsoft Learn: `https://learn.microsoft.com/windows/apps/windows-app-sdk/notifications/push-notifications/#limitations`.

App notifications can also be local to the user's PC. Let's discuss this type of notification next.

Local app notifications

Local app notifications do not involve the cloud and WNS is not involved in sending the notification. They originate from your app, are displayed to the user, and are handled by your app when the user acts on the toast notification. Users are familiar with these types of notifications from using Microsoft apps such as Outlook, Teams, and even the Microsoft Store app.

Sometimes, these notifications are informational, such as when the Store app displays a message after an app has been updated. The notifications can also prompt the user to take an action, such as snoozing an Outlook calendar reminder. In this case, the notification window contains a drop-down control that allows the user to select the snooze duration.

Later in this chapter, we'll add a local app notification to the **My Media Collection** app to prompt our users to add a new book to their collection. Now, we'll dive a little deeper into the implementation of raw push notifications and how they can be used to quietly receive a notification from the cloud.

Using raw push notifications in WinUI applications

As we discussed in the previous section, push notifications that are handled by the app without notifying the user are generated through WNS and Azure. In this section, we will briefly examine how these notifications can be leveraged in WinUI applications. The Azure configuration needed to get started is somewhat lengthy and not very interesting. Because the Azure Notification Hubs configuration for WNS is already well documented in the Azure docs on Microsoft Learn, you should review them before we get started: `https://learn.microsoft.com/azure/notification-hubs/notification-hubs-windows-store-dotnet-get-started-wns-push-notification`. It's also a good idea to familiarize yourself with the WNS overview in the Windows design documentation on Microsoft Learn: `https://learn.microsoft.com/windows/apps/design/shell/tiles-and-notifications/windows-push-notification-services--wns--overview`.

> **Note**
>
> The Azure documentation was written for UWP apps, but the configuration instructions work just as well for a WinUI 3 application.

Once the Azure configuration is complete, the steps to use notifications in a WinUI 3 app are similar to UWP but not exactly the same. For a detailed example of working with push notifications from the cloud, you can read this Microsoft Learn article: `https://learn.microsoft.com/windows/apps/windows-app-sdk/notifications/push-notifications/push-quickstart`. In this chapter, we are focusing on app notifications, and will add those to our sample app in the next section. The high-level steps you will need to complete are as follows:

1. Add the COM activation information to your `Package.appxmanifest` file. Here's an example:

    ```
    <Extensions>
      <!--Register COM activator-->
      <com:Extension Category="windows.comServer">
        <com:ComServer>
          <com:ExeServer Executable="MyApp\MyApp.
    exe" DisplayName="My App" Arguments="----
    WindowsAppRuntimePushServer:">
            <com:Class Id="[Azure AppId for App]" DisplayName="WinUI
    Push Notify" />
          </com:ExeServer>
        </com:ComServer>
      </com:Extension>
    </Extensions>
    ```

2. Register with `PushNotificationManager` in the `Microsoft.Windows.Push Notifications` namespace and subscribe to `PushNotificationChannel` for the notification type.

3. Add code to the App class to check whether the application was launched or activated from the background as a result of a push notification.

4. Create a WNS channel and register that channel with the WNS service. These are the HTTP endpoints that will receive the notification data to be pushed to your app.

5. Use a tool such as **Postman** (`https://postman.com/`) to send an HTTP POST request with the push notification data. You will need to get an access token for the request with your Azure tenant ID, app ID, and client secret. For more information, see this page: `https://learn.microsoft.com/azure/active-directory/develop/howto-create-service-principal-portal#get-tenant-and-app-id-values-for-signing-in`.

Those are the basic steps, but there's much more to be learned. Make sure you read all of the articles linked in this section to learn about the nuances of using raw push notifications in a WinUI application.

Now, let's learn more about app notifications and adding send-and-receive capabilities to our sample application.

Adding Windows app notifications with the Windows App SDK

In this section, we're going to add some local app notifications to the **My Media Collection** project. The code we'll add to the project is based on the Windows App SDK local app notification sample app created by the Microsoft Learn team. You can download the code for that project on GitHub: https://github.com/microsoft/WindowsAppSDK-Samples/tree/main/Samples/Notifications/App/CsUnpackagedAppNotifications.

We are adding two buttons to the MainPage in the app to trigger two types of notifications. One will have an image and some text. The second will add a text entry field to demonstrate how we can receive input from a user in the notification toast and act on it within our application.

> **Note**
>
> There is a lot of configuration and code required to implement notification handling. If you would like to open the completed solution and follow along, the code is available on GitHub: https://github.com/PacktPublishing/Learn-WinUI-3-Second-Edition/tree/main/Chapter08/Complete.

To get started, open your **MyMediaCollection** solution from the previous chapter or the starter solution for *Chapter 8* on GitHub: https://github.com/PacktPublishing/Learn-WinUI-3-Second-Edition/tree/main/Chapter08/Start:

1. The first step is to add some configuration to the `Package.appxmanifest` file to enable notification handling in the app. Start by adding two namespace declarations to the `Package` element:

   ```
   xmlns:com="http://schemas.microsoft.com/appx/manifest/com/
   windows10"
   xmlns:desktop="http://schemas.microsoft.com/appx/manifest/
   desktop/windows10"
   ```

2. Next, add an `Extensions` section inside the `Application` node, immediately after the `uap:VisualElements` section:

   ```
   <Extensions>
     <desktop:Extension Category="windows.
   toastNotificationActivation">
       <desktop:ToastNotificationActivation
   ToastActivatorCLSID="NEW GUID HERE" />
     </desktop:Extension>
     <com:Extension Category="windows.comServer">
       <com:ComServer>
   ```

```
      <com:ExeServer Executable="MyMediaCollection\
MyMediaCollection.exe" DisplayName="My Media Collection"
Arguments="----AppNotificationActivated:">
        <com:Class Id="SAME NEW GUID HERE" />
      </com:ExeServer>
    </com:ComServer>
  </com:Extension>
</Extensions>
```

Generate a new **GUID** and replace the two preceding highlighted sections of code with that GUID. It will be unique to your app. You can generate GUIDs in Visual Studio in the menu with **Tools | Create GUID**.

3. Next, we're going to create some shared code and helper classes. Your project is not going to compile without errors until we're finished with this section. First, create a new folder in your solution named `Helpers`.

4. Now create a new class named `NotificationShared` in the `Helpers` folder. Start by adding a constant and a struct to this class:

```
public const string scenarioTag = "scenarioId";
public struct Notification
{
    public string Originator;
    public string Action;
    public bool HasInput;
    public string Input;
};
```

The `Notification` struct will represent the data received in an app notification. `scenarioTag` is a constant that will be needed when each notification to send is being constructed.

5. Next, add the following static methods to the `NotificationShared` class. These will be used by the app to notify the UI when notifications are sent or received:

```
public static void CouldNotSendToast()
{
    MainPage.Current.NotifyUser("Could not send toast",
InfoBarSeverity.Error);
}
public static void ToastSentSuccessfully()
{
    MainPage.Current.NotifyUser("Toast sent successfully!",
InfoBarSeverity.Success);
}
public static void AppLaunchedFromNotification()
```

```
{
    MainPage.Current.NotifyUser("App launched from
notifications", InfoBarSeverity.Informational);
}
public static void NotificationReceived()
{
    MainPage.Current.NotifyUser("Notification received",
InfoBarSeverity.Informational);
}
public static void UnrecognizedToastOriginator()
{
    MainPage.Current.NotifyUser("Unrecognized Toast Originator
or Unknown Error", InfoBarSeverity.Error);
}
```

MainPage doesn't have a Current property, so this code won't compile yet. We'll take care of that soon. If Visual Studio didn't add the necessary using statements, make sure these are present in NotificationShared:

```
using Microsoft.UI.Xaml.Controls;
using MyMediaCollection.Views;
```

6. Now we are going to create two classes to represent the two types of notifications that the app will send and receive. First, create a new class named ToastWithAvatar and start by adding two constants to the class:

```
using Microsoft.Windows.AppNotifications.Builder;
using Microsoft.Windows.AppNotifications;
using MyMediaCollection.Views;
namespace MyMediaCollection.Helpers
{
    public class ToastWithAvatar
    {
        public const int ScenarioId = 1;
        public const string ScenarioName = "Local Toast with
Image";
    }
}
```

7. Next, add a method named SendToast to the class. This method will construct and show a Windows notification toast containing some text, an avatar image, and a button to display our app:

```
public static bool SendToast()
{
    var appNotification = new AppNotificationBuilder()
        .AddArgument("action", "ToastClick")
```

```
                    .AddArgument(NotificationShared.scenarioTag, ScenarioId.
ToString())
                    .SetAppLogoOverride(new System.Uri($"file://{App.
GetFullPathToAsset(" Square150x150Logo.scale-200.png")}"),
AppNotificationImageCrop.Circle)
                    .AddText(ScenarioName)
                    .AddText("This is a notification message.")
                    .AddButton(new AppNotificationButton("Open App")
                        .AddArgument("action", "OpenApp")
                        .AddArgument(NotificationShared.scenarioTag,
ScenarioId.ToString()))
                    .BuildNotification();
            AppNotificationManager.Default.Show(appNotification);
            // If notification is sent, it will have an Id. Success.
            return appNotification.Id != 0;
    }
```

8. Now add a `NotificationReceived` method, which will be invoked when this type of notification is received from Windows by our app. This method creates a `Notification` struct and calls a `NotificationReceived` method on `MainPage`, which we will create later in this section. We will also create the `ToForeground` method to bring our app to the front if it's hidden behind other windows or minimized:

```
public static void
NotificationReceived(AppNotificationActivatedEventArgs
notificationActivatedEventArgs)
{
    var notification = new NotificationShared.Notification
    {
        Originator = ScenarioName,
        Action = notificationActivatedEventArgs.
Arguments["action"]
    };
    MainPage.Current.NotificationReceived(notification);
    App.ToForeground();
}
```

9. The `ToastWithText` class will be similar to `ToastWithAvatar`, but it will add a call to `AddTextBox` in `AppNotificationBuilder` to create the input field in the Windows toast. It also adds the result of that user input to the `Notification` class created in `NotificationReceived`. To view the full code for this class, check out the completed solution on GitHub: `https://github.com/PacktPublishing/Learn-WinUI-3-Second-Edition/tree/main/Chapter08/Complete/MyMediaCollection/Helpers/ToastWithText.cs`.

10. Now it's time to create the NotificationManager class. This class will do exactly that – manage notifications. It will initialize and unregister notification receiving. It will do the actual sending and receiving of notifications. Create the NotificationManager class in the Helpers folder and start by adding the constructor and finalization code:

```csharp
using Microsoft.Windows.AppNotifications;
using System;
using System.Collections.Generic;
namespace MyMediaCollection.Helpers
{
    internal class NotificationManager
    {
        private bool isRegistered;
        private Dictionary<int,
Action<AppNotificationActivatedEventArgs>> notificationHandlers;
        public NotificationManager()
        {
            isRegistered = false;
            notificationHandlers = new Dictionary<int,
Action<AppNotificationActivatedEventArgs>>
            {
                { ToastWithAvatar.ScenarioId, ToastWithAvatar.
NotificationReceived },
                { ToastWithText.ScenarioId, ToastWithText.
NotificationReceived }
            };
        }
        ~NotificationManager()
        {
            Unregister();
        }
        public void Unregister()
        {
            if (isRegistered)
            {
                AppNotificationManager.Default.Unregister();
                isRegistered = false;
            }
        }
    }
}
```

11. Next, add the `Init` method that we'll call from the App class:

```
public void Init()
{
    AppNotificationManager notificationManager =
AppNotificationManager.Default;
    // Add handler before calling Register.
    notificationManager.NotificationInvoked +=
OnNotificationInvoked;
    notificationManager.Register();
    isRegistered = true;
}
```

12. `OnNotificationInvoked` is hooked up in the `Init` method. This will fire when notifications are received by the app. It makes different calls to `NotificationShared`, depending on whether the notification is recognized or not:

```
public void OnNotificationInvoked(object
sender, AppNotificationActivatedEventArgs
notificationActivatedEventArgs)
{
    NotificationShared.NotificationReceived();

    if (!DispatchNotification(notificationActivatedEventArgs))
    {
        NotificationShared.UnrecognizedToastOriginator();
    }
}
```

> **Note**
>
> If you have any unhandled exceptions in your code that process incoming notifications, they will also trigger this call to `NotificationShared.UnrecognizedToastOriginator`.

13. Finally, create the `ProcessLaunchActivationArgs` and `DispatchNotification` methods in `NotificationManager`:

```
public void
ProcessLaunchActivationArgs(AppNotificationActivatedEventArgs
notificationActivatedEventArgs)
{
    DispatchNotification(notificationActivatedEventArgs);
    NotificationShared.AppLaunchedFromNotification();
}
private bool
DispatchNotification(AppNotificationActivatedEventArgs
notificationActivatedEventArgs)
```

```
{
    var scenarioId = notificationActivatedEventArgs.
Arguments[NotificationShared.scenarioTag];
    if (scenarioId.Length != 0)
    {
        try
        {
            notificationHandlers[int.Parse(scenarioId)]
(notificationActivatedEventArgs);
            return true;
        }
        catch
        {
            // No matching handler
            return false;
        }
    }
    else
    {
        // No scenarioId provided
        return false;
    }
}
```

14. Now let's add the code to App.xaml.cs to initialize NotificationManager and handle some of the common calls. Let's start by adding the using statements that we'll need for the new code:

```
using Microsoft.Windows.AppLifecycle;
using Microsoft.Windows.AppNotifications;
using MyMediaCollection.Helpers;
using System.Runtime.InteropServices;
using WinRT.Interop;
```

15. Next, add a private notificationManager object, add DllImport to help bring the window to the foreground, and make m_window static:

```
[DllImport("user32.dll", SetLastError = true)]
static extern void SwitchToThisWindow(IntPtr hWnd, bool turnOn);
private NotificationManager notificationManager;
private static Window m_window;
```

> **Note**
>
> Be careful when choosing which Win32 APIs to use in your production WinUI applications. The `SwitchToThisWindow` API is documented as *"not suitable for general use,"* but it works for our purposes in a sample app. There are other APIs you can explore, including `ShowWindow`: https://learn.microsoft.com/windows/win32/api/winuser/nf-winuser-showwindow.

16. Next, add the following code to `OnLaunched` right before calling `m_window.Activate`. This gets the arguments passed to the app from the Windows notification:

```
var currentInstance = AppInstance.GetCurrent();
if (currentInstance.IsCurrent)
{
    AppActivationArguments activationArgs = currentInstance.
GetActivatedEventArgs();
    if (activationArgs != null)
    {
        ExtendedActivationKind extendedKind = activationArgs.
Kind;
        if (extendedKind == ExtendedActivationKind.
AppNotification)
        {
            var notificationActivatedEventArgs =
(AppNotificationActivatedEventArgs)activationArgs.Data;
            notificationManager.
ProcessLaunchActivationArgs(notificationActivatedEventArgs);
        }
    }
}
```

17. Next, add some code to the App constructor to initialize `NotificationManager` and handle the `AppDomain.CurrentDomain.ProcessExit` event to unregister the manager when the app closes:

```
public App()
{
    this.InitializeComponent();
    notificationManager = new NotificationManager();
    notificationManager.Init();
    AppDomain.CurrentDomain.ProcessExit += CurrentDomain_
ProcessExit;
}
private void CurrentDomain_ProcessExit(object sender, EventArgs
e)
{
```

```
            notificationManager.Unregister();
    }
```

18. The final items to be added to the App class are three static helper methods to get some application-related paths and the ToForeground method to bring the app to the front when it's hidden or minimized:

```
public static void ToForeground()
{
    if (m_window != null)
    {
        IntPtr handle = WindowNative.GetWindowHandle(m_window);
        if (handle != IntPtr.Zero)
        {
            SwitchToThisWindow(handle, true);
        }
    }
}
public static string GetFullPathToExe()
{
    var path = AppDomain.CurrentDomain.BaseDirectory;
    var pos = path.LastIndexOf("\\");
    return path.Substring(0, pos);
}
public static string GetFullPathToAsset(string assetName)
{
    return $"{GetFullPathToExe()}\\Assets\\{assetName}";
}
```

19. Now let's work on MainPage. Start in MainPage.xaml. We're going to add two buttons to send notifications and an InfoBar control to display messages at the bottom of the page when notifications are sent or received. Add another RowDefinition to the outermost Grid control:

```
<Grid.RowDefinitions>
    <RowDefinition Height="Auto"/>
    <RowDefinition Height="*"/>
    <RowDefinition Height="Auto"/>
    <RowDefinition Height="Auto"/>
</Grid.RowDefinitions>
```

20. Add two buttons to the beginning of StackPanel that contains the existing Button controls:

```
<StackPanel HorizontalAlignment="Right"
            Orientation="Horizontal">
```

```
<Button Command="{x:Bind ViewModel.SendToastCommand}"
        Content="Send Notification"
        Margin="8,8,0,8"/>
<Button Command="{x:Bind ViewModel.
SendToastWithTextCommand}"
        Content="Send Notification with Text"
        Margin="8,8,0,8"/>
...
</StackPanel>
```

21. Add an `InfoBar` control just before the closing tag for the outer `Grid`:

```
<InfoBar x:Name="notifyInfoBar" Grid.Row="3"/>
```

22. Next, open the `MainPage.xaml.cs` file, in which we need to add some code to handle the incoming notifications. The first thing we'll do is add a `using` statement for `MyMediaCollection.Helpers`.

23. Next, add the code to expose the current instance of `MainPage` so the notifications can be routed properly:

```
public static MainPage Current;
public MainPage()
{
    ViewModel = App.HostContainer.Services.
GetService<MainViewModel>();
    this.InitializeComponent();
    Current = this;
    Loaded += MainPage_Loaded;
}
```

24. Next, add some code to update `InfoBar` whenever notifications are sent or received. This is the code that will be called by the methods in the `NotificationShared` class:

```
public void NotifyUser(string message, InfoBarSeverity severity,
bool isOpen = true)
{
    if (DispatcherQueue.HasThreadAccess)
    {
        UpdateStatus(message, severity, isOpen);
    }
    else
    {
        DispatcherQueue.TryEnqueue(() =>
        {
            UpdateStatus(message, severity, isOpen);
```

```
        });
    }
}
private void UpdateStatus(string message, InfoBarSeverity
severity, bool isOpen)
{
    notifyInfoBar.Message = message;
    notifyInfoBar.IsOpen = isOpen;
    notifyInfoBar.Severity = severity;
}
```

The `DispatcherQueue` methods check whether the code has access to the UI thread. If not, `TryEnqueue` is used to queue the work to be performed when the UI thread is available. Otherwise, errors will be encountered when accessing UI elements from a background thread.

25. Create a `NotificationReceived` method to handle incoming notification information. This method parses through the incoming data and builds a message string to display:

```
public void NotificationReceived(NotificationShared.Notification
notification)
{
    var text = $"{notification.Originator}; Action:
{notification.Action}";
    if (notification.HasInput)
    {
        if (string.IsNullOrWhiteSpace(notification.Input))
            text += "; No input received";
        else
            text += $"; Input received: {notification.Input}";
    }
    if (DispatcherQueue.HasThreadAccess)
        DisplayMessageDialog(text);
    else
    {
        DispatcherQueue.TryEnqueue(() =>
        {
            DisplayMessageDialog(text);
        });
    }
}
```

The final code to add to `MainPage` is a simple method to display `ContentDialog` with the notification data:

```
private void DisplayMessageDialog(string message)
{
```

```
ContentDialog notifyDialog = new()
{
    XamlRoot = this.XamlRoot,
    Title = "Notification received",
    Content = message,
    CloseButtonText = "Ok"
};
notifyDialog.ShowAsync();
}
```

MainViewModel is the final class to be updated. We need to create two command methods for the new buttons to invoke when sending app notifications. Create two methods named SendToast and SendToastWithText:

```
[RelayCommand]
private void SendToast()
{
    if (ToastWithAvatar.SendToast())
        NotificationShared.ToastSentSuccessfully();
    else
        NotificationShared.CouldNotSendToast();
}
[RelayCommand]
private void SendToastWithText()
{
    if (ToastWithText.SendToast())
        NotificationShared.ToastSentSuccessfully();
    else
        NotificationShared.CouldNotSendToast();
}
```

Don't forget to add using MyMediaCollection.Helpers; to the list of using statements in MainViewModel.

We're ready to run the app and test the notifications. Start debugging and click the **Send Notification** button. You should see a toast appear in the lower-right portion of the main screen:

Figure 8.1 – A Windows toast notification

Bring another window in front of **My Media Collection** and then click **Open App** on the toast. The app should be brought back to the front of the screen and **ContentDialog** will display a message with information about the notification received:

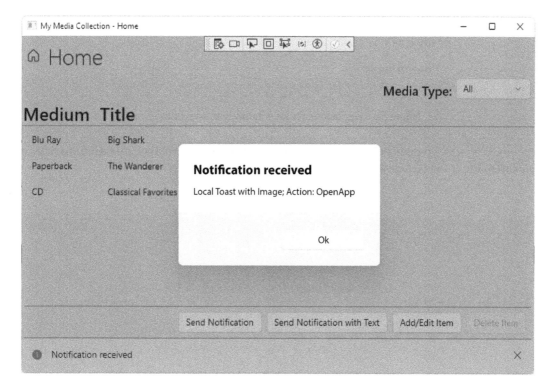

Figure 8.2 – Receiving an app notification

> **Note**
>
> If you click one of the buttons to send a notification multiple times without acknowledging the toast window, the toasts will not stack. The subsequent toasts will go straight to Windows' **Notifications Center**. Once they go there, it's not possible to use interactive fields such as a text box. In addition, if the user has *Do Not Disturb* or *Focus* mode enabled, all notifications will be suppressed and sent directly to **Notifications Center**.

Now click the **Send Notification with Text** button. When this toast appears, it will have a text box where you can **Enter a reply**:

Figure 8.3 – Displaying a toast window with a text box

Type `Hello world` and click the **Reply** button. Now, when **My Media Collection** displays **ContentDialog**, it will include the reply that was entered in the toast window:

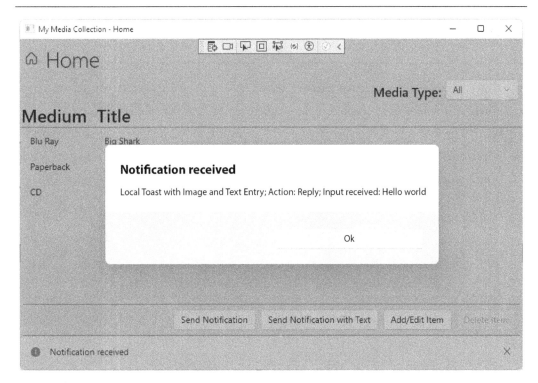

Figure 8.4 – Displaying the reply text from the toast window in our app

Now you're ready to start building notifications into your own WinUI applications. Let's wrap up the chapter and discuss what we've learned.

Summary

In this chapter, we learned about the types of Windows notifications available to WinUI developers in the Windows App SDK. We discussed how notifications can be used to save Windows resources, reduce the need for timers, and prompt users to act. We explored how to configure raw push notifications and added a local app notification to the **My Media Collection** sample app. You should now feel prepared to add any of these types of notifications to your own WinUI applications.

In the next chapter, we'll explore the **Windows Community Toolkit** (**WCT**) and learn how, together with the .NET Community Toolkit, you can save development time by leveraging existing helpers, styles, and controls.

Questions

1. What type of Windows notification can be used to initiate a data sync from the cloud?

2. Which type of notification doesn't rely on WNS?

3. Where do you register your app before configuring notification services in Azure?

4. Which Windows App SDK namespace contains the objects for working with app notifications?

5. Which class has methods to register and unregister your app for handling app notifications?

6. Which property can be set if you would like notifications from your app to disappear after a system reboot?

7. Can notifications from WNS prompt the user with a toast notification?

9

Enhancing Applications with Community Toolkits

The **Windows Community Toolkit (WCT)** and the **.NET Community Toolkit** are collections of open source libraries for Windows and .NET developers. The toolkits contain controls and libraries that can be leveraged by the **Windows UI Library (WinUI)**, **Universal Windows Platform (UWP)**, **.NET Multi-platform App UI (.NET MAUI)**, **Windows Presentation Foundation (WPF)**, and **Windows Forms (WinForms)** applications. In the **Microsoft Store**, there is a companion sample application for the WCT that developers can install to explore the controls and learn how to use them.

In this chapter, we will cover the following topics:

- Learning about the background and purpose of the toolkits
- Using the toolkit sample application to explore the controls available in the WCT
- Leveraging toolkit controls in a WinUI project
- Exploring the helpers, services, and extensions for Windows developers in the WCT
- Discovering what's available in the .NET Community Toolkit for WinUI developers

By the end of this chapter, you will understand the WCT and how it can boost your productivity when building Windows applications. You will also know how to incorporate its controls into your WinUI applications.

Technical requirements

To follow along with the examples in this chapter, the following software is required:

- Windows 10 version 1809 (build 17763) or newer
- Visual Studio 2022 or newer with the .NET desktop development workload configured for Windows App SDK development

The source code for this chapter is available on GitHub at `https://github.com/Packt Publishing/Learn-WinUI-3-Second-Edition/tree/master/Chapter09`.

Introducing the WCT

The WCT was created by Microsoft as an open source collection of controls and other helpers, tools, and services for Windows developers. It is primarily used by UWP developers but also adds value for WinUI, WinForms, and WPF developers. The toolkit is available to developers as a set of NuGet packages. There are over a dozen toolkit packages available on NuGet that can be installed independently, depending on the needs of your project. We will explore some of these packages throughout this chapter. Let's start by discussing the history of the WCT.

The toolkit was open sourced from the very beginning. It has long been available on GitHub at `https://github.com/CommunityToolkit/WindowsCommunityToolkit`, but the next generation of the toolkit is being hosted at `https://github.com/CommunityToolkit/Windows`. This new iteration of the toolkit is aimed toward helping WinUI 2, WinUI 3, and **Uno Platform** developers, but this new toolkit doesn't have any releases available yet. The toolkit is open to community contributions if you're interested in helping to move the project forward. The documentation for the WCT is available on *Microsoft Learn* at `https://learn.microsoft.com/windows/communitytoolkit/`.

Origins of the WCT

The WCT was first introduced as the **UWP Community Toolkit** in 2016. As the name implies, it was originally a toolkit solely for UWP developers. The toolkit was created to simplify UWP app development by providing controls and helpers that Windows developers frequently create for their own common libraries. The idea of creating a toolkit for XAML development is not a new one. There have been several other similar projects for other platforms, including the following:

- **WPF Toolkit** (`https://github.com/dotnetprojects/wpftoolkit`): A set of WPF open source controls and other components, originally hosted by Microsoft on **CodePlex**.

- **Extended WPF Toolkit** (`https://github.com/xceedsoftware/wpftoolkit`): An open source collection of controls maintained by **Xceed Software**, intended to complement the original WPF Toolkit.

- **Xamarin Community Toolkit** (`https://github.com/xamarin/Xamarin CommunityToolkit`): An open source collection of **Xamarin** controls, animations, behaviors, and effects for **Xamarin.Forms**. As Xamarin developers move to **.NET MAUI**, there is now a **.NET MAUI Community Toolkit** too (`https://github.com/CommunityToolkit/Maui`).

Microsoft, with help from the open source community, released regular updates to the toolkit, adding new and enhanced components and controls multiple times a year. In spring 2018, shortly before the release of v3.0, they announced the toolkit's new name: *Windows Community Toolkit*. This renaming signaled the team's intent to embrace all Windows developers moving forward.

WCT 3.0 included a legacy Microsoft Edge-based `WebView` control—not to be confused with `WebView2`, which we will cover later in this chapter—for WPF and WinForms applications. The release also added code samples to Visual Basic, which is still used in many legacy Windows desktop code bases.

Another purpose of the toolkit was to allow developers to work on new controls with the hope that some would be integrated into the Windows SDK at a later date (or alternatively, the WinUI libraries). This has happened with several controls over the years since the toolkit's introduction, including the `WebView` control.

Subsequent toolkit releases have continued to add value for both UWP and desktop developers, and these releases have been fueled by community contributions.

Reviewing recent toolkit releases

There have been several major releases of the WCT since version 3.0. It was WCT version 7.0 that first added WinUI 3 support.

In August 2018, WCT 4.0 added a `DataGrid` control, a feature long desired by UWP developers who were familiar with the `DataGrid` control available on the Silverlight and WPF platforms. This was quickly followed by a fall 2018 release of version 5. This release brought two major features to the toolkit, as follows:

- `WindowsXamlHost`: This control enabled a single UWP control to be wrapped and hosted within a WPF or WinForms control. Later, the `WindowsXamlHost` control would be known as XAML Islands, with the hosting API added to the Windows SDK. Several *wrapped controls* were also released, including `InkCanvas`, `MapControl`, and an update to the legacy `WebView` control.

- `TabView`: Behind `DataGrid`, a rich `TabView` control was probably the most requested control not yet available to UWP developers. The WCT `TabView` control included support for customizing, closing, and dragging and dropping tabs. `TabView` has also graduated to the WinUI 2 libraries, becoming available in WinUI 2.2 and later.

A year later, in fall 2019, WCT 6.0 brought XAML Islands controls to all WinForms, WPF, and C++ Win32 developers, adding support for .NET Core 3 clients. The other major improvement in this release was adding ARM64 development support. In June 2020, the team announced WCT 6.1, as well as upcoming previews of versions 7 and 8. Several previews of WCT 7.0 were released in 2020, and its final release came out in March 2021. The toolkit's 7.0 release included major project refactorings plus several major features. The most exciting feature was the first release of the **MVVM Toolkit**, which has since moved to the .NET Community Toolkit. We've made good use of the MVVM Toolkit in our **My Media Collection** project's `ViewModel` classes.

WCT 7.1 was released in September 2021. It added some helper classes for Microsoft Graph and the Microsoft Identity platform, as well as some new controls, behaviors, shadows, and styles. In November 2021, version 7.1.2 was released. This was announced as the final release to include updates to .NET libraries in the toolkit, as these are all moving to the .NET Community Toolkit. All subsequent 7.x releases have been UWP-only updates.

The newly released WCT 8.0 supports WinUI 3. Previously, creating WinUI 3 apps with .NET supported by WCT was only in preview in the new WCT repository. Trying these packages required building the toolkit libraries from source code as it has no published releases on GitHub. Now that they are available as stable NuGet packages, you can add them to your project as you would with any other package.

Now that we have covered some background and history of the WCT, we will take a quick look at some of the controls and components available in the toolkit.

Exploring the WCT Gallery app

As we mentioned earlier in this chapter, the **WCT Gallery app** is available from the Microsoft Store (`https://apps.microsoft.com/store/detail/windows-community-toolkit-gallery/9NBLGGH4TLCQ`). It can be installed on Windows 10 version 17763 or later, on Windows 11, or even on your Xbox, Surface Hub, or HoloLens device. As with the **WinUI 3 Gallery** app we discussed in *Chapter 5, Exploring WinUI Controls*, the toolkit sample app provides us with an easy way to navigate and explore the contents of the WCT.

Installing and launching the app

Let's get started:

1. Open the **Microsoft Store** app from the Windows Start menu and enter `windows community` in the **Search** box:

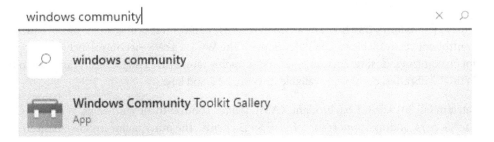

Figure 9.1 – Finding the app in the Microsoft Store

2. Select **Windows Community Toolkit Gallery** from the search results and click the **Install** button on the resulting page. Once the installation completes, the **Install** button will become an **Open** button. Open the WCT app from there or from the Windows Start menu:

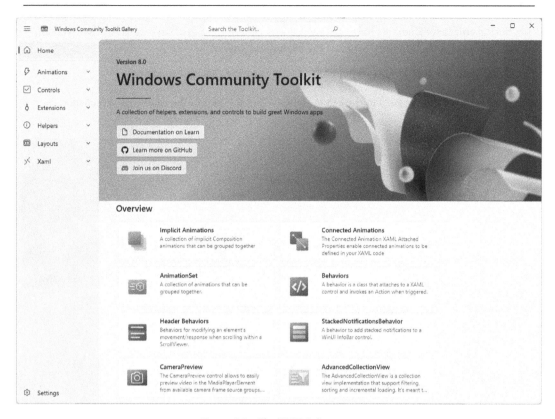

Figure 9.2 – The WCT Gallery app

The app opens to an overview page, where there are several highlighted controls, helpers, and behaviors. The top section also has some useful links to the WCT documentation, GitHub repository, and their Discord community.

The controls and other components are divided into seven sections on the left: **Animations**, **Controls**, **Extensions**, **Helpers**, **Layouts**, **Xaml**, and the app's **Settings**. With so many controls in the toolkit, we will explore just a few of them and leave the rest for you to explore on your own.

Controls

Click the **Controls** navigation item at the left of the app to display a list of controls. This is the largest section of the app, with the controls grouped by category, as follows:

- **Input**: These are custom input controls (for example, **RadialGuage**)
- **Layout**: Layout panels and related controls (for example, **HeaderedTreeView**)
- **Media**: Controls for working with media (for example, **CameraPreview**)
- **Sizers**: These are content sizing controls (for example, **GridSplitter**)

- **Status and Info**: Controls for updating the user on progress or status. In the current version of the app, the section only contains the **MetadataControl**

- **Text**: These are types of text input controls (for example, **RichSuggestBox**)

You can see some of the controls in the expanded navigation panel in the following screenshot:

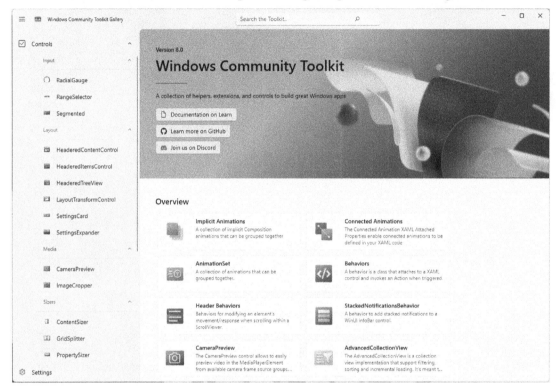

Figure 9.3 – The Controls menu expanded in the WCT Gallery app

Selecting one of these controls will open a page that contains several regions. The main panel is an interactive region where you can interact with the selected control. To the right of this panel, there are some drop-down boxes to update the control's behavior and a button where you can toggle between a **Light** or **Dark** theme, which will update the controls running in the panel.

The right panel contains several controls to modify the display and behavior of the current controls. The number of controls seen on the right panel will vary depending on the selected control. The **View Code** button expands a XAML editor with the markup for the code running in the main panel. You can change the markup here, and your changes will be reflected in the code running in the main panel. The **C#** tab will display the C# code for the control. Below the interactive section of the page, control's documentation from *Microsoft Learn* is displayed:

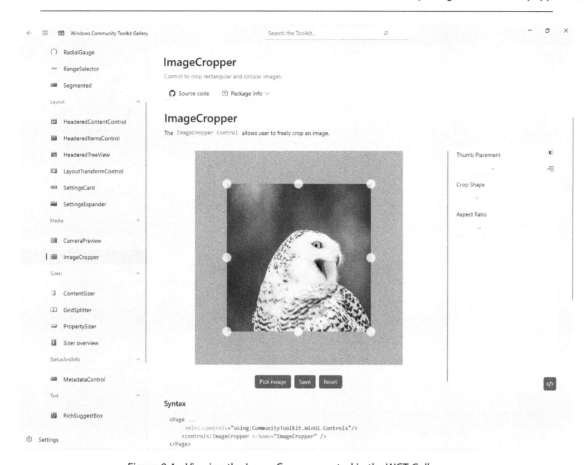

Figure 9.4 – Viewing the ImageCropper control in the WCT Gallery app

Take some time to explore the **ImageCropper** control and **MarkdownTextBlock** in the **Controls** section of the toolkit. Follow these steps:

1. Open the **ImageCropper** control and give it a try. Click the **Crop Shape** drop-down control, select **Circular**, and watch the cropped area change to a circle shape.

2. Next, select the **RangeSelector** control in the left panel. This control's page is similar, but on the main panel, there is a RangeSelector control where two sliders can be moved to select minimum and maximum points for the range. The **Minimum** and **Maximum** allowed values can be controlled from the right side of the panel as well:

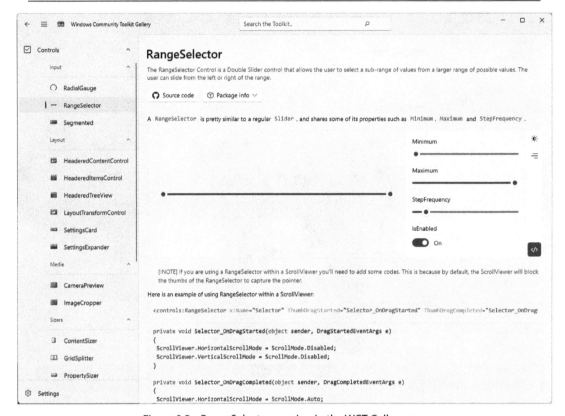

Figure 9.5 – RangeSelector running in the WCT Gallery app

3.   Scroll down to see an example use of the control.

There are many more controls you can explore in this part of the app. You should take some time to find out which might be useful in your next project.

Now that we have explored a couple of the controls in the sample app, let's try using them in a WinUI project.

Using controls from the toolkit

We explored a handful of the WCT controls in the sample app in the previous section. Now, it's time to use them in a WinUI project. To demonstrate some of the controls in action, we are going to create a new **WinUI 3 in Desktop** project.

> **Note**
>
> At the time of writing, the WCT controls are not recommended for use in production apps and have some caveats. To learn more about the current limitations, you can read this Microsoft blog post: `https://devblogs.microsoft.com/ifdef-windows/windows-community-toolkit-for-project-reunion-0-5/`.

Creating the WinUI project

To start our WCT project, you will have to launch Visual Studio and follow these steps:

1. Create a new project. Then, on the **Create a new project** page, enter `WinUI in Desktop` in the search field.

2. Several project types will be displayed, but one of the top results will be **Blank App, Packaged (WinUI 3 in Desktop)**. Select this project template for the language of your choice and click **Next**.

3. Name the project `HardwareSupplies` and click the **Create** button. The solution will be created and loaded into Visual Studio. The main **HardwareSupplies** project will have some familiar-looking components; that is, `App.xaml` and `MainWindow.xaml`:

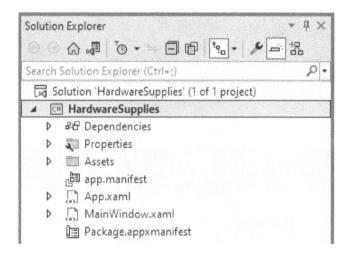

Figure 9.6 – The HardwareSupplies project in Visual Studio Solution Explorer

4. If you open the `MainWindow.xaml` file, you will see some simple starter markup. There is a `StackPanel` control containing a `Button` control named `myButton` with `Click Me` as its content. This is what the code looks like:

```
<StackPanel Orientation="Horizontal"
            HorizontalAlignment="Center"
            VerticalAlignment="Center">
```

```
    <Button x:Name="myButton"
          Click="myButton_Click">
       Click Me
    </Button>
</StackPanel>
```

5. The myButton control's Click event has a myButton_Click event handler in MainWindow.
    xaml.cs that changes the myButton variable's content to Clicked, as illustrated in the
    following code snippet:

```
private void myButton_Click(object sender, RoutedEventArgs e)
{
    myButton.Content = "Clicked";
}
```

6. Before we make any changes, run the application and test the button to make sure everything
    is working as expected:

Figure 9.7 – Running the HardwareSupplies app for the first time

Everything is working as expected. Next, we're going to add WCT package references to the project.

Referencing WCT packages

The primary control we need for the app is a DataGrid control that displays a list of hardware items.
We will also add a HeaderedContentControl control and a DropShadowPanel control to get
an idea of how those controls can be used. Most of the WCT controls are part of the **CommunityToolkit.
WinUI.UI.Controls** package, but DataGrid is in the **CommunityToolkit.WinUI.UI.Controls.
DataGrid** package. Open **NuGet Package Manager**, search for communitytoolkit.winui,
and add the latest version of those two packages to the project:

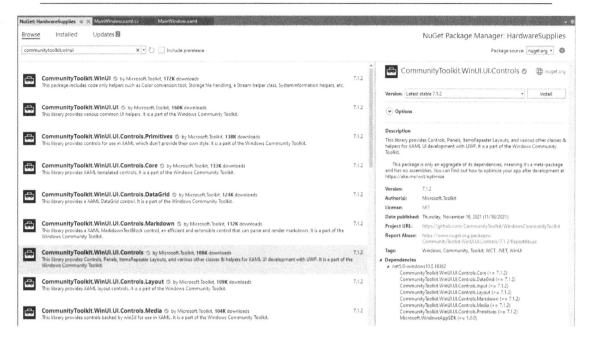

Figure 9.8 – Adding the WCT NuGet packages

After installing these two packages, close the package manager window and compile the project to ensure all the packages are downloaded. Next, we will set up some data for the `DataGrid` control.

Adding data to the DataGrid control

The most important part of any `DataGrid` control is the data being presented to the user. Before we start building the UI, we're going to build a small inventory of hardware data to display. Proceed as follows:

1. Start by adding a new class to the `HardwareSupplies` project named `HardwareItem`. The class will have six properties, as shown here:

    ```
    public class HardwareItem
    {
        public long id { get; set; }
        public string name { get; set; }
        public string category { get; set; }
        public int quantity { get; set; }
        public decimal cost { get; set; }
        public decimal price { get; set; }
    }
    ```

2. Next, open the `MainWindow.xaml.cs` file. Create a public property named `HardwareItems` and define it as an array of `HardwareItem`:

```
public HardwareItem[] HardwareItems { get; set; }
```

3. Now, create a new method named `PopulateItems`. This method will initialize the `HardwareItems` array and populate it with 12 items:

```
private void PopulateItems()
{
    HardwareItems = new HardwareItem[]
    {
        new HardwareItem { id = 1, name = "Wood Screw", category
= "Screws", cost = 0.02M, price = 0.10M, quantity = 504 },
        new HardwareItem { id = 2, name = "Sheet Metal Screw",
category = "Screws", cost = 0.03M, price = 0.15M, quantity = 655
},
        new HardwareItem { id = 3, name = "Drywall Screw",
category = "Screws", cost = 0.02M, price = 0.11M, quantity = 421
},
        new HardwareItem { id = 4, name = "Galvanized Nail",
category = "Nails", cost = 0.04M, price = 0.16M, quantity = 5620
},
        new HardwareItem { id = 5, name = "Framing Nail",
category = "Nails", cost = 0.06M, price = 0.20M, quantity =
12000 },
        new HardwareItem { id = 6, name = "Finishing Nail 2
inch", category = "Nails", cost = 0.02M, price = 0.11M, quantity
= 1405 },
        new HardwareItem { id = 7, name = "Finishing Nail 1
inch", category = "Nails", cost = 0.01M, price = 0.10M, quantity
= 1110 },
        new HardwareItem { id = 8, name = "Light Switch -
White", category = "Electrical", cost = 0.25M, price = 1.99M,
quantity = 78 },
        new HardwareItem { id = 9, name = "Outlet - White",
category = "Electrical", cost = 0.21M, price = 1.99M, quantity =
56 },
        new HardwareItem { id = 10, name = "Outlet - Beige",
category = "Electrical", cost = 0.21M, price = 1.99M, quantity =
90 },
        new HardwareItem { id = 11, name = "Wire Ties", category
= "Electrical", cost = 0.50M, price = 4.99M, quantity = 125 },
        new HardwareItem { id = 12, name = "Switch Plate -
White", category = "Electrical", cost = 0.21M, price = 2.49M,
quantity = 200 }
    };
}
```

The app now has a nice assortment of screws, nails, and electrical items to present in the `DataGrid` control.

4. Remove the `myButton_Click` event handler, as it's no longer needed.

5. Finally, call `PopulateItems` at the end of the `MainWindow` constructor:

```
public MainWindow()
{
    this.InitializeComponent();
    PopulateItems();
}
```

The data is ready to go. Let's move on and define the XAML markup for `MainWindow`.

Adding controls to the MainWindow control

The UI for our app will be simple. We will display the data in a `DataGrid` control with a drop shadow beneath some header text.

> **Note**
>
> The `DropShadowPanel` control will be removed from the toolkit in the future. You can consider using the `AttachedDropShadow` or `AttachedCardShadow` control as alternatives. For more information, read about **Attached Shadows**: `https://learn.microsoft.com/windows/communitytoolkit/helpers/attachedshadows`.

Proceed as follows:

1. Start by placing a `HeaderedContentControl` control inside a `Grid` control in `MainWindow.xaml`. Set the `Header` attribute to `Hardware Inventory`. This will display at the top of `MainWindow` control's content. Set `Margin` to 6 to leave some space around the edges of the control:

```
<Grid>
    <wct:HeaderedContentControl Header="Hardware Inventory"
                                Margin="6">
    </wct:HeaderedContentControl>
</Grid>
```

2. Don't forget to add a namespace definition for the WCT controls, as follows:

```
<Window
    x:Class="HardwareSupplies.MainWindow"
    xmlns="http://schemas.microsoft.com/winfx/2006/xaml/
presentation"
```

```
xmlns:x="http://schemas.microsoft.com/winfx/2006/xaml"
xmlns:local="using:HardwareSupplies"
xmlns:wct="using:CommunityToolkit.WinUI.UI.Controls"
xmlns:d="http://schemas.microsoft.com/expression/blend/2008"
xmlns:mc="http://schemas.openxmlformats.org/markup-
compatibility/2006"
mc:Ignorable="d">
```

3. Next, define a `DropShadowPanel` control as the content of `HeaderedContentControl`. `BlurRadius` defines the width of the blurred area of the drop shadow. A `ShadowOpacity` value of 1 indicates that the darkest part of the shadow will be completely opaque. Most of this will be behind the `DataGrid` control. The `OffsetX` and `OffsetY` values will shift the drop shadow over and down by 2 pixels. The `Color` attribute sets the color of the shadow. Setting `IsMasked` to `True` creates a more precise shadow but degrades performance. In our case, performance will not be a concern. Finally, we'll set `Margin` to 6 to leave some space to see the drop shadow:

```
<wct:HeaderedContentControl Header="Hardware Inventory"
                            Margin="6" x:Name="headerPanel">
    <wct:DropShadowPanel BlurRadius="8"
                         ShadowOpacity="1"
                         OffsetX="2"
                         OffsetY="2"
                         Color="Gray"
                         IsMasked="True"
                         Margin="6">
    </wct:DropShadowPanel>
</wct:HeaderedContentControl>
```

4. Lastly, add `DataGrid` as a child of `DropShadowPanel`. The grid will bind to the `HardwareItems` property we created. The `AutoGenerateColumns` property will create column headers using the names of the `HardwareItem` objects' properties. By setting `Background` and `AlternatingRowBackground` to `ThemeResource` styles, the grid will look great for Windows users who use either the **Light** or **Dark** theme. If you do not set any background colors, `DataGrid` will be transparent, and the gray drop shadow will obscure the contents of the grid:

```
<wct:DropShadowPanel BlurRadius="8"
                     ShadowOpacity="1"
                     OffsetX="2"
                     OffsetY="2"
                     Color="Gray"
                     IsMasked="True"
                     Margin="6">
```

```
<wct:DataGrid ItemsSource="{x:Bind HardwareItems}"
              AutoGenerateColumns="True"
              AlternatingRowBackground="{ThemeResource
SystemControlBackgroundListLowBrush}"
              Background="{ThemeResource
SystemControlBackgroundAltHighBrush}"/>
</wct:DropShadowPanel>
```

5. The app's code is complete. It's time to build and run the app to see how everything looks:

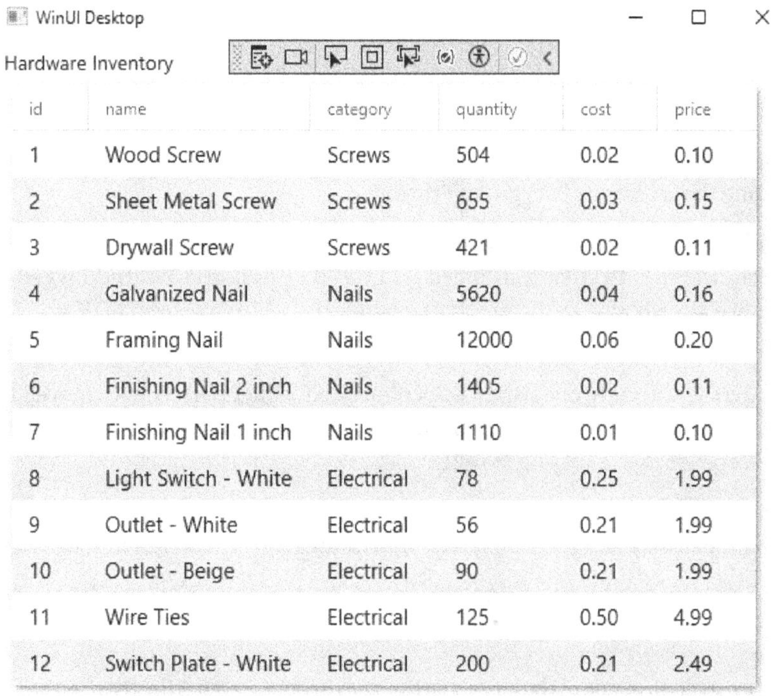
WinUI Desktop
Hardware Inventory
id | name | category | quantity | cost | price
1 | Wood Screw | Screws | 504 | 0.02 | 0.10
2 | Sheet Metal Screw | Screws | 655 | 0.03 | 0.15
3 | Drywall Screw | Screws | 421 | 0.02 | 0.11
4 | Galvanized Nail | Nails | 5620 | 0.04 | 0.16
5 | Framing Nail | Nails | 12000 | 0.06 | 0.20
6 | Finishing Nail 2 inch | Nails | 1405 | 0.02 | 0.11
7 | Finishing Nail 1 inch | Nails | 1110 | 0.01 | 0.10
8 | Light Switch - White | Electrical | 78 | 0.25 | 1.99
9 | Outlet - White | Electrical | 56 | 0.21 | 1.99
10 | Outlet - Beige | Electrical | 90 | 0.21 | 1.99
11 | Wire Ties | Electrical | 125 | 0.50 | 4.99
12 | Switch Plate - White | Electrical | 200 | 0.21 | 2.49

Figure 9.9 – The HardwareSupplies app running with data

Here, you can see that, with a little bit of code, we have a pretty nice-looking app to display some hardware inventory data. The header text, drop shadow, and rich `DataGrid` control work well together to create our UI.

Let's finish up our exploration of the WCT by looking at some of the other components available in the toolkit.

Exploring the toolkit's helpers, services, and extensions

We have discussed many of the controls in the WCT, but the toolkit contains much more than UI controls. In this section, we will return to the WCT sample app to explore some of the other components available in the toolkit. We'll start with some helper classes.

Helpers

Next to the controls in the toolkit, the **Helpers** section contains the largest number of components. As with the controls, the helpers are divided into categories in the sample app, as follows:

- **Data**: These helpers relate to loading and displaying data. Examples include **ImageCache**, **ObservableGroup**, and **Incremental Loading Collection**.

- **Developer**: These are helpers that are useful for developers and include **DispatcherQueueHelper** for updating the UI from a background thread.

- **Notifications**: These helpers provide customized ways of notifying users with Windows notifications and the Start menu. Included are **LiveTile**, **Toast**, and **WeatherLiveTileAndToast**. However, we already saw in the previous chapter that Windows App SDK now has built-in support for notifications in WinUI 3 apps. These toolkit helpers are useful for UWP developers.

- **Parser**: There is currently one parser helper included. Other parsers have moved to the .NET Community Toolkit. The **Win2d Path Mini Language Parser** helps when drawing with the CanvasGeometry class using **Win2D**.

- **State Triggers:** There are currently 10 state trigger helpers in the toolkit, including **IsNullOrEmptyStateTrigger**, **FullScreenModeStateTrigger**, and **RegexStateTrigger**.

- **Systems**: The 14 system helpers currently include **CameraHelper**, **NetworkHelper**, **PrintHelper**, and **ThemeListener**.

It's time to take a closer look at one of the helpers in the toolkit. Let's see what the SystemInformation helper class offers. This is a static class that contains a long list of useful information about the running application and the user's system. These are just a handful of the available properties:

- ApplicationName: The application's name

- ApplicationVersion: The application version

- AvailableMemory: The available system memory

- Culture: The current culture set in Windows

- DeviceFamily: The name of the user's device family

- DeviceModel: The model number of the current device

- FirstUseTime: The first time the app was launched

- `IsAppUpdated`: Indicates if this is the first time the app has been run after being updated

- `LaunchCount`: The number of times the app has been launched since a system reset

- `OperatingSystem`: The name of the operating system

- `OperatingSystemVersion`: The operating system version

There are many other helpers you can explore in the sample app. We'll finish up by reviewing some of the other tools in the **Extensions** area of the WCT sample app.

Extensions

The **Extensions** menu in the sample app contains several items that add extended properties to WinUI controls and extension methods to other classes. We will review **FrameworkElementExtensions** (formerly known as the **Mouse** extensions) and **StringExtensions** here.

FrameworkElementExtensions adds a property to any `FrameworkElement` control in order to set the mouse cursor to display when the mouse moves over that element:

```
<Button ui:FrameworkElementExtensions.Cursor="Wait"
        Content="Show Wait Cursor" />
<Button ui:FrameworkElementExtensions.Cursor="Hand"
        Content="Show Hand Cursor" />
<Button ui:FrameworkElementExtensions.Cursor="UniversalNo"
        Content="Show UniversalNo Cursor" />
```

StringExtensions contains a few extension methods related to string data, as follows:

- `IsEmail`: Determines whether a string is a valid email address format

- `IsDecimal`: Determines whether a string is a decimal value

- `IsNumeric`: Determines whether a string is a numeric value

- `IsPhoneNumber`: Determines whether a string contains a valid phone number format

- `IsCharacterString`: Determines whether a string contains only letters

- `DecodeHtml`: Returns a string with any HTML formatting, tags, comments, scripts, and styles removed

- `FixHtml`: Similar to `DecodeHtml`, it returns a string with all HTML formatting, comments, scripts, and styles removed

- `Truncate`: Truncates a string to a specified length, optionally adding an ellipsis

The `Truncate` extension includes two overloads. This code will truncate the `name` string so that it's no longer than 10 characters. It will truncate the `city` string to seven characters and add an ellipsis to the end of the string to indicate that it was truncated, as follows:

```
string name = "Bobby Joe Johnson";
string city = "San Francisco";
name.Truncate(10); // name will be "Bobby Joe "
city.Truncate(7, true); // city will be "San Fra..."
```

I encourage you to explore these extensions, and all the others in the WCT. The sample app is a great way to visually explore the toolkit and get ideas of how to integrate it into your own projects.

Before we wrap up, let's briefly discuss the .NET Community Toolkit.

.NET Community Toolkit features

The .NET Community Toolkit can be leveraged by all .NET developers. In *Chapter 3*, *MVVM for Maintainability and Testability*, we used the MVVM Toolkit, which is part of the .NET Community Toolkit. There are several other features of this toolkit, primarily targeting performance and diagnostics.

The **CommunityToolkit.Diagnostics** package is available for .NET developers or those frameworks that implement .NET Standard 2.0 or later. It includes two helper libraries, `Guard` and `ThrowHelper`.

`Guard` APIs are used to validate the arguments passed into your .NET methods. They are created to be fast, with minimal impact on the performance of your applications. Here are a few examples of their use:

```
public void TestData(decimal[] numbers, int size, string data)
{
    Guard.IsNotNull(numbers);
    Guard.IsInRangeFor(size, numbers);
    Guard.IsNotNullOrWhitespace(data);
}
```

You can view a complete set of helper methods in the *Microsoft Learn* documentation: `https://learn.microsoft.com/dotnet/api/microsoft.toolkit.diagnostics.guard#methods`.

The `ThrowHelper` class is a performant, efficient method of throwing exceptions. It's intended to work well with `Guard` helpers. The syntax is similar to the built-in way of throwing exceptions in .NET. This code could be used to throw an `ArgumentException` exception from our `TestData` method shown previously:

```
ThrowHelper.ThrowArgumentException<int>(nameof(size));
```

The **CommunityToolkit.HighPerformance** package includes helpers and extensions for code focused on high performance. Once again, the package is available for .NET and .NET Standard targets.

The following members are available in the **HighPerformance** package:

- `Span2D<T>`: This type has the same functionality as a `Span<T>` type but supports 2D memory.

- `Memory2D<T>`: This type has the same functionality as a `Memory<T>` type but supports 2D memory locations.

- `SpanOwner<T>`: This type is a stack-only buffer that leverages a shared memory pool to borrow memory only used in synchronous code.

- `MemoryOwner<T>`: This type is another buffer type. It implements `IMemoryOwner<T>` and is a lightweight wrapper around `ArrayPool<T>`.

- `StringPool`: This type is a configurable pool of `string` objects. It can improve performance when creating a large number of strings from buffers or streams.

- `ParallelHelper`: This helper class contains a set of APIs for working with parallel code in .NET. It has multiple overloads of the following helper methods: `For`, `For2D`, and `ForEach`. Each of these helper methods creates an optimized parallel loop.

- `Ref<T>`: This type is a stack-only type that stores a reference to a value. It can be used in place of a `ref  T` value in C# code, as they're not otherwise supported. There is also a `ReadOnlyRef<T>` type.

For an in-depth description of these types and scenarios for their use, you should check out the documentation on *Microsoft Learn*: `https://learn.microsoft.com/dotnet/communitytoolkit/high-performance/introduction`. The source code for the .NET Community Toolkit is available on GitHub: `https://github.com/CommunityToolkit/dotnet`.

Now, let's wrap up and review what we've learned in this chapter.

Summary

In this chapter, you learned about the controls, helpers, services, and other components available to WinUI developers in the WCT and the .NET Community Toolkit. We also practiced adding some of the WCT controls into a WinUI 3 project, leveraging the powerful `DataGrid` control. Finally, we installed and used the WCT sample app to discover the controls and components in the toolkit that we can use in our apps. Adding WCT packages to your application will provide controls with rich functionality and extensions that save you time.

In the next chapter, we will be working with the **Template Studio for WinUI** extension for Visual Studio to learn how you can quickly create a new WinUI app with rich controls and components included.

Questions

1. What was the original name of the WCT?

2. Which WCT legacy browser control can be used in WPF or WinForms apps?

3. Which WCT control can render markdown output?

4. Which helper in the WCT can manage and group items into an observable collection?

5. What is the name of the Visual Studio project template for running WinUI 3 apps?

6. Which of these was moved to the .NET Community Toolkit: `DataGrid` control, MVVM Toolkit, or `PrintHelper`?

7. Which extension class in the WCT contains methods to validate strings, including `IsEmail` and `IsPhoneNumber`?

8. Which WCT extension can update the Windows cursor at the control level?

10

Accelerating App Development with Template Studio

Starting a new project from scratch can be daunting. What are the best practices for application architecture and project layout? **Template Studio for WinUI** is an open source project that began as **Windows Template Studio** for UWP and WPF applications. Each version of Template Studio is an extension for Visual Studio. It now supports WinUI, and variations have been created that will also generate **.NET MAUI** and **Uno Platform** projects.

In this chapter, we will cover the following topics:

- Discover what Template Studio is and how it can help developers create new WinUI projects while following best patterns and practices

- Review the history of Windows Template Studio and UWP applications

- Create a new project with Template Studio for WinUI and the MVVM Toolkit

- Learn about other variations of Template Studio

By the end of this chapter, you will understand the origins of the current Template Studio extensions for Visual Studio. You'll also have enough familiarity with Template Studio for WinUI to choose it when starting your next WinUI 3 project. You will also know where you can go to suggest enhancements, submit issues, or improve the project by submitting your own changes to the open source project.

Technical requirements

To follow along with the examples in this chapter, please refer to the *Technical requirements* section of *Chapter 2, Configuring the Development Environment and Creating the Project*.

The source code for this chapter is available on GitHub here: `https://github.com/PacktPublishing/Learn-WinUI-3-Second-Edition/tree/master/Chapter10`

Overview of Template Studio for WinUI

Template Studio for WinUI is an open source extension for Visual Studio that enhances the experience of creating a new WinUI 3 project. Microsoft currently has three versions of the Template Studio extension available:

- **Template Studio for WinUI (C#)** – This is the extension we will use in this chapter. There are also plans for a C++ version of Template Studio for WinUI.

- **Template Studio for WPF** – The WPF version of Template Studio is similar to the WinUI extension. It creates a .NET WPF project.

- **Template Studio for UWP** – This version is the updated extension that was originally named Windows Template Studio.

The code and documentation for the Template Studio projects are available on GitHub: `https://github.com/microsoft/TemplateStudio`. The team also maintains a release roadmap on GitHub that you can monitor: `https://github.com/microsoft/TemplateStudio/blob/main/docs/roadmap.md`.

Creating a new project with one of the Template Studio extensions launches an enhanced wizard-style experience where you can select the type of project you want to create and the design pattern to follow (such as MVVM). You can also select some pre-defined pages and other features to include in your project, as well as a unit test project. We will step through the full experience and discuss the options in the next section.

Template Studio for WinUI is installed like any other Visual Studio extension. If you aren't familiar with the process, you can either download the **VSIX** package from the Visual Studio Marketplace (`https://marketplace.visualstudio.com/items?itemName=TemplateStudio.TemplateStudioForWinUICs`) or you can search for and add it in the **Manage Extensions** dialog box in Visual Studio.

Template Studio for WinUI (C#)

Microsoft | ⤓ 36,588 installs | ★ ★ ★ ★ ★ (7) | Free

Template Studio accelerates the creation of new WinUI apps using a wizard-based UI.

Download

Overview   Rating & Review

Template Studio for WinUI accelerates the creation of new WinUI apps using a wizard-based UI.

Projects created with this extension contain well-formed, readable code and incorporate the latest development features while implementing proven patterns and leading practices. The generated code includes links to documentation and TODO comments that provide useful insight and guidance for turning the generated projects into production applications.

To get started, install the extension, then select the corresponding Template Studio project template when creating a new project in Visual Studio. Name your project, then click Create to launch the Template Studio wizard.

Categories

Tools   Coding   Other

Tags

MVVM   WinUI   XAML   Template Studio   Templates

Works with

Visual Studio 2022 (amd64), 2022 (Arm64)

Resources

License

Copy ID

Project Details

○ microsoft/TemplateStudio

● Last Commit: 3 weeks ago

⋔ 6 Pull Requests

❶ 165 Open Issues

More Info

Version   5.4

Released on   4/28/2022, 6:28:48 PM

Last updated   5/16/2023, 4:36:58 PM

Publisher   Microsoft

Report   Report Abuse

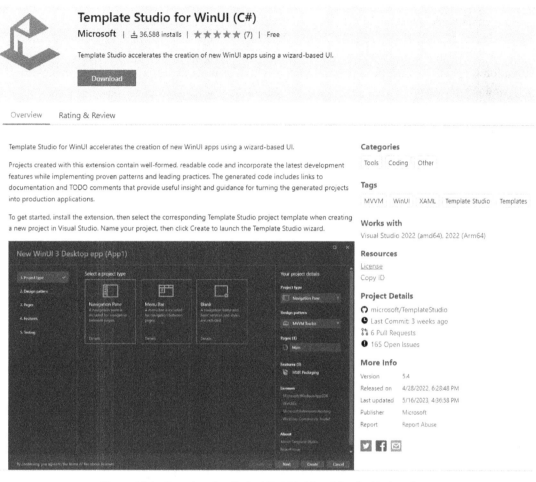

Figure 10.1 – Template Studio for WinUI in Visual Studio Marketplace

We'll be using the **Manage Extensions** dialog to install the extension in this chapter. For detailed information on managing extensions in Visual Studio, see this documentation on Microsoft Learn: `https://learn.microsoft.com/visualstudio/ide/finding-and-using-visual-studio-extensions`.

> **Note**
>
> If you're curious about the inner workings of a Visual Studio extension package, or VSIX, you can read more about them on Microsoft Learn: `https://learn.microsoft.com/visualstudio/extensibility/anatomy-of-a-vsix-package`

The code that is generated by the extension continues to guide you as you proceed to build out the newly created project. There are *TODO* comments with guidance about where you add your own code and helpful links to documentation that explains the concepts and controls used in the code. The extension is updated frequently to reflect the latest WinUI features, practices, and recommendations for Windows developers.

Contributions to the Template Studio projects on GitHub are all reviewed to ensure they follow good coding style, fluent design, and helpful comments throughout.

Now that we have reviewed some basics of Template Studio for WinUI, let's dive right in and create a new project with the extension.

Starting a new WinUI project with Template Studio

In this section, we are going to create a new WinUI project with Template Studio for WinUI. We'll install the extension, create the project with several pages and features selected, and then run the project to explore what is provided before we add any of our own code. In the next section, we'll dive a little deeper into the generated code to see where we would start extending and enhancing the project if we were building a production application:

1. To start, open Visual Studio and select **Continue without code** to open the IDE without loading a solution:

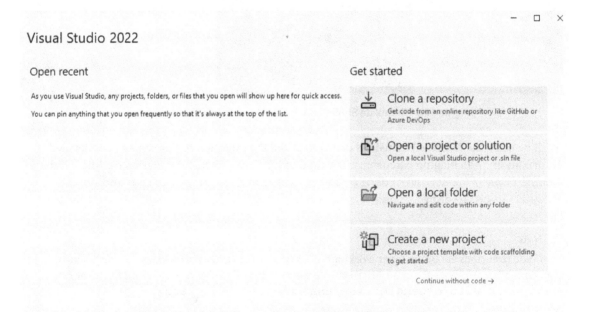

Figure 10.2 – The Visual Studio 2022 launch dialog

2. In the menu, select **Extensions | Manage Extensions** to open the **Manage Extensions** dialog:

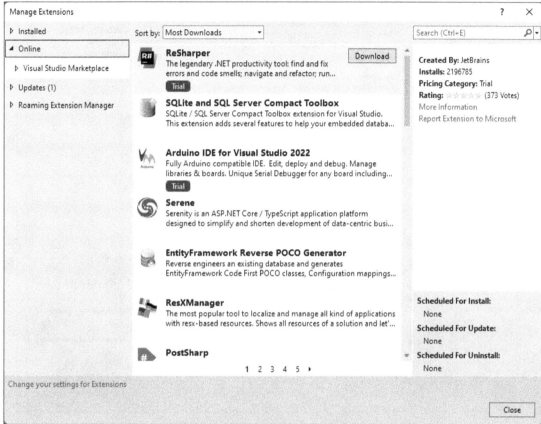

Figure 10.3 – The Manage Extensions dialog in Visual Studio

3. In the **Search** field, search for `template studio`. In the list of search results, select **Download** on **Template Studio for WinUI (C#)**:

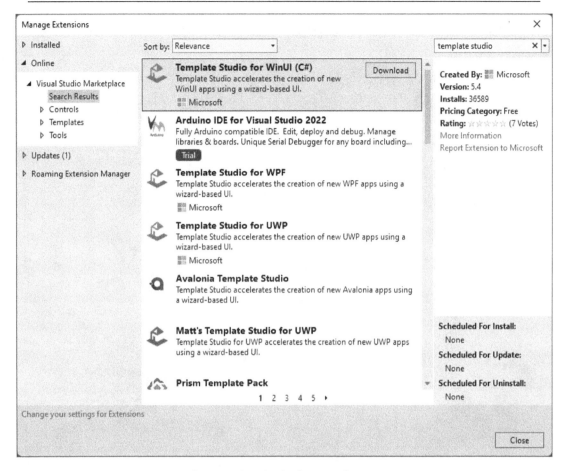

Figure 10.4 – Installing Template Studio for WinUI from Manage Extensions

You will need to restart Visual Studio to complete the extension's installation.

4. After the installation completes, launch Visual Studio and select **Create a new project**.

5. On the **Create a new project** screen, if you don't see **Template Studio for WinUI** in the list of templates, search for template studio. The new project template should appear first in the list of results:

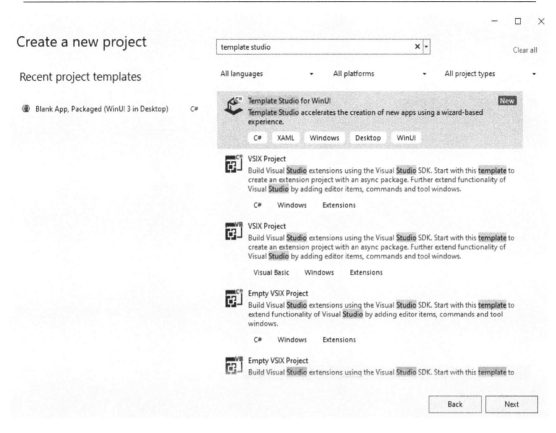

Figure 10.5 – Selecting Template Studio for WinUI to create a new project

6. Select **Next** and, on the **Configure your new project** screen, give the project a name such as `TemplateStudioSampleApp`.

7. Click **Create** to continue. Instead of the Visual Studio IDE immediately loading, you will be presented with the Template Studio wizard:

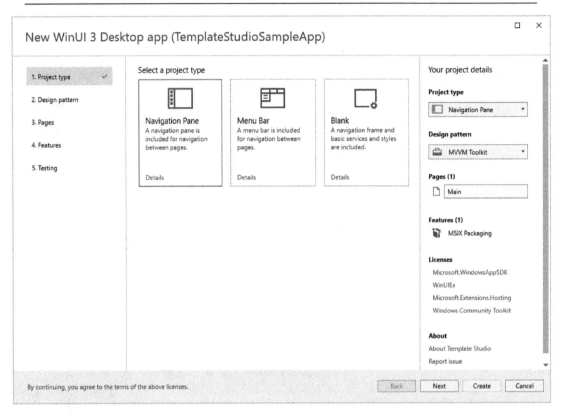

Figure 10.6 – The first page of the Template Studio for WinUI wizard

The first page of the wizard prompts you to select a project type. The choices are **Navigation Pane**, **Menu Bar**, or **Blank**. You can select **Details** on any of the choices to read more about each option. Select the **Navigation Pane** option. This layout leverages the `NavigationView` control that we discussed in *Chapter 5, Exploring WinUI Controls*. It's also the navigation method used in the WinUI 3 Gallery app.

8. Select **Next** to continue. On the **Design pattern** screen, the only available option is **MVVM Toolkit**. Some versions of Template Studio offer other MVVM frameworks or a **Code Behind** option. For WinUI 3, we only have one choice:

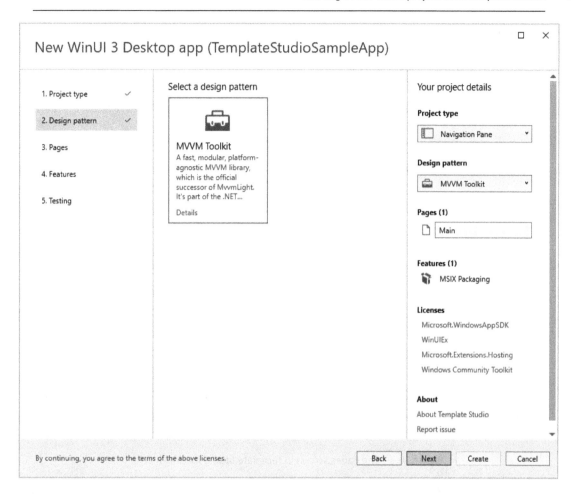

Figure 10.7 – The Design pattern screen

You'll also notice that the right pane contains the **Your project details** heading and the options that have been selected so far. When you're more familiar with Template Studio, you will be able to review these options and click **Create** to finish the wizard without visiting each screen if you're satisfied with the default selections.

9. Click **Next** and review the **Pages** screen:

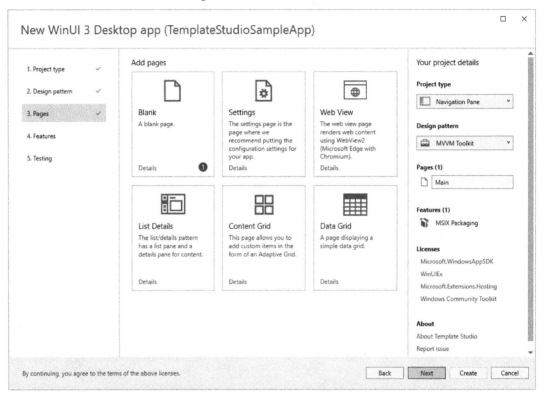

Figure 10.8 – The Pages screen in Template Studio for WinUI

By default, one **Blank** page has been selected. The default name of this page is **Main**. You can change the names of any pages in the **Your project details** panel.

10. Let's select several other page types to review in the next section. Select **Data Grid**, **List Details**, **Web View**, and **Settings**. You can select more if you like:

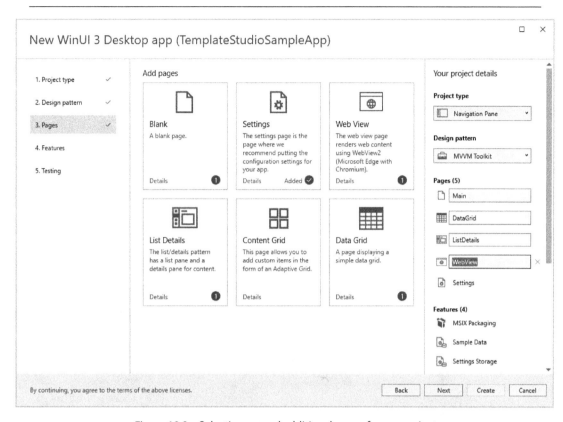

Figure 10.9 – Selecting several additional pages for our project

Any of the pages can be renamed except for **Settings**. We'll leave the default names.

11. Click **Next** to move on to the **Features** screen:

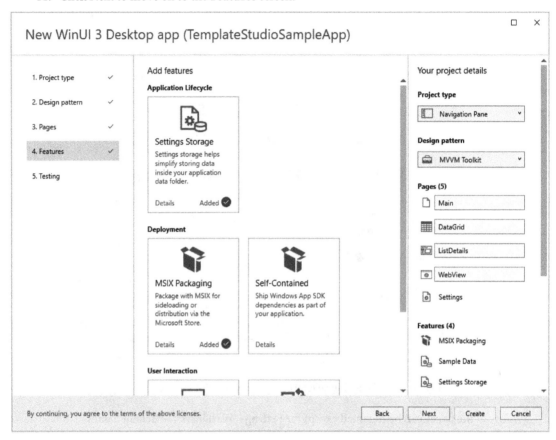

Figure 10.10 – Exploring the Features screen of Template Studio for WinUI

The default selections on the **Features** screen are **Settings Storage**, **MSIX Packaging**, and **Theme Selection**. We'll leave those defaults selected. If you want to include the Windows App SDK dependencies with your project, you can select **Self-Contained**. This is useful if you are going to distribute your app manually with an **xcopy deployment**. We'll discuss deployment options in *Chapter 14, Packaging and Deploying WinUI Applications*. The other unselected option is **App Notifications**. We have already explored notifications in *Chapter 8, Adding Windows Notifications to WinUI Applications*. If you want to learn more about any of the features, select **Details**.

12. Click **Next** to move on to the final step of the wizard, **Testing**:

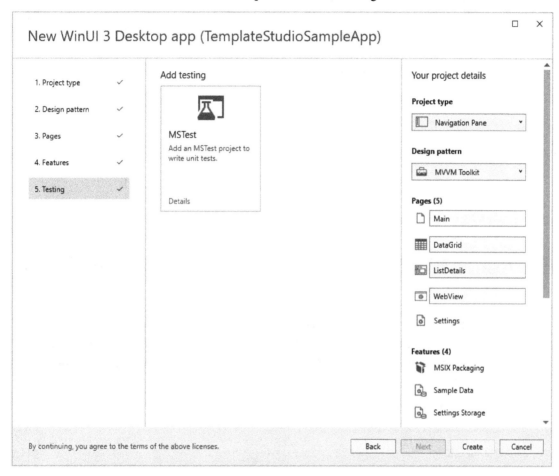

Figure 10.11 – The Testing screen of the Template Studio for WinUI wizard

13. The only option on the **Testing** screen is **MSTest**. Select it to add a unit test project to your solution.

14. We've reached the end of the wizard. Select **Create** to create the solution and launch the Visual Studio IDE:

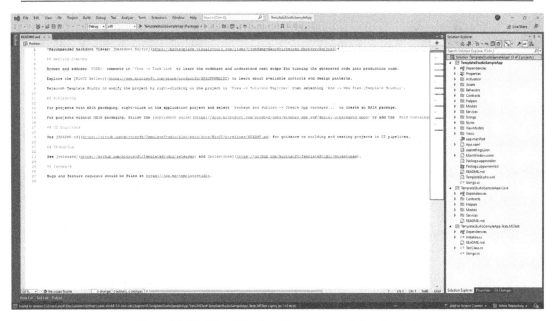

Figure 10.12 – Visual Studio with our new solution loaded

15. The markdown file named README.md will be opened by default. If you want to view a formatted preview of the markdown, you can select the **Preview** button at the top of the editor window:

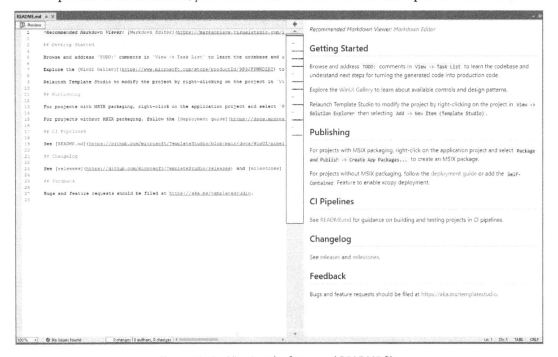

Figure 10.13 – Viewing the formatted README file

The solution contains three projects: **TemplateStudioSampleApp**, **TemplateStudioSampleApp. Core**, and **TemplateStudioSampleApp.Tests.MSTest**. We'll discuss the purpose and contents of each of these projects in the next section:

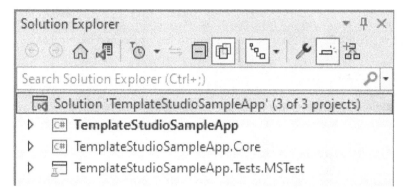

Figure 10.14 – Viewing the projects in Solution Explorer

16. It's finally time to run the application. Start debugging and ensure that there are no compile-time or runtime errors when launching it:

Figure 10.15 – Running the TemplateStudioSampleApp solution

Everything should run as expected, and you can try navigating to each page with the `NavigationView` controls on the left. The **Settings** button will always appear at the bottom of the navigation bar.

Now that we have a working application, let's take some time to understand what's been generated for us.

Exploring the code generated by Template Studio

It's time to review the contents of the newly generated **TemplateStudioSampleApp** solution. There is a lot of code created for us in the three projects, so we won't be exploring every file. We'll discuss each folder, explore a few of the important files, and make some minor code changes along the way. Each project has its own README.md file with an overview of the project and its purpose.

Exploring the Core project

The **TemplateStudioSampleApp.Core** project is a class library project targeting .NET 7. This is where you would place any code that is intended to be shared across projects. The project contains four folders:

- Contracts: Interfaces for the services in the project are kept here in a Services subfolder. Any new interfaces needed in this project should be created here.

- Helpers: This folder contains a Json helper class with methods to convert between **JSON** strings and .NET objects. Add your own common helper classes to this folder.

- Models: There are some sample model classes in this folder that are used to populate company and order data on the DataGridPage and ListDetailPage views.

- Services: This folder contains FileService and SampleDataService classes. The FileService class reads and writes files with classes in the .NET System.IO and System.Text namespaces. The SampleDataService creates static data to populate the model classes for the UI. Any other shared services can be added here.

> **Note**
> It's possible that the Template Studio extensions may be updated to create .NET 8 libraries by the time this book is published.

Next, let's explore the largest project in the solution, **TemplateStudioSampleApp**.

Exploring the main project

The main project, **TemplateStudioSampleApp**, is the largest of the three projects in the solution. It contains all the user interface markup and logic. You will probably recognize the files in the root of the project, after working with other WinUI projects. **App.xaml**, **MainWindow.xaml**, and **Package. appxmanifest** are all there, along with C# code-behind files for each XAML file.

The contents of the **Views** and **ViewModels** folders also contain files that you would expect to find there. We have a corresponding Page and ViewModel class for each page that we selected when configuring the project with the Template Studio wizard. There are also ShellPage and ShellViewModel classes for handling the navigation between child pages. **ShellPage.xaml** contains the NavigationView control and is the direct child of MainWindow.

Next, let's go through the contents of the remaining folders:

- `Activation`: This folder contains the `ActivationHandler`, `DefaultActivation Handler`, and `IActivationHandler` classes. They are helpers that use the `INavigationService` to navigate to the selected page inside the `Frame` hosted within `ShellPage`. If you needed to change the default activation behavior, you would create a new handler that inherits from `ActivationHandler`.

- `Assets`: This contains the graphical assets for the project. The `Assets` folder is present in every WinUI project.

- `Behaviors`: This folder contains an enum named `NavigationViewHeaderMode`, which specifies the appearance of the navigation bar, and `NavigationViewHeaderBehavior`, which contains the logic to implement these modes. The behavior class inherits from `Behavior<NavigationView>`. Any other custom WinUI behaviors would be added here.

- `Contracts`: This is where you keep your interfaces for the project. The two subfolders, `Services` and `ViewModels`, contain interfaces for eight existing classes in those corresponding project folders.

- `Helpers`: Any helper classes specific to this project are kept here. Some of the helpers provided by default include `NavigationHelper`, `SettingsStorageExtensions`, and `TitleBarHelper`. The `SettingsStorageExtensions` helper class leverages members of the `Windows.Storage` and `Windows.Storage.Streams` namespaces to read and write user settings.

- `Models`: The sample data models are kept in the **Core** project, but there's also one model class in this project. The `LocalSettingsOptions` class stores the name and location of the settings file. Any other UI-specific model classes would be added here.

- `Services`: There are seven service classes in the `Services` folder. You can probably determine the purpose of each by its name: `ActivationService`, `LocalSettings Service`, `NavigationService`, `NavigationViewService`, `PageService`, `ThemeSelectorService`, and `WebViewService`. You should take some time to review the code in these services.

- `Strings`: This folder holds language-specific `Resources.resw` files to localize any string values displayed in your application. The English language resource file can be found in the `en-us` folder. For more information about localization, you should read *Localize your WinUI 3 app* on Microsoft Learn: `https://learn.microsoft.com/windows/apps/winui/winui3/localize-winui3-app`.

- Styles: This folder contains three files with XAML ResourceDictionary elements: FontSizes.xaml, TextBlock.xaml, and Thickness.xaml. Let's look at the contents of FontSizes.xaml as an example:

```
<ResourceDictionary
    xmlns="http://schemas.microsoft.com/winfx/
      2006/xaml/presentation"
    xmlns:x="http://schemas.microsoft.com/winfx/
      2006/xaml">
    <x:Double x:Key="LargeFontSize">24</x:Double>
    <x:Double x:Key="MediumFontSize">16</x:Double>
</ResourceDictionary>
```

By centralizing how your app defines a large or medium font size, you can change this later without having to modify multiple XAML views. If you are using a TextBlock or RichTextBlock, the other option for font sizing is to use the **XAML type ramp** (discussed in *Chapter 7, Fluent Design System for Windows Applications*) defined in the XAML theme resources: https://learn.microsoft.com/windows/apps/design/style/xaml-theme-resources#the-xaml-type-ramp.

Before we move on to explore the **MSTest** project, let's look inside the App.xaml.cs file. Everything in here should look familiar to you. The project is using the IHostBuilder.ConfigureServices method to add the ActivationHandler and all services, views, and ViewModel classes to the DI container. The services and core services are added as singleton objects while all the other classes are added with AddTransient.

The App class also has a handy helper method to fetch an instance from the DI container:

```
public static T GetService<T>() T : class
{
    if ((App.Current as App)!.Host.Services.GetService
      (typeof(T)) is not T service)
    {
        throw new ArgumentException($"{typeof(T)} needs to
          be registered in ConfigureServices within
            App.xaml.cs.");
    }
    return service;
}
```

This encapsulates some exception-handling logic in case the requested type cannot be found, reducing the need to repeat this code throughout the application.

Notice how each class has helpful comments with links to Microsoft Learn resources for any related APIs or other topics. The App class has links to .NET dependency injection, logging, and other learning resources.

Let's finish this section with a quick look at the **MSTest** project that was created by Template Studio.

Exploring the MSTest project

The **TemplateStudioSampleApp.Tests.MSTest** project contains a single test class named TestClass, a README.md file, and Initialize and Usings classes. You should read the README.md file carefully. It contains information about the project, testing UI elements, dependency injection, and mocking. There are examples of how to leverage DI and mocks to test the SettingsViewModel without actually reading or writing any settings to the filesystem.

The TestClass contains examples of test initialization and cleanup at the class and test level, as well as two sample test methods: TestMethod and UITestMethod:

```
[TestMethod]
public void TestMethod()
{
    Assert.IsTrue(true);
}
[UITestMethod]
public void UITestMethod()
{
    Assert.AreEqual(0, new Grid().ActualWidth);
}
```

Any test method decorated with the UITestMethod attribute will run on the UI thread. The generated code does not test any members of the **TemplateStudioSampleApp** or **TemplateStudioSampleApp.Core** projects yet. It's up to you to add your own test methods to do that. You can get started by reading the Visual Studio unit testing documentation on Microsoft Learn: https://learn.microsoft.com/visualstudio/test/getting-started-with-unit-testing.

In the next section, we will discuss some other Template Studio extensions created by Microsoft and one from a third party.

Template Studio extensions for other UI frameworks

We've taken a deep dive into the Template Studio for WinUI extension, but what about the UI frameworks? As we mentioned earlier in the chapter, Microsoft also maintains extensions for Template Studio for WPF and Template Studio for UWP. In fact, they even have a **Microsoft Web Template Studio** available: https://github.com/microsoft/WebTemplateStudio. It supports

React, **Angular**, or **Vue.js** for the frontend and **Node.js**, **Flask**, **Molecular**, and **ASP.NET Core** as backend frameworks. If you're interested in web development, you should check it out.

There is also an extension called **MAUI App Accelerator** (`https://marketplace.visualstudio. com/items?itemName=MattLaceyLtd.MauiAppAccelerator`), which is a Template Studio version for .NET MAUI. We'll remain focused on WinUI and WPF templates in this chapter. The final two we'll review are Template Studio for WPF and the Template Studio-style wizard that comes with the Uno Platform extension for Visual Studio. Let's start with WPF.

Template Studio for WPF

The Template Studio for WPF extension (`https://marketplace.visualstudio.com/ items?itemName=TemplateStudio.TemplateStudioForWPF`) is similar to its WinUI counterpart. It has one additional step in the wizard (**Services**), and there are a few different options on some of the pages. One of the project types available to WPF developers is the **Ribbon** type. This creates a shell with a Microsoft Office-style ribbon control at the top in place of the standard menu control you would get in a **MenuBar**-type project.

The **Design pattern** screen allows you to select **Code Behind** or **Prism**, in addition to the **MVVM Toolkit** option. While the **Page** options are the same as WinUI, the **Features** screen has an option with the ability to show multiple views in separate windows. The **Services** screen has two identity-related options: **Forced Login** and **Optional Login**. Finally, the **Testing** screen has seven different options, rather than just **MSTest**. The additional testing frameworks provided are **NUnit**, **xUnit**, and **Appium** (for UI tests), and there are options to add test projects for the main project and the **Core** library project.

The generated projects have the same folder structure as the WinUI projects. Here's an example of a generated WPF project with an empty ribbon control:

Figure 10.16 – A WPF project created by Template Studio

Let's finish up by taking a look at the Template Studio wizard provided by the Uno Platform extension.

Template Studio for Uno Platform

Uno Platform (`https://platform.uno/`) is a UI framework that uses WinUI XAML and .NET code, and it can create applications to target virtually every available device platform today: Windows, iOS, Android, macOS, Tizen, web (with **WebAssembly**), and even Linux. The Uno Platform extension for Visual Studio (`https://marketplace.visualstudio.com/items?itemName=unoplatform.uno-platform-addin-2022`) includes a new project wizard that is based on the Template Studio code.

If you install the extension in Visual Studio and create a new project with the **Uno Platform App** template, clicking the **Create** button from the **Configure your new project** screen will launch the wizard:

Figure 10.17 – The Uno Platform new project screen

From here, you can simply select **Create** to accept all the defaults and generate a new solution. However, if you select the **Customize** button on the **Default** startup type, you will get the full wizard experience:

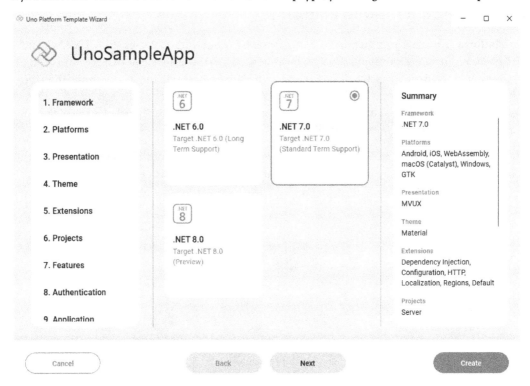

Figure 10.18 – The Uno Platform new project wizard

From here, you can select from options in 10 different categories. Even though the wizard is styled a bit differently, you can see that it has the same origins as the Template Studio extensions. We will get into the details of each step of the wizard when we build an Uno Platform app in *Chapter 13, Take Your App Cross-Platform with Uno Platform*. If you create a new Uno Platform project with the defaults and run the **UnoApp1.Wasm** project, you'll see your app running in the browser by leveraging WebAssembly:

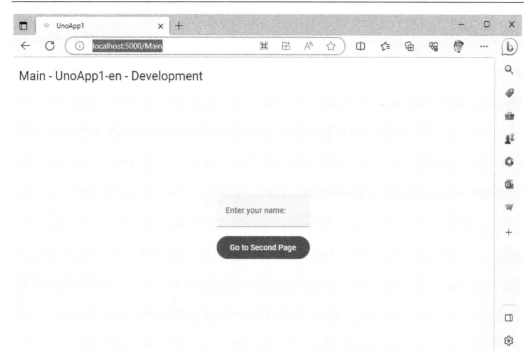

Figure 10.19 – Running an Uno Platform app in the browser

That's very cool! Now let's wrap up and review what we've learned in this chapter.

Summary

In this chapter, we learned how the Template Studio for WinUI extension can save time and promote good patterns and practices when starting a new WinUI project. We stepped through the creation of a new WinUI project with the wizard and explored the generated code in the new solution. Understanding the structure and purpose of the solution's components will make it easier to extend it for your own projects. We wrapped things up by discussing the Template Studio extensions that are available for other UI frameworks such as WPF and Uno Platform.

In the next chapter, *Chapter 11, Debugging WinUI Apps with Visual Studio*, we will explore the tools and options provided by Visual Studio to make .NET and XAML developers' lives easier.

Questions

1. Which unit test framework is used when creating a test project in Template Studio for WinUI?

2. Which project type in Template Studio for WinUI implements a `NavigationView` control?

3. What was the previous name of Template Studio for UWP?

4. Which MVVM framework is used by Template Studio for WinUI when generating a project?

5. What file format is used for Visual Studio extensions?

6. Which Template Studio extension could you use to create a new project if you needed to include Linux as one of your target platforms?

7. Which folder contains all the interfaces for the main project generated by Template Studio for WinUI?

Part 3:
Build and Deploy
on Windows and Beyond

This part rounds out your WinUI knowledge by exploring techniques to debug, build, and deploy WinUI 3 applications. You will explore the extensive debugging tools Visual Studio has to offer WinUI developers. Then, you will see how you can host a web application inside a WinUI application, leveraging Blazor, Visual Studio Code, GitHub Actions, and the WebView2 control. We'll also learn how to migrate a WinUI project to Uno Platform to run on multiple platforms, including Android and the web with WebAssembly. Finally, you'll learn about the options to build and deploy WinUI applications with Visual Studio, the Microsoft Store, and Microsoft's command-line installer, Windows Package Manager (WinGet).

This part has the following chapters:

- *Chapter 11, Debugging WinUI Applications with Visual Studio*
- *Chapter 12, Hosting a Blazor Application in WinUI*
- *Chapter 13, Take Your App Cross-Platform with Uno Platform*
- *Chapter 14, Packaging and Deploying WinUI Applications*

11

Debugging WinUI Applications with Visual Studio

Good debugging skills are essential for developers. While .NET developers need to know how to use features including breakpoints and the **Output** and **Immediate** windows, WinUI project debugging adds another set of tools and techniques to master. There are issues that can arise in the UI layer with data binding, layout, and resources. You will learn how to use **Live Visual Tree** and **Live Property Explorer** and how to discover data binding errors with Visual Studio's **XAML Binding Failures** window.

In this chapter, we will cover the following topics:

- How to debug WinUI applications and work with breakpoints in ViewModels and service classes

- How to debug data binding failures by leveraging the **XAML Binding Failures** window in Visual Studio and avoid common problems when binding to collections

- Explore the **Live Visual Tree** window in Visual Studio to find layout problems in your XAML

- Discover and use **Live Property Explorer** to get and set data in your XAML elements at runtime

By the end of this chapter, you will be comfortable with debugging common problems typically encountered by WinUI developers while developing applications. You'll be able to use these skills while building applications with other XAML frameworks, such as .NET MAUI, WPF, and UWP, too.

Technical requirements

To follow along with the examples in this chapter, the following software is required:

- Windows 10 version 1809 (build 17763) or newer or Windows 11

- Visual Studio 2022 or later with the .NET Desktop Development workload configured for Windows App SDK development

The source code for this chapter is available on GitHub at this URL: `https://github.com/PacktPublishing/Learn-WinUI-3-Second-Edition/tree/master/Chapter11`.

Debugging in Visual Studio

There are several fundamental areas of debugging WinUI applications that we will be covering in this section. Some of these techniques are applicable to debugging other types of .NET applications, whereas others are specific to XAML and WinUI development. Throughout the book, we've run our projects with Visual Studio, which is an example of a local debugging session. We will explore other ways to debug local applications as well as remote applications.

Simple mistakes in XAML markup are not always apparent when we're writing it, and this kind of problem is not detected by the compiler. In this section, we will see how to detect and avoid XAML markup issues and how to adhere to best practices.

Let's get started by taking a closer look at debugging local applications.

Debugging local applications

Open the **Ch11-MyMediaCollection** project from GitHub and compile it to make sure you have downloaded all the referenced NuGet packages. This is the WinUI 3 project that we've been building throughout the previous chapters. Run the application to make sure everything works as expected.

> **Note**
>
> If you have experience in developing and debugging WPF or UWP applications, you're probably familiar with **XAML Designer** in Visual Studio. There is no designer support for WinUI 3 applications at this time. It's unclear if or when this feature will be added. There is some discussion on GitHub about this topic here: `https://github.com/microsoft/microsoft-ui-xaml/issues/5917`. As one of the comments in the issue suggests, you can try to work around this limitation by leveraging **XAML Hot Reload** in Visual Studio to make changes to the XAML file while debugging. While there are some limitations to this approach (see `https://github.com/microsoft/microsoft-ui-xaml/issues/7043`), most simple XAML changes will be reflected in the running app when saving. For more information about XAML Hot Reload, see the Microsoft Learn documentation: `https://learn.microsoft.com/visualstudio/xaml-tools/xaml-hot-reload`.

For our first walk-through, let's look at how to debug a local application installed on your PC.

Debugging a locally installed application

We have been running and debugging our Visual Studio solutions throughout this book. Now we will see how you can debug an application that you have already installed in Windows.

You have previously run several projects while reading this book. Unless you uninstalled them, each should appear as an installed app package that you can debug. Let's start with the steps:

1. Start by selecting **Debug | Other Debug Targets | Debug Installed App Package** in Visual Studio. The **Debug Installed App Package** window will appear:

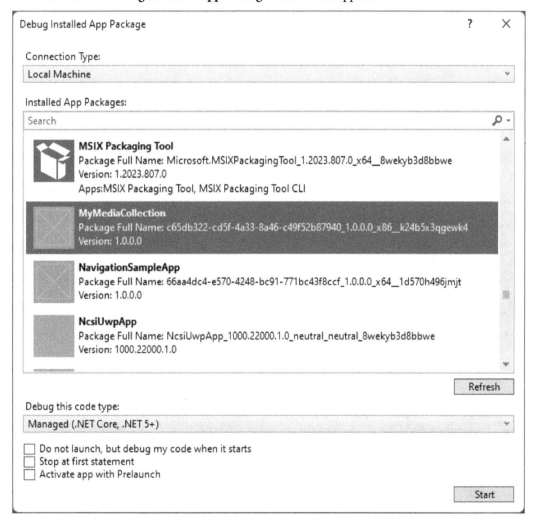

Figure 11.1 – The Debug Installed App Package window

This window will show all the installed packages on your Windows PC. Some names will be familiar, such as **Microsoft.WindowsTerminal**, **Fluent XAML Theme Editor**, or **Microsoft Defender**. Others will only be listed by their application ID. You can select some of these other applications to debug, but without debug symbols, you won't be able to hit any breakpoints or step through the code. Let's find one of our applications.

2. If you have debugged the **MyMediaCollection** app on your machine, it will appear in the list. So, let's search for `MyMediaCollection`. The **MyMediaCollection** application will appear in the search results. If you do not see it, make sure you have run the application from Visual Studio at least once. This step is necessary to package and deploy the application to Windows.

3. Select it and click **Start**. The application will run, and Visual Studio will start debugging.

    If you don't want to start debugging immediately, you can select the **Do not launch, but debug my code when it starts** checkbox. Now, Visual Studio will start debugging when you start the application from the **Start** menu or any other method.

Another way to start debugging an installed local application is by attaching it to a running application:

1. First, run the app from the **Start** menu, and in Visual Studio, go to **Debug | Attach to Process**.

2. In the **Attach to Process** window, find the `ApplicationFrameHost.exe` process with the title that matches the application you want to debug. This is the process that hosts every packaged WinUI and UWP application on Windows:

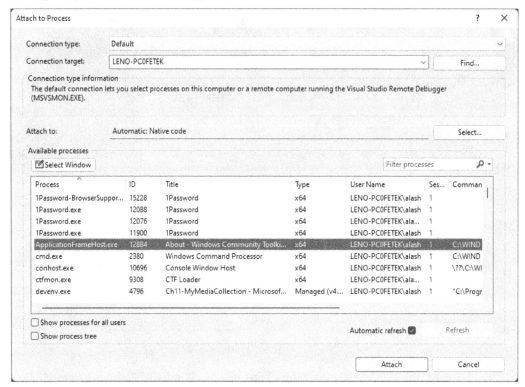

Figure 11.2 – Attaching to a running process to debug a packaged application

3. Click **Attach** and begin debugging as usual.

These are different ways to start a debugging session on a local application, but what if you want to debug your application running on another machine? Let's examine those options next.

Debugging remote applications

There are many reasons why you might want to debug an application on a remote machine. Sometimes you can only reproduce an error on one device. Perhaps there is an issue that only occurs on a specific device type or screen size. If you were working with a UWP project, there are some devices, such as Xbox, where you have to use remote debugging.

> **Note**
>
> Before starting any remote debugging session, ensure that the target device has **developer mode** enabled. For more information about activating developer mode, you can read this Microsoft Docs article: `https://learn.microsoft.com/windows/apps/get-started/enable-your-device-for-development`.

To debug a remote installed application, you will use Visual Studio's **Debug Installed App Package** window again:

1. Open the window from **Debug | Other Debug Targets | Debug Installed App Package**.

2. Change **Connection Type** to **Remote Machine**:

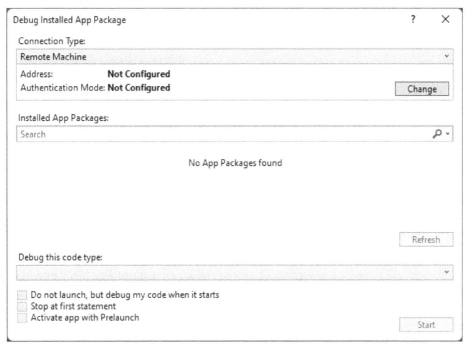

Figure 11.3 – Debugging an application package on a remote machine

3. Click the **Change** button in the **Connection Type** section to open the **Remote Connections** window.

4. Visual Studio will attempt to discover other Windows devices and list them in the **Auto Detected** section. If you see the device you want, select it to continue. If the device you want to debug isn't shown, enter its IP address in the **Address** field in the **Manual Configuration** section and click **Select**:

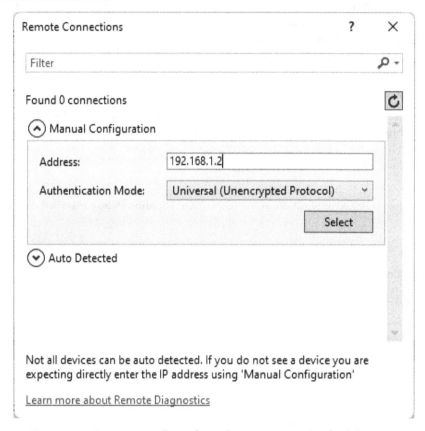

Figure 11.4 – Enter a manually configured remote connection for debugging

5. When you return to the previous window, you can select the application to debug from the list of installed app packages on the selected device.

6. Click **Start** to begin debugging, just as we did with the locally installed application in the previous section.

These techniques will allow you to connect to other Windows machines. For UWP applications, this includes other device types, such as Xbox, HoloLens, Surface Hub, and Windows IoT devices. Debugging options and resources can also be accessed from the **Debug** tab of the project's **Properties** page. Select **Open debug launch profiles UI** to open the **Launch Profiles** window:

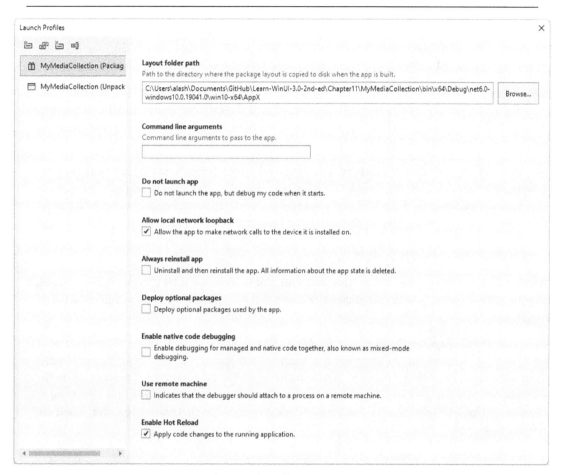

Figure 11.5 – The Launch Profiles window in Visual Studio

Let's shift gears and examine some common mistakes that can cause rendering issues in your application's UI.

Common XAML layout mistakes

There are many kinds of mistakes that XAML developers can make while coding the UI. Some of them won't be caught by the compiler. If you have a syntax error or an invalid x:Bind expression, these will fail while compiling, but many other issues will not.

The first source of common XAML layout mistakes we will explore is the Grid control.

Grid layout issues

Some mistakes related to the Grid control revolve around its rows and columns. Forgetting to set Grid.Row or Grid.Column on child controls leads to overlapping or obscured elements at runtime. Similar issues can be seen when setting these values incorrectly or when working with `Grid.RowSpan` and `Grid.ColumnSpan`. One mistake that's not always immediately apparent is setting `Grid.Row` or `Grid.Column` to a value that's beyond the defined number of rows or columns.

Open **MainPage.xaml** in the **MyMediaCollection** project and remove the `Grid.Row` attribute from the `Border` control containing the `Button` controls at the bottom of the page. If you run the application, you will see the buttons move to the top of the page and overlap the controls in the header area.

Now restore the `Grid.Row` attribute but change the value to 5. If this were the last row in the grid, everything would look fine even though `Grid` only has four rows. Since 5 is greater than the number of available rows, the control is added to the last row in `Grid`. However, because we have `InfoBar` below the buttons in the fourth row, the buttons and the `InfoBar` overlap.

Problems when applying style

XAML `Style` resources are another common source of unintentional UI changes. When creating `Style` in `Resource`, you should be aware of how it will be applied to controls within the scope of that `Resource`.

Open **ItemDetailsPage.xaml** and review the `Page.Resources` section. This is where we created three `Style` elements for the current page. Each has a different `Target` type: `TextBlock`, `TextBox`, and `ComboBox`. However, they won't be applied to every control of those types on the `Page` because we also gave each `Style` an `x:Key`. That means that `Style` will only be applied to elements of that type when the `Style` property is explicitly set to that named resource. These are referred to as *explicit styles*:

```
<TextBlock Text="Name:" Style="{StaticResource
    AttributeTitleStyle}"/>
```

If you remove `x:Key` from `Style` in `Page.Resources`, that *implicit style* will apply to every control of the specified `Target` type on the `Page`, unless those controls have another explicit `Style` set. In a large application with styles declared at different scopes (`Application`, `Page`, or control), it can sometimes be difficult to determine which style has been applied to a control. We will see how to do this later in the chapter when discussing Visual Studio's **Live Property Explorer** window. It's a best practice to have implicit styles always inherit from an explicit style. This enables developers to inherit from a default style and reduces repeated implicit style attributes across elements.

Next, we will look at a third-party extension that can help find common XAML problems through **static code analysis**.

Improving your XAML with static code analysis

There is a free, open source extension for Visual Studio that, among other things, adds support for static code analysis to XAML files. **Rapid XAML Toolkit** (`https://rapidxaml.dev/`) provides

XAML analyzers and code fixes for common issues and provides support for adding your own custom XAML analyzers.

> **Note**
>
> At the time of writing, Rapid XAML Toolkit for Visual Studio 2022 has not yet been released. It is being developed and should be available by the time you read this book. The current example illustrates how to use the extension currently available for Visual Studio 2019.

Let's install the tool in Visual Studio and see what kind of issues it can identify in a WinUI project:

1. In Visual Studio, go to **Extensions | Manage Extensions**.

2. The **Manage Extensions** window will appear. Ensure **Visual Studio Marketplace** is selected and search for `rapid xaml`:

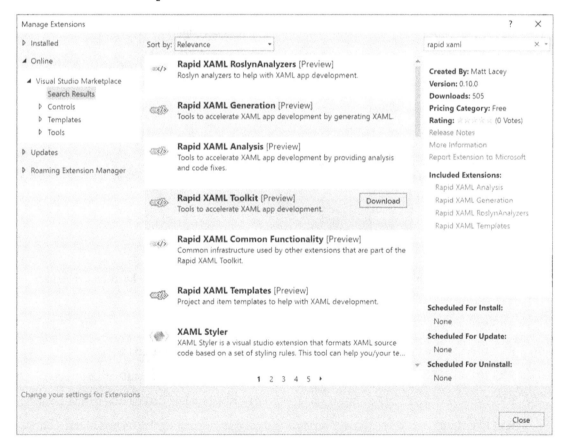

Figure 11.6 – Installing Rapid XAML Toolkit

3.   Click **Download** to queue the extension for installation. When the download completes, you can close the **Manage Extensions** window and restart Visual Studio to complete the installation.

4.   Now, when you view the **Error List** window in Visual Studio, there are a handful of warnings from Rapid XAML's analyzers:

Figure 11.7 – Viewing the new warnings from Rapid XAML Toolkit

5.   Open **ItemDetailPage.xaml**, place your cursor over one of the green squiggles created by the code analyzer, and click the lightbulb icon:

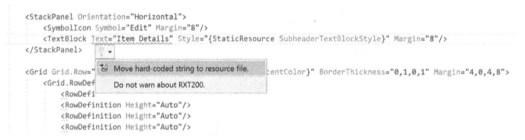

Figure 11.8 – View the quick fix for a code analyzer warning

Alternatively, you can right-click on the XAML and select **Rapid XAML | Move hard-coded string to resource file.** to fix all warnings of this type.

This is a list of other analyzers that are provided by the toolkit:

- **RXT101**: Use of a `Grid.Row` value without a corresponding `RowDefinition`

- **RXT102**: Use of a `Grid.Column` value without a corresponding `ColumnDefinition`

- **RXT103**: Use of a `Grid.RowSpan` value without a corresponding `ColumnDefinition`

- **RXT104**: Use of a `Grid.ColumnSpan` value without a corresponding `ColumnDefinition`

- **RXT150**: `TextBox` does not have `InputScope` specified

- **RXT160**: The `SelectedItem` binding should probably be `TwoWay`

- **RXT200**: The hardcoded string value that should be a resource
- **RXT300**: `Entry` does not have a `Keyboard` specified
- **RXT300**: Password entry does not have a `MaxLength` specified
- **RXT300**: `Image` lacks accessibility consideration
- **RXT300**: `ImageButton` lacks accessibility consideration
- **RXT401**: Handle both `Checked` and `Unchecked` events for a `CheckBox`
- **RXT402**: Use `MediaPlayerElement` in place of `MediaElement`
- **RXT451**: `x:Uid` should begin with an uppercase character
- **RXT452**: `Name` should begin with an uppercase character
- **RXT999**: Unknown error – something went wrong when parsing the XAML document

Rapid XAML Toolkit has many other features outside of analyzers and code fixes, and new features and analyzers are being added frequently. To see a list of upcoming features and fixes being considered, you can view the issues on GitHub: `https://github.com/mrlacey/Rapid-XAML-Toolkit/issues`.

> **Note**
> Community-driven projects like this are always looking for contributors. It's a great way to get started with the open source community.

Another related topic that can be a common source of developer angst is debugging data binding. Let's see how we can avoid some common pitfalls in the next section.

Pinpointing data binding failures

While debugging data binding problems is not as difficult in WinUI and UWP as it is in WPF (if you use `x:Bind`-compiled bindings), there are still some *gotchas* to avoid. In this section, we will look at what can go wrong in views and ViewModels and how you can diagnose and fix the problems.

Common mistakes in data binding

If you use `x:Bind`, the compiler will evaluate whether you're binding to a valid source and can give you the peace of mind of knowing that your views and ViewModels are hooked up correctly, but there is still a lot that can go wrong. Let's review a few of the most common mistakes.

Selecting the best binding mode

We have seen in previous chapters that the default mode for most controls with `x:Bind` is `OneTime`, while the default for `Binding` is `OneWay`. Defaulting to `OneTime` helps with performance as many read-only properties are only ever set when the view is first created. However, if you forget to change this for controls bound to data that changes as the user is interacting with the page, you may not immediately realize why the data in the UI isn't updating.

When you're binding controls that need data to flow in both directions, remember to set `Mode` to `TwoWay`. We used this in the **MyMediaCollection** project with the `ComboBox.SelectedItem` property to filter the collection by media type.

Triggering PropertyChanged notifications

By binding to a ViewModel that properly implements `INotifyPropertyChanged` for all its public properties, issues related to `PropertyChanged` are not common. Using MVVM Toolkit makes it even simpler. Problems can still arise if ViewModel code outside of one of these properties updates the property's value by setting the `private` backing variable. This will update the property's value without notifying the view. If you are using MVVM Toolkit, it will call out this issue when it generates its code in the hidden partial class. You can avoid this by always using the `public` property to update the value. If there is a good reason for not updating the property directly, then a `PropertyChanged` event should be manually triggered for that property after updating the value. It is a best practice to use the `nameof` method in C# to ensure you use a property name that exists. Misspelled property names will be caught at compile time and highlighted in the editor. You can also use `CallerMemberNameAttribute` in .NET: `https://learn.microsoft.com/dotnet/api/system.runtime.compilerservices.callermembernameattribute`. An exception will be raised if your application tries to raise a property change notification for a property that does not exist.

Working with ObservableCollection<T>

`ObservableCollection<T>` serves an important role. Lists in the view will stay synchronized with the collections if they are used correctly. There are a few practices to avoid when using observable collections.

Do not replace the entire value of an observable collection. The element on the view bound to the property will still be bound to the original collection. Any subsequent changes to the collection will not be reflected in the view. While you can work around this by triggering a `PropertyChanged` notification, this can have performance implications with larger collections. It can also be jarring to the user, as most controls will reset the current view to the beginning of the list. Set ViewModel properties that use `ObservableCollection<T>` to be read-only to avoid accidentally resetting the entire collection. The one exception to this is if you know the collection will be completely repopulated. Removing and re-adding a large number of items individually in a list can result in a poor user experience.

Do not use LINQ to modify observable collections. LINQ expressions do not operate by calling the Add and Remove methods on the observable collections. They do not even return ObservableCollection<T>. If you use LINQ and convert the results back to ObservableCollection<T>, you will be back to replace the entire collection, which was just discussed.

Here is an example using LINQ. This will cause the view to stop receiving CollectionChanged notifications because LINQ does not return an ObservableCollection:

```
_entryList = from entry in _entryList
             where entry.Lastname.StartsWith("J")
             select entry;
```

This example does the same thing. It removes any entries with a Lastname starting with J. By using the Remove method and not changing the entire collection, the CollectionChanged events are preserved:

```
for (int i = _entryList.Count - 1; i >= 0; i--)
{
    Entry entry = _entryList[i];
    if (!entry.Lastname.StartsWith("J"))
    {
        _entryList.Remove(entry);
    }
}
```

Finally, it's best not to use observable collections for lists that do not change. The extra overhead they bring is not needed for static data. Bind to an IList<T>, IEnumerable<T>, or better yet, a traditional array of items instead. Check out this *C# 101* video to learn when to leverage arrays, lists, and collections in .NET: https://learn.microsoft.com/shows/csharp-101/csharp-arrays-list-and-collections.

Using the XAML Binding Failures window

Visual Studio 2019 version 16.7 introduced the new **XAML Binding Failures** window and a **Binding failures** indicator on the in-app toolbar. These are for failures in Binding, not x:Bind, as those issues are checked and caught by the compiler. Clicking the red indicator will take you to the **XAML Binding Failures** window while debugging. Binding failures were always available in the **Output** window while debugging, but they could be difficult to find. The new, dedicated window provides sorting and searching. Similar failures are also grouped to make it easy to address related items together:

Figure 11.9 – Checking the in-app toolbar for binding failures

Let's give it a try. Open the **XamlDebugging** solution from the GitHub repository for this chapter and follow along with these steps:

1. Open **MainWindow.xaml** and review the XAML. `Window` contains a `StackPanel` with two `TextBox` child elements:

    ```
    <StackPanel DataContext="Test" Background="LightGray">
        <TextBox x:Name="Text1"
                 Text="{Binding Path=SomeText,
                   Mode=TwoWay}"/>
        <TextBox Text="{Binding ElementName=Text1,
            Path=Text, Mode=OneWay}"/>
    </StackPanel>
    ```

    `DataContext` does not exist, so what do you think will be reported in the binding failures? Let's find out!

2. Run the application and look at the in-app toolbar. There is an indication that we have one binding failure.

3. Click the red indicator on the toolbar to open the **XAML Binding Failures** window in Visual Studio:

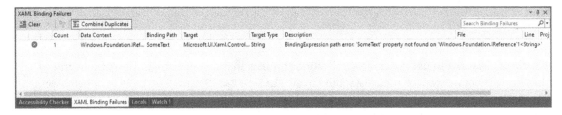

Figure 11.10 – The XAML Binding Failures window

The **Description** text in the window tells us **BindingExpression path error: 'SomeText' property not found on 'Windows.Foundation.IReference`1<String>'**. This is useful information. It would be more useful if there was something telling us directly that the data context itself is not valid. However, if you had a dozen controls using this data context, and all the bindings were failing, it would become clear that there is a problem with the data context and not the individual bindings.

4. Let's make sure the other binding is working correctly. Enter some text into the first `TextBox`:

Figure 11.11 – Binding TextBoxes with ElementName

The text you enter should be duplicated in the second `TextBox` as your type. Our binding to `ElementName` is working as expected.

I will leave fixing the data source as an exercise for you. Add a valid data source to the code behind it and see whether the binding error is cleared up.

Now, let's explore a few other XAML debugging tools available from the in-app toolbar.

Debugging live data with Live Visual Tree and Live Property Explorer

While the **XAML Binding Failures** window is new to Visual Studio, the in-app toolbar has been available to XAML developers since 2015. The toolbar floats over the active window in your application while you are debugging. There are several parts to the toolbar:

- **Go to Live Visual Tree**: Opens the **Live Visual Tree** window.
- **Show in XAML Live Preview**: This opens the **XAML Live Preview** window in Visual Studio.
- **Select Element**: Allows you to select an element in **Live Visual Tree** by clicking on it in the active window.
- **Display Layout Adorners**: This will highlight the element in the UI that is currently selected in **Live Visual Tree**.
- **Track Focused Element**: While the **Live Visual Tree** window is open, toggling this on will indicate in **Live Visual Tree** which element currently has focus on the UI.
- **Binding failures**: Indicates the number of current binding failures and opens the **XAML Binding Failures** window when clicked.
- **Scan for Accessibility Issues**: This opens the **Accessibility Checker** window and runs an accessibility check on the UI elements currently visible.
- **Hot Reload**: Indicates whether **XAML Hot Reload** is currently available. Clicking it will open the documentation on Microsoft Learn.

Let's explore a few of the most commonly used debugging tools. If you wish to get more information on the remaining tools, you can visit this page about XAML tools on Microsoft Learn: `https://learn.microsoft.com/visualstudio/xaml-tools/`. Or, view this *Visual Studio Toolbox* episode about using the XAML tools in Visual Studio: `https://learn.microsoft.com/shows/visual-studio-toolbox/new-xaml-features-in-visual-studio`. We'll start with XAML Hot Reload.

Coding with XAML Hot Reload

XAML Hot Reload is a simple but powerful feature. Before Visual Studio 16.2, it was known as **XAML C# Edit & Continue**. Hot reload has been available to web developers for a while longer, and the name change for XAML helps to clear up some confusion for developers familiar with the concept in web development. The idea of hot reload is that you can make changes to your UI and the changes are reflected in the running application without having to stop debugging and recompile. Let's try it with the **XamlDebugging** solution:

1. Start by running the application again. Make sure that the **Hot Reload** indicator in the toolbar shows that it is enabled. It should only be disabled if you are running an unsupported project type.

2. Now let's make a change to **MainWindow.xaml**. We're going to change the Background color of StackPanel to LightGray:

```
<StackPanel DataContext="Test"
            Background="LightGray">
    <TextBox x:Name="Text1"
             Text="{Binding Path=SomeText,
                Mode=TwoWay}"/>
    <TextBox Text="{Binding ElementName=Text1,
        Path=Text, Mode=OneWay}"/>
</StackPanel>
```

3. Save the file and look at the running application:

Figure 11.12 – Changing the UI without restarting the application

The background of the window is now light gray.

This is a huge time-saver when building a new UI. For a list of known limitations, see this Microsoft Learn article: https://learn.microsoft.com/troubleshoot/developer/visualstudio/tools-utilities/xaml-hot-reload-troubleshooting#known-limitations.

Now let's look at another powerful debugging tool, the **Live Visual Tree** window.

Debugging with Live Visual Tree and Live Property Explorer

The **Live Visual Tree** window allows developers to explore the elements in the current window of an application's XAML **visual tree**. It is available to UWP and WinUI applications and other XAML frameworks. Let's step through using **Live Visual Tree** and related XAML debugging tools:

1. While debugging the **XAMLDebugging** project, open the **Live Visual Tree** window. The visual tree contains the hierarchy of controls in the window with the **Show Just My XAML** button selected by default in the **Live Visual Tree** window's toolbar:

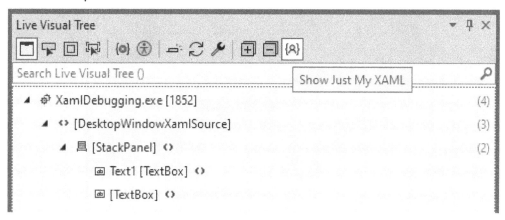

Figure 11.13 – Viewing Live Visual Tree for the XamlDebugging project (Show Just My XAML selected)

2. If you want to view the entire visual tree for your window, de-select **Show Just My XAML** on the toolbar and the tree will refresh:

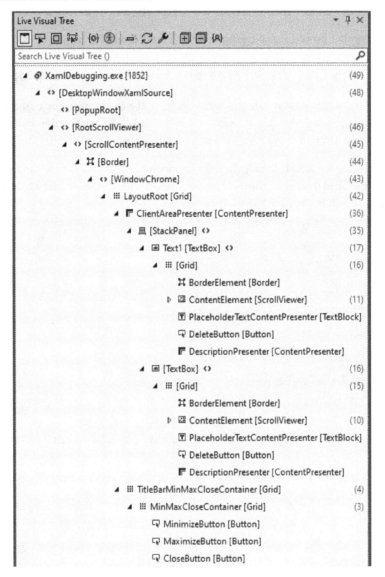

Figure 11.14 – Viewing Live Visual Tree for the XamlDebugging project (all XAML)

There's a lot more going on here. With **Show Just My XAML** de-selected, you can see the elements that make up each control. These are the contents of the **control templates**. A TextBox is made up of 17 child elements with a Grid at the root of its template. This is a great way to learn how the controls we use are composed. Working with and modifying these templates is beyond the scope of this chapter, but I encourage you to explore them on your own. *Chapter 7, Fluent Design System for Windows Applications,* has additional information on using default styles and theme resources. This Microsoft Learn article on control templates is another great place to start: `https://learn.microsoft.com/windows/apps/design/style/xaml-control-templates`. For now, let's switch back to the **Show Just My XAML** view.

3. From **Live Visual Tree**, right-click on a node to navigate to the XAML markup for the selected item by selecting **View Source**.

4. Next, right-click a node and select **Show Properties** to show the **Live Property Explorer** window, where you can inspect the current properties of the selected element. You can see how the properties are grouped based on where they have been set. Here, some are set by **Local** changes and others are set based on the **Style** for a **TextBox**. If you had multiple levels of inherited explicit styles and an implicit style, those would all be grouped here:

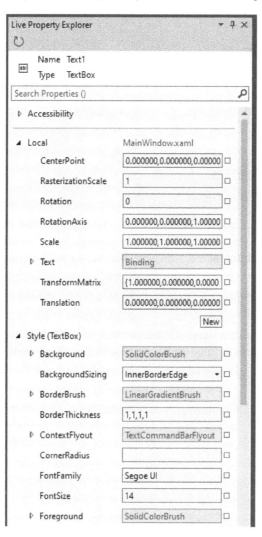

Figure 11.15 – Viewing the Live Property Explorer window for the Text1 TextBox

5. Look at the **Text** property of **Text1**. The value is **Binding**, meaning that the value is set to a `Binding` markup extension. Expand the **Text** property node to view the details of the binding:

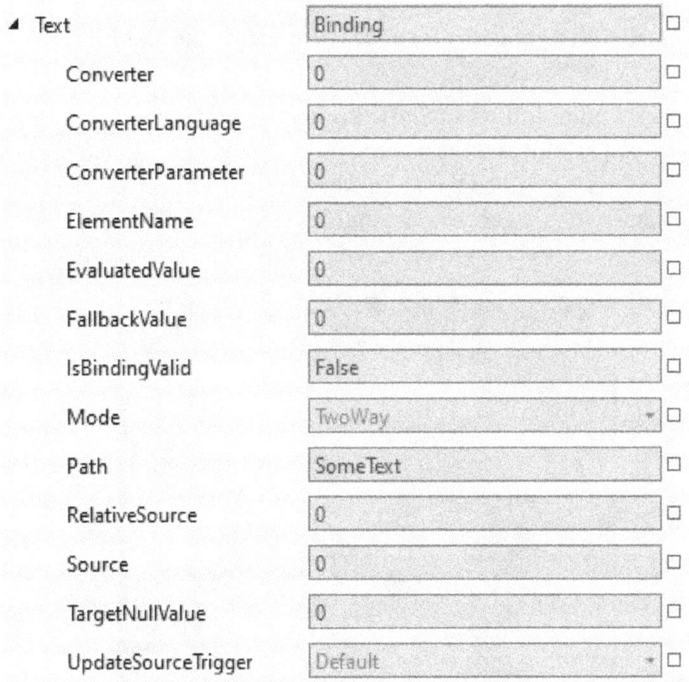

⊿ Text	Binding	☐
Converter	0	☐
ConverterLanguage	0	☐
ConverterParameter	0	☐
ElementName	0	☐
EvaluatedValue	0	☐
FallbackValue	0	☐
IsBindingValid	False	☐
Mode	TwoWay ▾	☐
Path	SomeText	☐
RelativeSource	0	☐
Source	0	☐
TargetNullValue	0	☐
UpdateSourceTrigger	Default ▾	☐

Figure 11.16 – View the binding details for the Text property of Text1

There is some very helpful information here. We can see the **Path** and **Mode** that were set in the XAML, the ones we did not set, and yet others that are read-only. **IsBindingValid** is **False** in this project, but it may be **True** if you fixed your data context from the previous section. When the binding is valid, **EvaluatedValue** will contain the current value for the **Text** property.

6. Select the second `TextBox` element in the tree and view the **Live Property Explorer** window. You can see that the default value for **Background** is **SolidColorBrush**.

7. Expand the **Background** node to view the resource details:

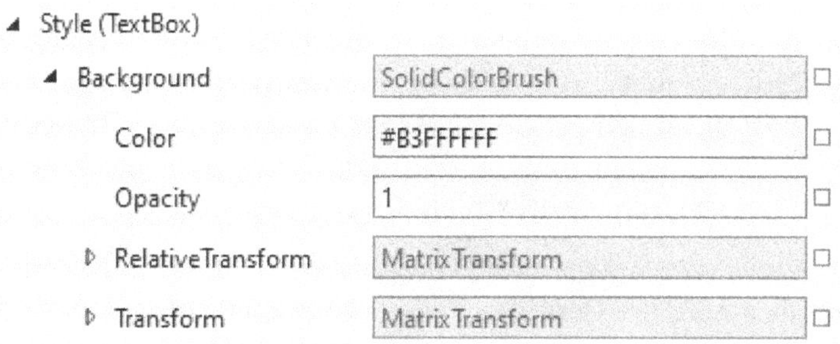

▲ Style (TextBox)

   ▲ Background   SolidColorBrush   ☐

        Color   #B3FFFFFF   ☐

        Opacity   1   ☐

        ▷ RelativeTransform   MatrixTransform   ☐

        ▷ Transform   MatrixTransform   ☐

Figure 11.17 – Viewing the property details of Page.Background

8. Try changing the **Color** property to white and see what happens in the XAML code and to the running application. The UI in the app should update, but the XAML file will remain unchanged.

9. Next, try adding markup to `MainWindow` to set the `MaxWidth` property of the second `TextBox` to `100`. What happens in **Live Property Explorer**? Can you find this property and value? Try using the search field. You can remove the `MaxWidth` when you're finished.

10. Returning to **Live Visual Tree**, you can view the depth of the visual tree to the right of each node's name. Remember that this number is not the true depth of the visual tree when **Show Just My XAML** is enabled. It is the depth of the visible nodes. This is important to note because the depth and complexity of the visual tree impact the performance of the UI rendering. `Grid` is more complex than `StackPanel`. `StackPanel` is preferred for layout if you are simply laying out a few elements horizontally or vertically. This unidirectional layout is what `StackPanel` was built to handle. As a rule of thumb, you should use the right control for the job and always keep performance in mind.

11. Now select the active node from the tree in your XAML file and enable **Select Element in the Running Application** from the toolbar. The **Track Focused Element** button on the toolbar will highlight the current tree node in the application's window at runtime. This option is also available from the in-app toolbar.

12. To toggle the in-app toolbar on/off, you can use the **Enable in-app Toolbar** button on the **Live Visual Tree** toolbar.

I encourage you to spend some time in these windows the next time you are debugging your application. Use them to help find issues with binding, resources, or custom control templates.

Now let's wrap up the chapter and review what we've learned.

Summary

In this chapter, we have covered some essential tools and techniques for debugging your XAML applications. We learned how to debug installed applications on a local or remote PC. If you are developing WPF or UWP applications, tools such as **Live Visual Tree**, **Live Property Explorer**, and **Rapid XAML Toolkit** will all work for those projects as well. Leveraging these tools will shorten the time you spend debugging and help you deliver higher-quality software.

In the next chapter, we will explore the `WebView2` browser control. You will learn how to use `WebView2` to embed an ASP.NET Core Blazor **single-page application (SPA)** inside a WinUI 3 desktop application.

Questions

1. How can you debug a UWP application that is running on an Xbox?

2. How can you debug an application that is currently running on your machine?

3. How can you launch an application package installed on a remote machine for debugging?

4. What feature in Visual Studio allows you to change XAML properties at runtime and see them reflected in the running application?

5. Which window will show a hierarchy of the elements in the current window?

6. What is the default binding mode for most control properties with `x:Bind`?

7. Where can you view the runtime properties for the control currently selected in **Live Visual Tree**?

12

Hosting a Blazor Application in WinUI

Blazor is a web framework from Microsoft that allows .NET developers to create C# web applications with little to no JavaScript code. Server-side Blazor applications were introduced with ASP.NET Core 3.0, and ASP.NET Core 3.2 added the ability to create client-side Blazor web apps with **WebAssembly** (**Wasm**). Wasm (`https://webassembly.org/`) allows runtimes such as .NET and Java to run in web applications in the browser, and it is supported by all modern browser engines. By leveraging the `WebView2` control in WinUI 3, Windows developers can run a cloud-hosted Blazor application inside their WinUI client application. These options are changing a bit in .NET 8 with the introduction of **rendering modes**. We'll discuss these new modes and the advantages of each.

In this chapter, we will cover the following topics:

- Learning some basics of client-side .NET development with ASP.NET Core and Blazor
- Creating a new Blazor application with **Visual Studio Code** and the **.NET command-line interface** (**CLI**)
- Deploying Blazor applications to the **Azure Static Web Apps** service
- Creating a WinUI application to host a Blazor application in a `WebView2` browser control

By the end of this chapter, you will understand how to create a new Blazor application, deploy it to the cloud, and use the application as a **single-page application** (**SPA**) inside the WinUI `WebView2` control.

Technical requirements

To follow along with the examples in this chapter, the following software is required:

- Windows 10 version 1809 (build 17763) or later or Windows 11.
- Visual Studio 2022 or later with the .NET Desktop Development workload configured for Windows App SDK development.

- **Visual Studio Code** (**VS Code**) with the following extensions: C# Dev Kit and Debugger for Microsoft Edge.

- Windows Terminal (which was built with WinUI) or your preferred command-line tool. You can also use the **Terminal** window in VS Code.

- To create the Blazor project, install .NET 7 SDK or later.

The source code for this chapter is available on GitHub at this URL: `https://github.com/ PacktPublishing/-Learn-WinUI-3/tree/master/Chapter12`.

Getting started with ASP.NET Core and Blazor

Blazor is a web development framework that provides C# developers with an alternative to JavaScript when building client-side web applications. Blazor is a part of **ASP.NET Core** and was first introduced with ASP.NET Core 3.0. Let's start by exploring a brief history of **ASP.NET** and ASP.NET Core.

A brief history of ASP.NET and ASP.NET Core

ASP.NET was Microsoft's .NET-based web development framework that was first released in 2002. The early versions of ASP.NET used a client development model called **Web Forms**, which was intended as a web equivalent of **Windows Forms** (**WinForms**) client applications. Web Forms was popular with .NET web developers but did not adhere to many web development best practices and patterns. Many developers were critical of the large amount of **ViewState** data sent over the wire with every server request and response.

In response to Web Forms criticism, the ASP.NET team released ASP.NET MVC in 2009. Web applications built with ASP.NET MVC follow the **Model-View-Controller** (**MVC**) pattern. The new framework was well-received by the .NET community and is still a popular choice with web developers today. ASP.NET was also one of the first Microsoft frameworks to be released as open source. In 2012, ASP.NET MVC 4 was released as open source under the Apache License 2.0.

As the .NET team continued to embrace open source software, they also decided to make a fresh start with a new, open source, and cross-platform version of .NET called **.NET Core**. Microsoft released .NET Core 1.0 in 2016 with runtimes available for Windows, macOS, and Linux. With the release of .NET Core came a new web framework called **ASP.NET Core**. ASP.NET Core 1.0 included project templates to build web applications and Web API projects. The web applications were built with the MVC pattern, the **Razor** syntax for building a rich UI, and CSS for styling pages.

The ASP.NET team continued to add more features to ASP.NET Core over the next several years, including the following:

- **Razor Pages**: Razor Pages projects were introduced with ASP.NET Core and offer a simple alternative to ASP.NET Core MVC

- **SignalR**: A framework for real-time web communication; SignalR is integral to client-server communication in Blazor server applications

- **Identity (previously Identity Core)**: Supports login functionality in ASP.NET Core applications and manages authentication resources such as users, passwords, roles, tokens, and so on

> **Note**
>
> This book will not provide a detailed tutorial on ASP.NET Core development. If you want to learn more about building web applications with ASP.NET Core, see *ASP.NET Core 5 for Beginners*, by *Andreas Helland, Vincent Maverick Durano, Jeffrey Chilberto, and Ed Price, Packt Publishing* (`https://www.packtpub.com/product/asp-net-core-5-for-beginners/9781800567184`).

But where does Blazor fit into the ASP.NET Core development picture? Let's explore that next.

What is Blazor?

Blazor is a framework for building web applications with .NET and C#. Prior to .NET 8, there were three hosting models from which developers could choose when starting a new Blazor project:

- **Blazor Server**: Introduced with ASP.NET Core 3.0, the server model executes application logic on the server with UI updates pushed to the client through SignalR connections.

- **Blazor WebAssembly**: Delivered later with ASP.NET Core 3.2, this execution model runs solely on the client, sandboxed and running on the browser's UI thread via Wasm.

- **Blazor Hybrid**: This is a newer type of Blazor app that combines web and native client technologies. In this model, Razor components run in .NET on the client and render web user interfaces to the native client with interop and WebView technology that is seamless to the user. Hybrid apps can be used with .NET MAUI, WPF, and WinForms clients.

In .NET 8 and later, the Blazor team has evolved these hosting models into rendering modes. There are now three modes you can choose when developing with Blazor:

- **Server mode**: The equivalent of the server hosting model from previous versions.

- **WebAssembly mode**: The client-side mode that leverages Wasm.

- **Auto mode**: The new Auto mode combines the best of the previous two modes. It will run in WebAssembly mode if the client runtime components can be downloaded quickly enough. Otherwise, it falls back to Server mode.

So, which mode should you choose for your next Blazor application? Luckily, with .NET 8, you don't have to choose the same mode for the entire application anymore. The modes can be selected at the component level by setting the @rendermode attribute. That component-level decision will depend on your project's requirements, but it's likely that many applications will start to leverage Auto mode.

> **Note**
>
> At the time of writing, .NET 8 is still only available as developer previews. We will build the application in this chapter with .NET 7 and the Blazor WebAssembly hosting model. You will be able to build the same kind of app with .NET 8 and the WebAssembly mode.

Here are some of the pros and cons of the server and Wasm hosting models:

Blazor Hosting Models

	Blazor Server	Blazor WebAssembly
Pros	• Smaller initial download • Full .NET API available • App code stays on server • Better performance on resource-limited devices • Robust debugging	• No .NET needed on server • Serverless deployments • Workload distributed to clients; increased scalability • Leverages client capabilities • Offline execution as a Progressive Web App (PWA)
Cons	• No offline support • Higher latency • Clients rely on server connections; less scalability • ASP.NET Core server hosting required • No serverless	• Limited by browser capabilities • Runtime included in initial download; slower first load • .NET runtime limited on Wasm compared for full .NET API set • Client-side debugging complicated in production

Figure 12.1 – Blazor hosting model pros and cons

The Blazor server hosting model was released first and has the most mature tooling and debugging support. It is a great choice if you plan to host the server on a service that supports ASP.NET Core and your users may be using browsers that do not have Wasm support.

In this chapter, we are going to focus on client-side Blazor applications. So, why choose this model, and how does it work?

WebAssembly and client-side .NET development

The primary benefits of the client-side hosting model with Wasm are the option of serverless deployment and the ability for clients to work offline. The offline support means your Blazor application can be configured as a **Progressive Web Application (PWA)** and downloaded to PCs, tablets, and phones. You can learn more about PWAs from Mozilla's developer documentation: https://developer. mozilla.org/en-US/docs/Web/Progressive_web_apps.

The reasons that Blazor client applications can run as PWAs are the reasons why we want to use it in a `WebView2` control in our WinUI application. Once the web application has loaded in the browser host, all in-memory execution and interactions can occur regardless of any interruptions in network connectivity. If connectivity, scalability, and server hosting are not concerns in your project, then the Blazor server model could certainly be used.

Simple Blazor Wasm applications can be hosted as *static resources* on a web server. You can also host Blazor Wasm applications on ASP.NET Core web hosting solutions. Doing this enables sharing code with other web solutions on the server and more advanced routing scenarios to support deep linking within the application. With .NET 8, using a host with ASP.NET Core support allows you to take advantage of the new Auto mode or choose to only use Wasm mode in some components that lend themselves to offline use.

With the Wasm model, when clients make their first request to the server, the entire application and .NET runtime are sent to the browser in the response, and the entire application runs on the client side. There is no shared server-side code in this mode. The runtime and application are then loaded on top of Wasm on the UI thread:

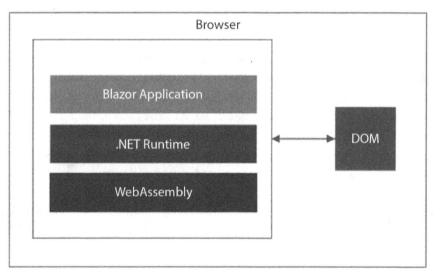

Figure 12.2 – The Blazor Wasm model running in the browser

Now that you have a little background on ASP.NET Core and Blazor applications, let's create a Blazor Wasm project and get some hands-on experience with the framework.

Creating a Blazor Wasm application

It's time to start building the Blazor application that we'll be running in our WinUI application. We are going to use the .NET CLI and VS Code to create the Blazor project. You can also use Visual Studio 2022 if you prefer the experience of a full-featured IDE:

1. Start by opening a Command Prompt with your Terminal application of choice. I will be using Windows Terminal (https://apps.microsoft.com/store/detail/windows-terminal/9N0DX20HK701) with PowerShell 7.3 (https://learn.microsoft.com/powershell/scripting/overview):

Figure 12.3 – Running PowerShell 7.3 in Windows Terminal

2. Use the terminal to change the current folder to the location where you keep your projects. My location will be C:\Users\alash\source\repos.

3. Use the following command to create a new Blazor WebAssembly project named BlazorTasks and hit *Enter*: dotnet new blazorwasm -o BlazorTasks. The .NET CLI will create the new project, and you should see a message indicating it has completed successfully:

```
The template "Blazor WebAssembly App" was created successfully.
This template contains technologies from parties other than Microsoft, see https://aka.ms/aspnetcore/7.0-third-party-not
ices for details.

Processing post-creation actions...
Restoring C:\Users\alash\source\repos\BlazorTasks\BlazorTasks.csproj:
  Determining projects to restore...
  Restored C:\Users\alash\source\repos\BlazorTasks\BlazorTasks.csproj (in 6.61 sec).
Restore succeeded.
```

Figure 12.4 – The .NET CLI successfully creates a Blazor WebAssembly App project

4. Navigate to the new BlazorTasks folder that .NET just created. If you have VS Code (https://code.visualstudio.com/) installed, you can enter code . at the command line to open the current folder in VS Code:

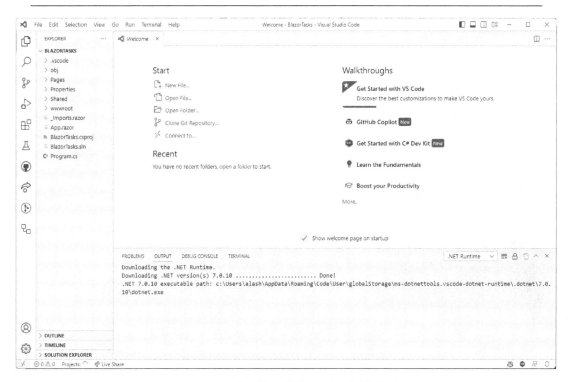

Figure 12.5 – The BlazorTasks project in VS Code

You may see some activity in the **OUTPUT** window as VS Code downloads some debugging and editing tools relevant to the project. If you are presented with a **Do you trust the authors of the files in this folder?** dialog, select the **Yes, I trust the authors** button to continue.

5. Switch to the **Terminal** window in VS Code. If the window isn't visible at the bottom of your editor, you can click **Terminal | New Terminal** from the menu.

6. Type `dotnet run` in the Terminal. You can also use *F5* to run in VS Code as you are accustomed to using in Visual Studio. When the compilation completes, you can view the running `BlazorTasks` application by navigating to `https://localhost:5240/` in your browser (the port number will be displayed in the **TERMINAL** window):

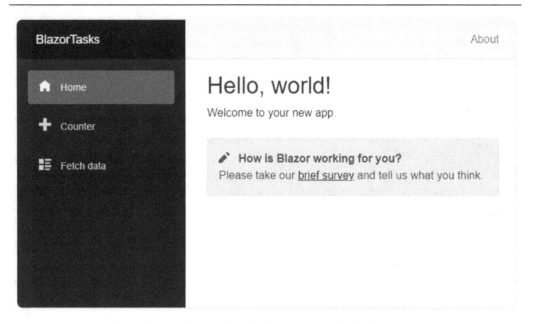

Figure 12.6 – Running the BlazorTasks project for the first time

The default project template has three navigation options in the left pane: **Home**, **Counter**, and **Fetch data**. As you navigate from page to page, all the execution logic is running within the browser. There are no round trips to an ASP.NET Core server instance.

7. You can open the developer tools in your browser by pressing *F12*. You will see that there is no activity on the **Network** tab of the developer tools while navigating to the **Counter** tab in the application and clicking the **Click me** button several times:

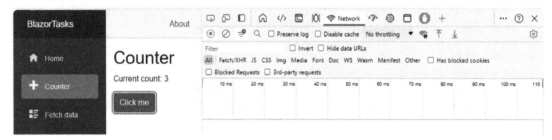

Figure 12.7 – Viewing network activity in the BlazorTasks application

8. Finally, when you are done exploring the application, you can close your browser and hit *Ctrl + C* in the VS Code **TERMINAL** window to stop debugging the application.

Now that we have created and tested the project, let's start coding a new task page for the application.

Building a simple application for tracking tasks

In this section, we are going to create a new task page for the application that will appear in the left navigation below the **Fetch data** item. If you like, you can remove the other components from the project. I am going to keep them there to test the navigation in the deployed application hosted in WinUI:

1. Start by adding a `Tasks` component to the project. Do this by entering `dotnet new razorcomponent -n Tasks -o Pages` in the VS Code **TERMINAL** window. This will create a `Tasks` Razor component in the `Pages` folder.

2. Double-click `Tasks.razor` in the `Pages` folder in the **Explorer** window to open it in the editor. As an alternative to the Explorer window, the C# Dev Kit extension should have added a **Solution Explorer** view to the bottom of the left pane. Use this view if you like. The file contains the following code:

    ```
    <h3>Tasks</h3>
    @code {
    }
    ```

    Razor files contain a combination of HTML markup and C# code, with the HTML at the top of the file, and the C# inside the `@code` block at the bottom of the file. We'll see how these two sections can interact as we move along.

3. Add `@page "/tasks"` as the first line of the `Tasks.razor` file. This will allow the application to route to the page using `/tasks` on the URL.

4. Before we add the page contents, let's add the new navigation item for it. Open `NavMenu.razor` from the `Shared` folder in **Explorer**.

5. Inside the `<nav>` element, add a new `<div>` before the closing `</nav>` tag:

    ```
    <div class="@NavMenuCssClass nav-scrollable"
      @onclick="ToggleNavMenu">
        <nav class="flex-column">
    ...
            <div class="nav-item px-3">
                <NavLink class="nav-link" href="tasks">
                    <span class="oi oi-list-rich" aria-
                        hidden="true"></span> Tasks
                </NavLink>
            </div>
        </nav>
    </div>
    ```

6. Run the application with `dotnet run` to make sure the new menu option appears and you can navigate to the new page with the **Tasks** header:

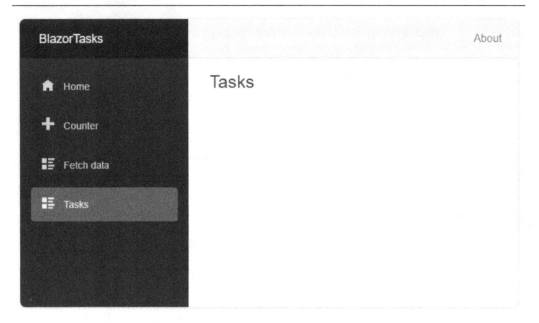

Figure 12.8 – Navigating to the new Tasks page

7. Next, use **File | New File** at the root of the project and name the file `TaskItem.cs`. This will be the model class for tasks. Add the following code to the new file:

```
namespace BlazorTasks
{
    public class TaskItem
    {
        public string? Name { get; set; }
        public bool IsComplete { get; set; }
    }
}
```

8. Open `Tasks.razor` and add the following code to create an unordered list of tasks by iterating over a list of tasks contained in the `@code` block:

```
@page "/tasks"
<h3>Tasks</h3>
<ul>
    @foreach (var task in taskList)
    {
        <li>@task.Name</li>
    }
```

```
</ul>
<input placeholder="Enter new task..." />
<button>Add task</button>
@code {
    private IList<TaskItem> taskList = new
      List<TaskItem>();
}
```

Notice how Razor files allow you to blend C# code and HTML markup. We have a C# `foreach` within `<ul>`, and inside `foreach`, we're adding `<li>` elements that again contain C# code to get each `task.Name`. This is powerful stuff. We've also added an `input` field to enter a new task and a `button` to add the task. We'll add some code to make `button` functional next.

9. Add a `newTask` private variable and a new method to the `@code` block named `AddTask`. This method will add a new task to the `taskList` collection:

    ```
    private string newTask;
    private void AddTask()
    {
        if (!string.IsNullOrWhiteSpace(newTask))
        {
            taskList.Add(new TaskItem { Name = newTask });
            newTask = string.Empty;
        }
    }
    ```

10. Finally, add some data binding code to the `input` and `button` elements on the page. The `input` will bind to the `newTask` variable, and the `onclick` event of `button` will trigger the `AddTask` method to run:

    ```
    <input placeholder="Enter new task..." @bind="newTask"
      />
    <button @onclick="AddTask">Add task</button>
    ```

11. Now, run the application and test the controls. You should be able to add some tasks to the list:

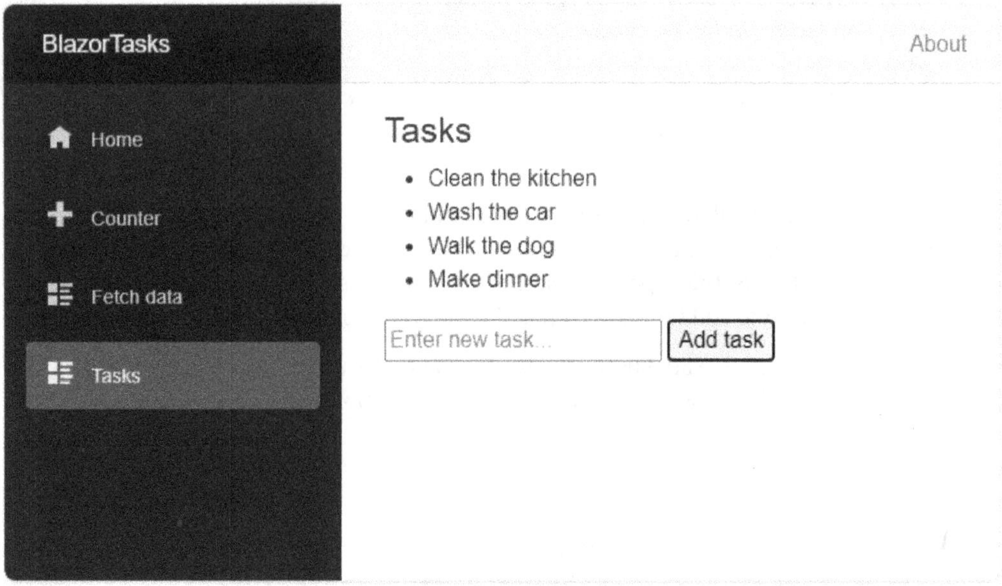

Figure 12.9 – Adding some tasks to the task list in BlazorTasks

This works great, but now that we have some tasks to do, we don't have any way to mark them as done. Let's take care of that next.

12. The first step is to make each list item checkbox that users can check when they complete a task. We are also binding task.Name to an input field so users can edit the name of each task:

```
<ul>
    @foreach (var task in taskList)
    {
        <li>
            <input type="checkbox"
              @bind="task.IsComplete" />
            <input @bind="task.Name" />
        </li>
    }
</ul>
```

13. Next, in case the list gets lengthy, let's use some data binding to display the number of incomplete tasks as part of the page header:

```
<h3>Tasks - (@taskList.Count(task =>
    !task.IsComplete)) Incomplete</h3>
```

14. Run the application again, and start working on your task list:

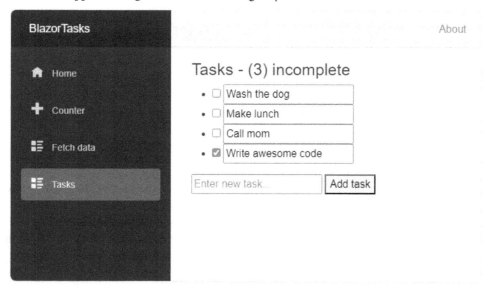

Figure 12.10 – Adding and completing tasks in the BlazorTasks application

You may have noticed that the tasks do not save between sessions. The `taskList` is an in-memory collection for now. To persist it between sessions, you would need to add service calls to save the data in a server-side data store. Creating this service is beyond the scope of this chapter, and I will leave it as an exercise for you.

> **Note**
>
> All of these steps can also be taken with Visual Studio or Visual Studio for Mac if you prefer using a full-featured IDE. This Microsoft Learn documentation page has information on how to debug a Blazor Wasm app in both of these tools, as well as VS Code: `https://learn.microsoft.com/aspnet/core/blazor/debug`.

Now that we have a functioning task-tracking web client, we can move on to the next step. It's time to deploy our Blazor app to the cloud.

Exploring Blazor Wasm deployment options

Running and debugging the Blazor project locally is great while we're developing the solution, but when it's time to share your application with the world, we will need to host it in the cloud. There are many cloud hosting options for typical ASP.NET Core applications, and Blazor Wasm applications have even more. Sites that run entirely on the client can be hosted as static files on the server, meaning that the server simply serves up the files when it receives a request. There is no server-side execution required.

Let's start by reviewing some of the available hosting options for Blazor WebAssembly deployments.

Deployment options for Blazor Wasm projects

There are several hosting options for our Blazor project. We are going to discuss a few of the most popular solutions today: **GitHub Pages**, **Azure App Service**, **Azure Static Web Apps**, and two options on **Amazon Web Services** (**AWS**). For an in-depth exploration of options either hosted with ASP. NET Core or as static files, Microsoft Learn has a great article: `https://learn.microsoft. com/aspnet/core/blazor/host-and-deploy/webassembly`.

Amazon Web Services

With AWS, a Blazor Wasm site can be hosted with ASP.NET Core in **Elastic Container Service** (**ECS**) (`https://aws.amazon.com/ecs/`) and **Fargate**. The ECS solution uses **Docker** to create the container to be hosted in the cloud. The site is then served through Fargate (`https:// aws.amazon.com/fargate/`), the AWS compute engine for containers. To read more about this solution for ASP.NET Core projects, the AWS blog has a great article detailing the steps: `https:// aws.amazon.com/blogs/compute/hosting-asp-net-core-applications-in-amazon-ecs-using-aws-fargate/`.

For a static hosting option with AWS, static pages can be hosted using **Amazon S3** storage (`https:// aws.amazon.com/s3/`) and **CloudFront** (`https://aws.amazon.com/cloudfront/`). An Amazon S3 bucket is a cloud file storage solution. Your `wwwroot` folder will be copied to S3 storage, and CloudFront handles serving the static files from the S3 bucket. This article details how to create and deploy a Blazor Wasm application in AWS: `https://aws.amazon.com/blogs/ developer/run-blazor-based-net-web-applications-on-aws-serverless/`.

Now, let's see how to serve static files through **GitHub**.

GitHub Pages

GitHub Pages (`https://pages.github.com/`) are static websites served directly from GitHub repositories. You can maintain your site on GitHub and configure **GitHub Actions** to deploy the site to GitHub Pages. Microsoft MVP Niels Swimburghe has a step-by-step guide for deploying Blazor Wasm projects to GitHub Pages on his personal blog: `https://swimburger.net/blog/dotnet/ how-to-deploy-aspnet-blazor-webassembly-to-github-pages`. GitHub Pages are free, but *standard* user accounts can only host pages from the *default* GitHub branch.

In the next section, we will be using GitHub Actions with our project to deploy to Azure. But now, let's review two of the available Azure hosting solutions.

Azure App Service

Azure App Service (`https://azure.microsoft.com/products/app-service/`) is a great option to use if you want your Blazor app hosted on an ASP.NET Core web server. There are Windows and Linux servers available with App Service, but currently, only Windows instances are supported with Blazor WebAssembly apps. Microsoft Learn has extensive documentation on deploying ASP.NET Core applications to App Service: `https://learn.microsoft.com/aspnet/core/host-and-deploy/azure-apps/`.

Now, let's look at another Azure option. This one is specifically for deploying static sites such as Blazor Wasm.

Azure Static Web Apps

Azure Static Web Apps (`https://azure.microsoft.com/products/app-service/static/`) is a service to host and serve static web applications such as Blazor Wasm. It offers easy deployment through GitHub Actions, free SSL certificates, custom domains, and easy integration with **Azure Functions**.

For full documentation on Static Web Apps, including information about using it with other SPA websites, Microsoft Learn has documentation, guides, and **Training** (`https://learn.microsoft.com/training/`) content available at `https://learn.microsoft.com/azure/static-web-apps/`.

We are going to use Static Web Apps to host our Blazor application. Let's do that now!

Publishing Blazor to Azure Static Web Apps hosting

In this section, we are going to host our `BlazorTasks` application in the cloud by pushing the source to GitHub, creating an Azure Static Web Apps app, and configuring GitHub Actions to publish the app to Azure with every commit to the main branch. Let's start by pushing our code to GitHub.

Pushing the project to GitHub

To push your code to a GitHub repository, you can either use the Git CLI (`https://git-scm.com/downloads`) or the **GitHub Desktop** (`https://desktop.github.com/`) application. We will use GitHub Desktop in this example:

1. Download and install GitHub Desktop. When the installation is complete, launch the application.
2. If your local project is not part of a Git repository yet, choose **File | New Repository**. If you already have a local repository for your project, you can skip to the next step:

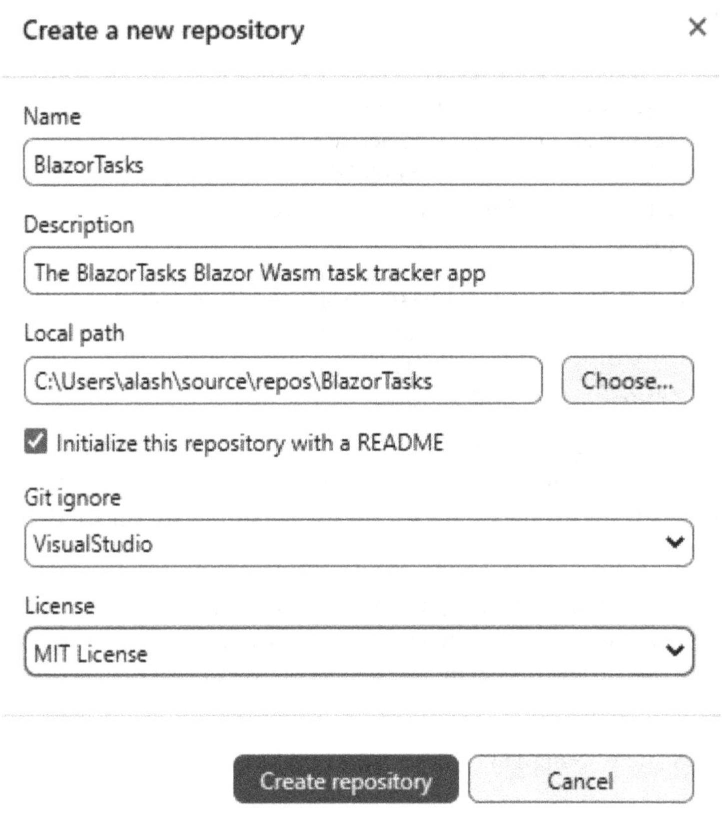

Create a new repository   ✕

Name

| BlazorTasks |

Description

| The BlazorTasks Blazor Wasm task tracker app |

Local path

| C:\Users\alash\source\repos\BlazorTasks | | Choose... |

☑ Initialize this repository with a README

Git ignore

| VisualStudio   ⌄ |

License

| MIT License   ⌄ |

| Create repository | | Cancel |

Figure 12.11 – Creating a new local GitHub repository for the BlazorTasks application

Name the repository something like `BlazorTasksWasm` or `BlazorTasks`, optionally add a description, and browse to **Local path** for your project. It's a good practice to have a README, a **Git ignore** file, and **License**. So, choose each of these options. When you're done, click **Create repository**. After completing this step, move ahead to *step 4*.

3. If you created your Blazor project in a local Git repository, you can select **File | Add Local Repository**. Browse to the folder where you have the `BlazorTasks` project and select it. If you do not have a Git repository there yet, the application will prompt you to create one:

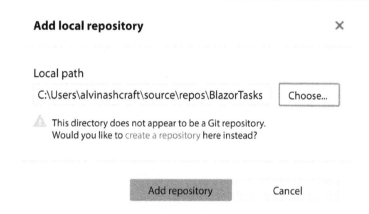

Figure 12.12 – Adding a local repository

4.   In this step, we'll publish the local repository to GitHub. If you don't have a GitHub account, you can create one at `https://github.com/`. When you're ready to go, make sure your `BlazorTasksWasm` repository is selected for **Current repository** and click the **Publish repository** button:

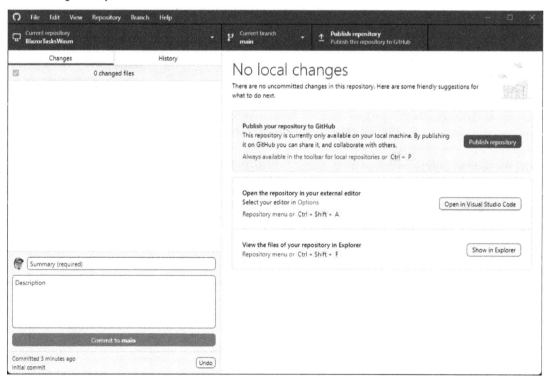

Figure 12.13 – Publishing the local repository to GitHub

If you have the **Keep this code private** option on the dialog that appears, you can uncheck it.

5.   View the repository on GitHub to make sure it has been published correctly:

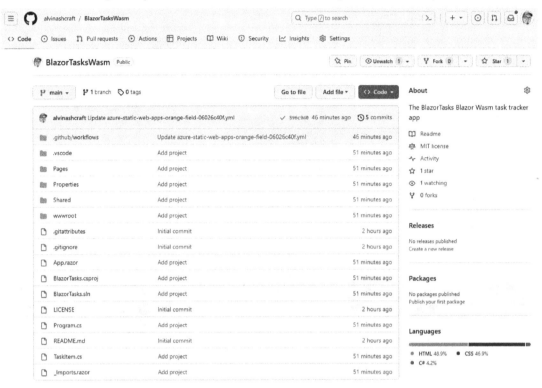

Figure 12.14 – The BlazorTasks code on GitHub

Now, the code is ready to be published to Azure. Let's do that next.

Creating an Azure Static Web Apps resource

Let's walk through creating a new Azure Static Web Apps app:

1.   To start, if you don't have an Azure account yet, you can create a free trial account at `https://azure.microsoft.com/`. The site will walk you through the steps to create a new account.

2. Log in to the Microsoft account associated with your Azure account at `https://portal.azure.com/`.

3. From the portal home page, click **Create a resource** at the top under **Azure services**.

4. On the **New** page, search for `static` and select **Static Web App**:

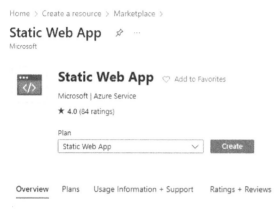

Figure 12.15 – Creating a new Static Web App

5. Click **Create**. On the **Create Static Web App** page, select your free trial subscription. You will also need to select a resource group. Resource groups are a way to group a related set of Azure resources. Create a new **Resource Group** and name it `BlazorTasksWasm`. Give the resource a name, select a **Region** option that makes sense for you or your users, and select the **Free** option for **SKU**. Choose **GitHub** for **Deployment details**. We'll link to GitHub in the next step:

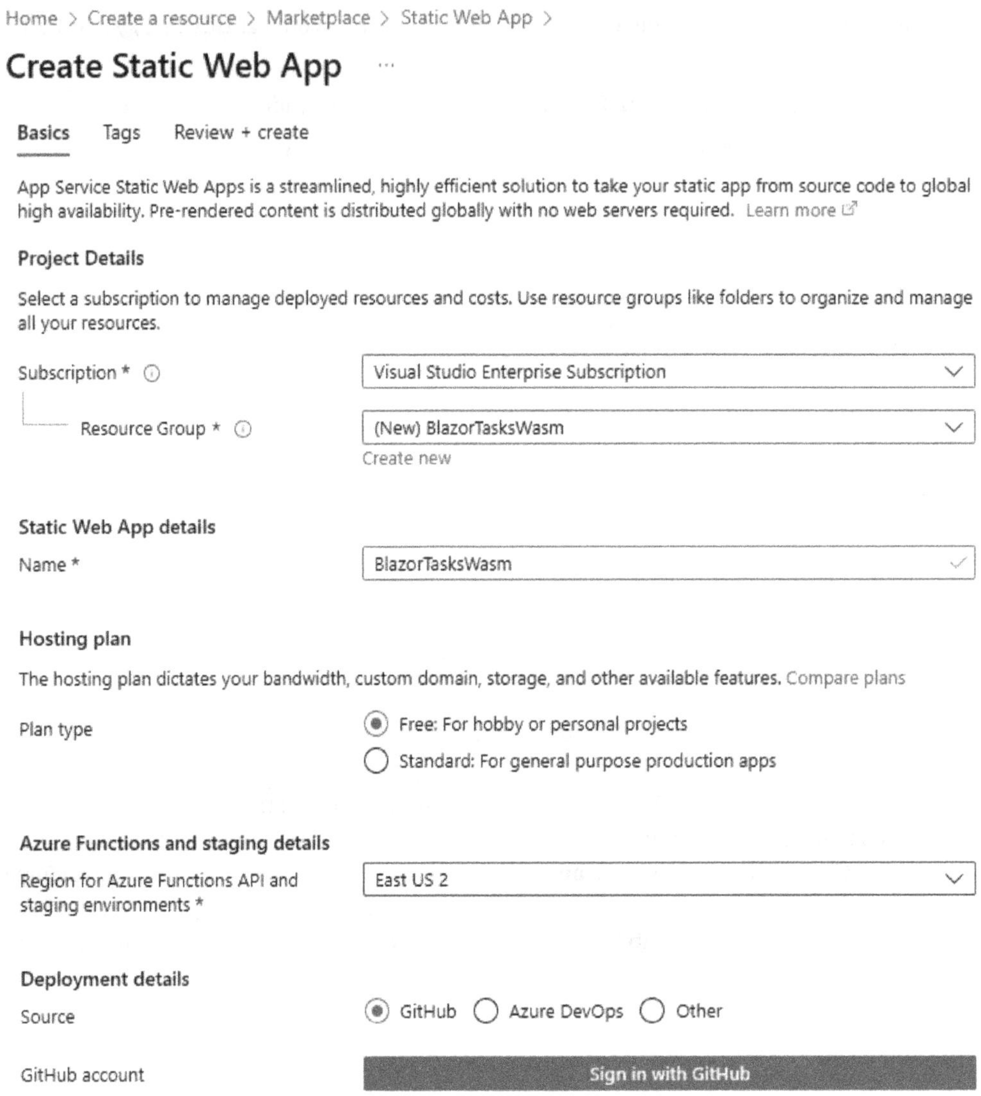

Home > Create a resource > Marketplace > Static Web App >

Create Static Web App   ...

Basics   Tags   Review + create

App Service Static Web Apps is a streamlined, highly efficient solution to take your static app from source code to global high availability. Pre-rendered content is distributed globally with no web servers required.   Learn more ⬀

Project Details

Select a subscription to manage deployed resources and costs. Use resource groups like folders to organize and manage all your resources.

Subscription * ⓘ

Visual Studio Enterprise Subscription	⌄

Resource Group * ⓘ

(New) BlazorTasksWasm	⌄

Create new

Static Web App details

Name *

BlazorTasksWasm	✓

Hosting plan

The hosting plan dictates your bandwidth, custom domain, storage, and other available features. Compare plans

Plan type

◉ Free: For hobby or personal projects

◯ Standard: For general purpose production apps

Azure Functions and staging details

Region for Azure Functions API and staging environments *

East US 2	⌄

Deployment details

Source   ◉ GitHub ◯ Azure DevOps ◯ Other

GitHub account

Sign in with GitHub

Figure 12.16 – Configuring the new Static Web Apps resource

6. Next, click the **Sign in with GitHub** button to link your GitHub account. Linking the accounts is necessary for the GitHub files to be deployed to the Azure site. After it has linked your accounts, select the **Organization**, **Repository**, and **Branch** names for your BlazorTasksWasm repository:

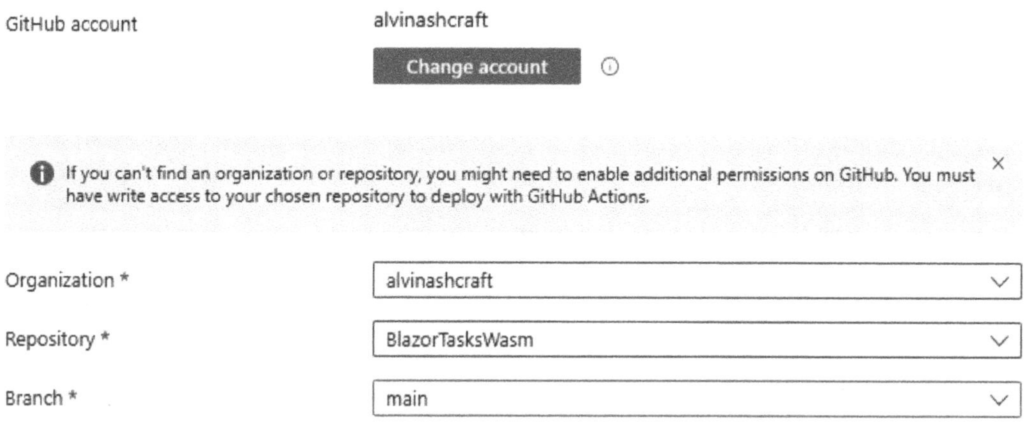

GitHub account   alvinashcraft

Change account   ⓘ

ⓘ If you can't find an organization or repository, you might need to enable additional permissions on GitHub. You must   ✕
have write access to your chosen repository to deploy with GitHub Actions.

Organization * | alvinashcraft   ⌄ |

Repository * | BlazorTasksWasm   ⌄ |

Branch * | main   ⌄ |

Figure 12.17 – Entering GitHub details for the Static Web Apps resource

7. In the **Build Details** section, select **Blazor** from the **Build Presents** dropdown. **App location** will be . (*just a dot*), **Api location** can be left blank, and **Output location** will be wwwroot.

8. Click **Review + create**. Review the **Summary** page to make sure everything looks correct and click **Create**. Azure will take a few minutes to create the new resource. When it's done, you can click **Go to resource**.

The Static Web Apps resource is ready to go. Azure created our GitHub Actions deployment for us. Let's review what it did and then review the website.

Publishing an application with GitHub Actions

Typically, this is where we would configure GitHub Actions to build our project in the GitHub repository and publish it to the Azure resource. However, the Azure Static Web App configuration took care of that step for us. Let's review what it did:

1. Navigate to your project on GitHub and click the **Actions** tab. You will see that Azure has created a workflow named **Azure Static Web Apps CI/CD**:

Figure 12.18 – Viewing the workflows for BlazorTasks

2. Select the **Azure Static Web Apps CI/CD** workflow and click the `.yml` file hyperlink that appears just under the **Azure Static Web Apps CI/CD** title. The `.yml` file will appear in an editor.

3. Review the file contents. You'll see a section for `build_and_deploy_job`. This step will take the latest committed code, build it, and deploy it to the app service that we configured in Azure.

4. You can verify that the site has been published to Azure by navigating to the `BlazorTasksWasm` resource in the Azure portal and clicking on the URL for the site:

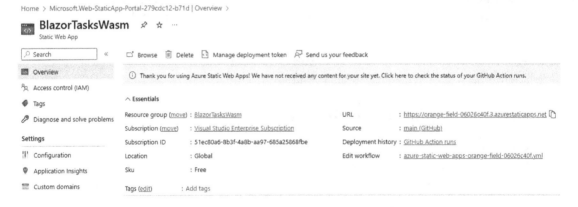

Figure 12.19 – The BlazorTasks resource home page in the Azure portal

5. The Blazor site will open in a new tab in your browser. Click the **Tasks** item in the navigation menu and verify that the application works as expected:

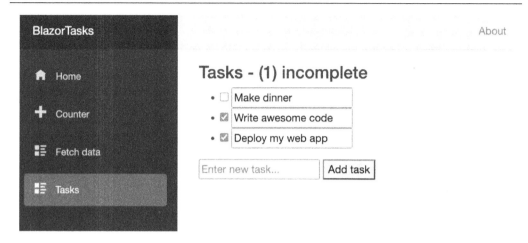

Figure 12.20 – Running BlazorTasks in the static cloud

We now have a public-facing static website running the Blazor Wasm application. Now, we're ready to run the web application inside a WinUI project.

Hosting your Blazor application in the WinUI WebView2

We're on the home stretch. We created a Blazor Wasm application, pushed the source code to GitHub, and Azure configured GitHub Actions to publish the application to Azure Static Web Apps with every commit. The last step is to create a simple WinUI 3 project and add a `WebView2` control to **MainWindow**:

1. You can start by either creating a new **Blank App, Packaged (WinUI in Desktop)** named `BlazorTasksHost` in Visual Studio or opening the starter project from GitHub: https://github.com/PacktPublishing/-Learn-WinUI-3/tree/master/Chapter12/Start/BlazorTasksHost.

2. Open `MainWindow.xaml` and update the window to host `Grid` that contains the `WebView2` control. Set the `Source` property to the URL of your `BlazorTasksWasm` site:

    ```
    <Grid>
        <WebView2 Source="https://you-custom-url-
            0af06780d.azurestaticapps.net/"/>
    </Grid>
    ```

3. Remove the unused button click event handler in `MainWindow.xaml.cs` to prevent compilation errors.

4. Run the application, and you'll see the `BlazorTasksWasm` application load as if it were a Windows application:

Figure 12.21 – Running BlazorTasksWasm in a WinUI application

You can test the app in the web view. Because it's all client-side code, you can even disconnect from your network and keep using the app. The **Tasks** page will continue to function offline.

Now, any updates you make to the Blazor application will be immediately pushed to all your users when you commit to GitHub. This is a compelling way for web developers to reach more Windows users.

> **Note**
>
> If you would like to explore Blazor and WinUI integration further, you can check out this blog post by Thomas Claudius Huber. In the post, he experiments with calling a method in the Blazor app from the WinUI host application by executing a script through the `WebView2` control: `https://www.thomasclaudiushuber.com/2020/02/18/hosting-blazor-app-in-winui-3-with-webview-2-and-call-blazor-component-method-from-winui/`.

Let's wrap up with a summary of what we've covered in this chapter.

Summary

In this chapter, we learned about ASP.NET Core Blazor. You created a simple task-tracking application with Blazor Wasm and published it to Azure Static Web Apps with GitHub Actions. From here, you could use ASP.NET Core Identity to integrate an application login and save the task data to **Azure SQL**, **Azure Cosmos DB**, or another cloud-based data store. This would allow personalizing the task list for each user and saving its state. We created a WinUI 3 application to run the Blazor client on Windows, but you could also send users directly to your site or create a JavaScript-based PWA for desktop and mobile clients. For more information about creating a PWA with Blazor WASM, check out this Microsoft blog post: `https://devblogs.microsoft.com/visualstudio/building-a-progressive-web-app-with-blazor/`.

> **Note**
> To learn more about building web applications with Blazor, you can read *Web Development with Blazor* by Jimmy Engstrom. Here's the Amazon link: `https://www.amazon.com/dp/1803241497/`

In the next chapter, *Chapter 13, Take Your App Cross-Platform with Uno Platform*, we will explore what **Uno Platform** can do for WinUI developers.

Questions

1. What is the name of the Blazor hosting model in .NET 7 and earlier that runs all application logic in the browser?

2. Which Blazor hosting model is less scalable?

3. What is the name of the syntax used in Blazor UI files?

4. Which .NET CLI command will compile and run the project in the current folder?

5. What is the name of GitHub's product that hosts static websites?

6. Which Azure product hosts static websites?

7. What WinUI 3 control can load web content in a Chromium-based browser control?

8. What is the name of GitHub's **Continuous Integration/Continuous Delivery** (CI/CD) solution?

13

Take Your App Cross-Platform with Uno Platform

Uno Platform allows developers to write XAML markup and C# code in a single code base and deploy the application to multiple platforms. Uno currently supports iOS, Android, Windows, macOS, Linux, Tizen, and the web (with **WebAssembly**). Uno Platform uses the same XAML syntax as WinUI, allowing WinUI developers to easily make the jump to Uno while reusing much of their existing XAML and C# code. We will look at how the **My Media Collection** sample app can be adapted to run on some of these other platforms with Uno Platform.

In this chapter, we will cover the following topics:

- The history of Uno Platform and discuss its current capabilities
- How to configure Visual Studio to create Uno Platform projects
- Adapting existing WinUI views and ViewModels for reuse in Uno projects
- Running and debugging an Uno Platform application on Android using the **Windows Subsystem for Android (WSA)**
- Running your application in the browser natively with WebAssembly

By the end of this chapter, you will understand how to take a WinUI application built with the Windows App SDK and port it to multiple platforms outside the Windows ecosystem with Uno Platform.

Technical requirements

To follow along with the examples in this chapter, the following software is required:

- Windows 11 version 22000.0 or later with WSA installed from the Microsoft Store. To use WSA, 16 GB of RAM is recommended.

- Visual Studio 2022 or later with the **.NET Desktop Development** workload configured for Windows App SDK development.

- If you want to build and run an iOS or macOS version of the sample application, you will need a Mac running macOS 12.5 or later with Xcode 14 or later installed from the App Store.

- To target Android devices, you can install the **.NET Multi-platform App UI development** workload in the Visual Studio Installer. This will install a supported version of the **Android SDK**.

An overview of Uno Platform

Uno Platform is an open source UI framework that installs as an extension to Visual Studio. It is cross-platform, with the ability to target Windows, iOS, Android, macOS, Linux, and WebAssembly. With a single C# and WinUI XAML code base, you can target all of these platforms. While the Uno Platform team recommends Visual Studio for the best experience, you can build Uno applications with Visual Studio Code or the **JetBrains Rider** IDE. The pros and cons of each development environment are discussed on Uno Platform's **Get Started** documentation: `https://platform.uno/docs/articles/get-started.html?tabs=windows#select-your-development-environment`.

Uno Platform was first released in May 2018 and has been growing in popularity in recent years. They have also added to their supported platforms and shifted from UWP to WinUI 3 in their XAML support. This year, in their 4.10.13 release, they even added support for embedding **.NET MAUI** controls within Uno Platform apps, with support for an extensive number of third-party controls. We won't be covering .NET MAUI embedding in this chapter, but you can explore this exciting feature in their documentation: `https://platform.uno/docs/articles/external/uno.extensions/doc/Overview/Maui/MauiOverview.html`.

Speaking of .NET MAUI, you are probably wondering why a developer may choose Uno Platform over Microsoft's cross-platform successor to **Xamarin.Forms**. One reason why WinUI developers would choose Uno Platform is *familiarity*. Uno apps are created with WinUI XAML, so there is no learning curve. The .NET MAUI XAML is slightly different than WinUI. If targeting Linux and web browsers is important to you, .NET MAUI applications cannot currently target either of these platforms, whereas Uno Platform can. If you or the designers in your company use **Figma** to create user interfaces, you'll find the Uno Platform Figma plugin will give your team a great head-start when building your next application.

Uno Platform is open source. On their GitHub repository (`https://github.com/unoplatform/uno`), you can track open issues, submit pull requests to improve the framework, or get insights into their latest releases. If you want to try Uno Platform before getting it installed and building your first app, you can open their interactive **Uno Playground** in your browser at `https://playground.platform.uno/#wasm-start`:

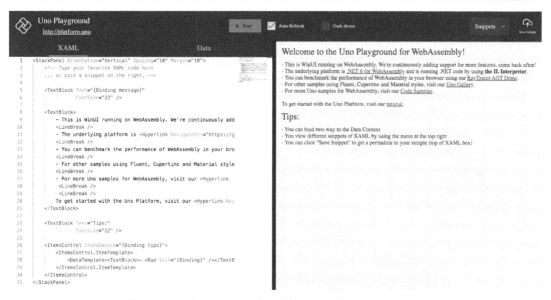

Figure 13.1 – Exploring the Uno Playground in a web browser

The Uno Playground sample app runs interactively in the browser with WebAssembly. You can make changes to the XAML in the left panel and watch it update the preview on the right in real time.

The other browser-based resource you can explore is the **Uno Gallery** (`https://gallery.platform.uno/`). In the Uno Gallery, you can explore controls, theming capabilities, and other UI and non-UI features of Uno Platform. For example, on the gallery's page for the **Button** control, you can see how the control will be rendered in different styles – **Material**, **Fluent**, or **Cupertino** designs:

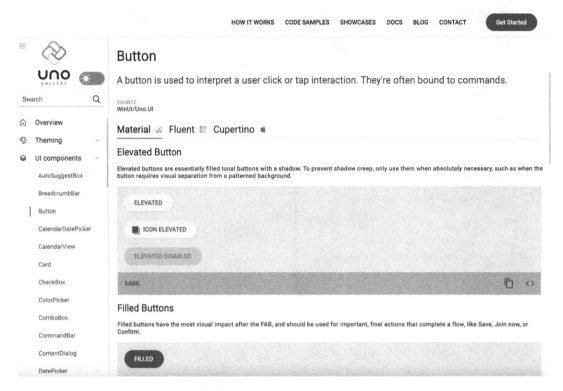

Figure 13.2 – Exploring the Button control in the Uno Gallery

Spend some time reviewing these online resources before we continue to create our first project with Uno Platform.

Creating your first Uno Platform project

In this section, we are going to create a new Uno Platform project that will be the basis of our cross-platform version of the *My Media Collection* application that we created in several of the earlier chapters of this book. Before we can create a new Uno Platform project, we need to install the extension:

1. Start by opening Visual Studio and go to **Extensions | Manage Extensions** to open the **Manage Extensions** window.

2. In the **Search** field, search for Uno Platform.

3. The **Uno Platform** extension should be the first result. Click **Install** and restart Visual Studio to complete the installation.

4. When you open Visual Studio again, select **Create a new project**.

5. In the **Search for templates** field, enter Uno Platform. You will get several results for the different Uno Platform project types.

6. Select the **Uno Platform App** template and click **Next**.

7. Name the project `UnoMediaCollection` and select **Create**. This will launch **Uno Platform Template Wizard**:

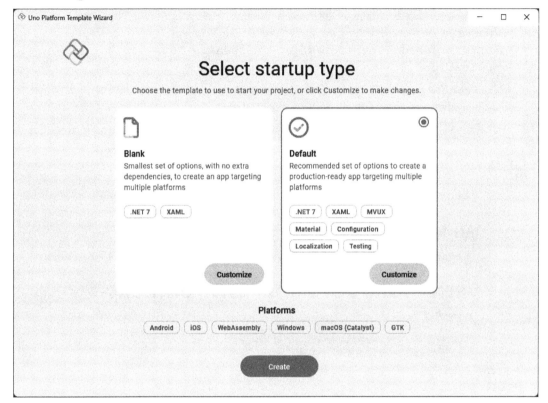

Figure 13.3 – Uno Platform Template Wizard

8. On the **Select startup type** page, select the **Customize** button on the **Default** type.

    This will open the detailed steps of the wizard. From here, you can configure all of the available Uno Platform options. We will leave most of these as default, but let's step through each page.

9. On the **Framework** page, the default is currently **.NET 7.0**, but it may be **.NET 8.0** when you are reading this book. You can leave the default selection.

10. On the **Platforms** page, we are going to only work with **Windows**, **Android**, and **WebAssembly**. You can unselect the other platforms.

11. On the **Presentation** page, select **MVVM**. The default is **MVUX**, but we want to bring our ViewModel classes over from the existing `MyMediaCollection` application.

12. On the **Theme** page, select **Fluent** to use the same Fluent design of the original application.

13. On the **Extensions** page, you can remove **Localization** and change **Navigation** to **Blank**.

14. You can uncheck the **Unit Tests** and **UI Tests** options on the **Testing** page. We won't get into testing in this chapter.

15. You can leave the default settings on the **Projects**, **Features**, **Authentication**, and **Application** pages. To learn more about these options, you can review the Uno Platform documentation: `https://platform.uno/docs/articles/get-started-vs-2022.html#create-an-application`.

16. Click **Create** to generate the projects and start working with them in Visual Studio. If Visual Studio prompts you to reload any projects, click **Reload**.

17. Follow the **Verify your developer environment** steps on the Uno welcome screen in Visual Studio:

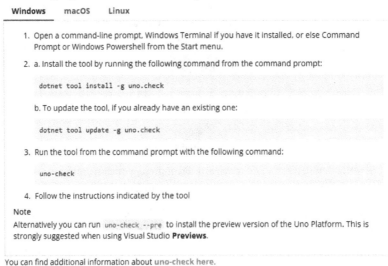

Figure 13.4 – Uno Platform welcome screen

The uno-check command-line utility does a great job of diagnosing potential development environment issues and automatically fixing them. You should allow it to fix any issues it identifies before continuing. You may need to reboot your system after it's done. Do this and open the project again before continuing to the next step.

18. Make sure the UnoMediaCollection.Windows project is set as the startup project and start debugging. The app should launch and display a window containing a **Hello Uno Platform** message:

Figure 13.5 – Running UnoMediaCollection as a Windows app

That's it! We've got a running app to use as our starting point. In the next section, we will learn more about the structure of the projects as we reuse code from the MyMediaCollection project to enhance UnoMediaCollection.

Migrating WinUI XAML markup and code to Uno Platform

In this section, we are going to take the UnoMediaCollection solution that we created in the previous section and migrate the code from an earlier version of MyMediaCollection. This will give us a cross-platform version of the application that we will run on Windows, Android, and WebAssembly in the sections ahead.

In order to keep things simple for our first project, we are going to migrate the code from the completed `MyMediaCollection` solution found in the completed code for *Chapter 5, Exploring WinUI Controls*. If you don't have a copy of that code, you can get it from GitHub here: `https://github.com/PacktPublishing/Learn-WinUI-3-Second-Edition/tree/main/Chapter05/Complete`. The easiest way to follow along with the instructions is to download the solution, but you can also create each class in the Uno Project solution and copy and paste the WinUI project code from the GitHub editor.

We are going to use the code from *Chapter 5* because the SQLite database hasn't been added yet at this point. Adding code with file access to a Uno Platform project is possible but more complicated. It requires writing some **platform-specific code**. This code will be conditionally executed, depending on the platform where the application is currently running. Using SQLite on most platforms is relatively straightforward, but local file access on WebAssembly is not as easy. You can read more about platform-specific code on Uno Platform in their documentation: `https://platform.uno/docs/articles/platform-specific-csharp.html`.

If working offline is not a concern, the best option for data access across all these platforms is to create a lightweight web service to handle your data access. Doing this also means adding an identity solution to ensure each user is accessing their own data. Uno Platform has some documentation on consuming a web API, if you're interested in pursuing this option on your own: `https://platform.uno/docs/articles/howto-consume-webservices.html`.

Now, let's start our WinUI project migration to Uno Platform.

Migrating the WinUI project code

It's time to get started with our cross-platform transformation of `MyMediaCollection`. We'll start by importing the C# classes from the old project:

1. Start by opening the `UnoMediaCollection` solution from the previous section and create four new folders in the `UnoMediaCollection` project: `Enums`, `Interfaces`, `Model`, and `ViewModels`. We'll also be adding classes from the `Services` folder, but that folder already exists in the new project:

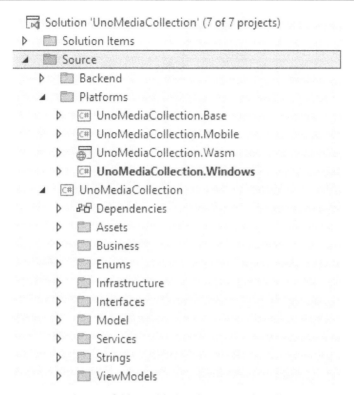

Figure 13.6 – The new folders added to the UnoMediaCollection project

2. Right-click the Enums folder and select **Add** | **Existing Item**. Browse to the Enums folder in the WinUI MyMediaCollection project, select the ItemType.cs and LocationType. cs files, and click **Add**.

3. Open each newly added file and change the namespace to UnoMediaCollection.Enums.

4. We're going to repeat these steps for each of the remaining folders. Next, add the existing IDataService.cs and INavigationService.cs files to the Interfaces folder.

5. In IDataService, change the namespace to UnoMediaCollection.Interfaces and update the using statements to the following:

```
using UnoMediaCollection.Enums;
using UnoMediaCollection.Model;
```

You can remove any other using statements, as they're part of the **global usings** in the project.

6. In INavigationService, you can update the namespace to UnoMediaCollection. Interfaces and remove the using System; statement.

7. Add the existing MediaItem.cs and Medium.cs files to the Model folder.

8. Modify MediaItem to look like this (changes highlighted):

```
using UnoMediaCollection.Enums;
namespace UnoMediaCollection.Model
{
    public class MediaItem
    {
        public int Id { get; set; }
        public string? Name { get; set; }
        public ItemType MediaType { get; set; }
        public Medium? MediumInfo { get; set; }
        public LocationType Location { get; set; }
    }
}
```

9. Modify the Medium class to look like this:

```
using UnoMediaCollection.Enums;
namespace UnoMediaCollection.Model
{
    public class Medium
    {
        public int Id { get; set;  }
        public string? Name { get; set; }
        public ItemType MediaType { get; set; }
    }
}
```

10. Add the existing DataService.cs and NavigationService.cs files to the Services folder.

11. In DataService, update the namespace to UnoMediaCollection.Services and update your using statements to only contain these three statements:

```
using UnoMediaCollection.Enums;
using UnoMediaCollection.Interfaces;
using UnoMediaCollection.Model;
```

12. In NavigationService, update the namespace to UnoMediaCollection.Services and change the accessor of the AppFrame variable from private static to internal static. We'll need to set this value from App.cs later. Also, update the using statements to contain only these two statements:

```
using UnoMediaCollection.Interfaces;
using System.Collections.Concurrent;
```

13. Add the existing `ItemDetailsViewModel.cs` and `MainViewModel.cs` files to the `ViewModels` folder.

14. In `ItemDetailsViewModel`, change the namespace to `UnoMediaCollection.ViewModels` and modify the `using` statements to contain these four statements:

```
using UnoMediaCollection.Enums;
using UnoMediaCollection.Interfaces;
using UnoMediaCollection.Model;
using System.Collections.ObjectModel;
```

15. In `MainViewModel`, change the namespace to `UnoMediaCollection.ViewModels` and update the `using` statements to contain only these four statements:

```
using Microsoft.UI.Xaml.Input;
using UnoMediaCollection.Interfaces;
using UnoMediaCollection.Model;
using System.Collections.ObjectModel;
```

All the changes so far are relatively simple. The Uno Platform project already uses the NuGet packages that we referenced in the WinUI project, so the code is very compatible.

16. Before we move on to the two views, let's make the necessary changes to `App.cs`. We need to set up `NavigationService` and register our services and ViewModel classes with the IoC container. First, add these three `using` statements to the App class:

```
using UnoMediaCollection.Interfaces;
using UnoMediaCollection.Services;
using UnoMediaCollection.ViewModels;
```

17. Rename the `Host` variable to `HostContainer` to match the name from our WinUI project and make it `internal static`:

```
internal static IHost? HostContainer { get; private set; }
```

18. Add the following code to the beginning of the `OnLaunched` method, right before the `builder` object is created:

```
var navigationService = new NavigationService(new Frame());
navigationService.Configure(nameof(MainPage), typeof(MainPage));
navigationService.Configure(nameof(ItemDetailsPage),
typeof(ItemDetailsPage));
```

This creates the `navigationService` class, which will later be registered in the IoC container and registers the two views for navigation. I've highlighted the one difference from the code in the original WinUI project. We're temporarily passing `new Frame()` into the constructor. Later in the method, we'll set `AppFrame` to the `rootFrame` created toward the end of the `OnLaunched` method.

19. Next, update the `ConfigureServices` block in `OnLaunched` to look like this:

```
.ConfigureServices((context, services) =>
{
    services.
AddSingleton<INavigationService>(navigationService);
    services.AddSingleton<IDataService, DataService>();
    services.AddTransient<MainViewModel>();
    services.AddTransient<ItemDetailsViewModel>();
})
```

This registers our classes with the IoC container just like we did in our WinUI project.

20. Update the `Host` = `builder.Build();` line of code in `OnLaunched` to `HostContainer` = `builder.Build();`.

21. Finally, immediately before the `MainWindow.Activate();` call at the end of `OnLaunched`, add this line of code to update the `AppFrame` static variable in `NavigationService`:

```
NavigationService.AppFrame = rootFrame;
```

That's everything we need to add and update except for the two views. The code won't compile successfully yet because we referenced `ItemsDetailsPage` in `OnLaunched` but haven't added it yet. We'll take care of that in the next section.

Migrating the WinUI XAML views

In this section, we'll finish the additions and changes to the `UnoMediaCollection` project and run the Windows version of the application. Let's start with `ItemDetailsView`:

1. Right-click the `UnoMediaCollection` project and select **Add | New Item**.

2. In the **Add New Item** dialog, select **Uno Platform** from **C# Items** on the left panel, choose the **Page (Uno Platform Windows App SDK)** template, name it `ItemDetailsPage.xaml`, and click **Add**:

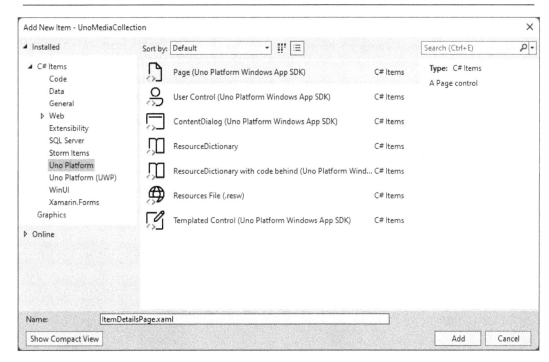

Figure 13.7 – Adding the ItemDetailsPage to the project

3. Open `ItemDetailsPage.xaml.cs` and replace the contents of the class with the following code from the WinUI project:

```
public ItemDetailsPage()
{
    ViewModel = App.HostContainer.Services.
GetService<ItemDetailsViewModel>();
    this.InitializeComponent();
}
public ItemDetailsViewModel ViewModel;
protected override void OnNavigatedTo(NavigationEventArgs e)
{
    base.OnNavigatedTo(e);
    var itemId = (int)e.Parameter;
    if (itemId > 0)
    {
        ViewModel.InitializeItemDetailData(itemId);
    }
}
```

Note that we're not migrating any of the user settings code following the `InitializeComponent` call in the constructor. We'll keep things simple for our first migration attempt.

4. You can also remove all `using` statements from the `ItemDetailsPage` class except for the following:

```
using UnoMediaCollection.ViewModels;
```

5. Open `ItemDetailsPage.xaml` and replace the child contents of the `Page` with the contents of the `Page` from the `ItemDetailsPage.xaml` in the WinUI project. Do not replace the `Page` itself because the namespaces differ.

6. Remove this `SplitButton.Resources` block because we won't be using `TeachingTip`. We removed the code behind that relies on saving user preferences to the filesystem. Without that, it would appear every time the page opens:

```
<SplitButton.Resources>
    <TeachingTip x:Name="SavingTip"
                 Target="{x:Bind SaveButton}"
                 Title="Save and create new"
                 Subtitle="Use the dropdown button option to
save your item and create another.">
    </TeachingTip>
</SplitButton.Resources>
```

7. Open `MainPage.xaml.cs` and add the following `using` statement:

```
using UnoMediaCollection.ViewModels;
```

8. The contents of the `MainPage` class will be similar to `ItemDetailsPage`:

```
public MainPage()
{
    ViewModel = App.HostContainer.Services.
GetService<MainViewModel>();
    this.InitializeComponent();
}
public MainViewModel ViewModel;
protected override void OnNavigatedTo(NavigationEventArgs e)
{
    base.OnNavigatedTo(e);
    if (e.NavigationMode == NavigationMode.Back)
    {
        ViewModel.PopulateData();
    }
}
```

This is slightly different than the implementation of `MainPage` in the WinUI project. We added an override of `OnNavigatedTo`. On some platforms, the list of items on `MainPage` was not updating after adding an item on `ItemDetailsPage`. Calling `PopulateData()` on `MainViewModel` when the user is navigating `Back` solved the behavior. This was an issue on both Android and WebAssembly. The Windows project worked as expected.

9. Open `MainPage.xaml` and replace the entire child contents of the `Page` from the `Page` in `MainPage.xaml`. Like we did in `ItemDetailsPage.xaml`, be careful not to replace the `Page` itself due to namespace differences.

10. Finally, add the following `using` declaration to the `Page` element in `MainPage`:

```
xmlns:model="using:UnoMediaCollection.Model"
```

The `MediaItem` model class is referenced by `DataTemplate` in our `ListView` and requires this `using` declaration.

Those are all the changes needed to get the application ready to run with Uno Platform. We didn't have to change our XAML controls at all, outside of removing `TeachingTip`.

Let's run the Windows version of the application to make sure everything works as expected. Make sure `UnoMediaCollection.Windows` is set as the startup project and run the application. It should look something like this when it launches:

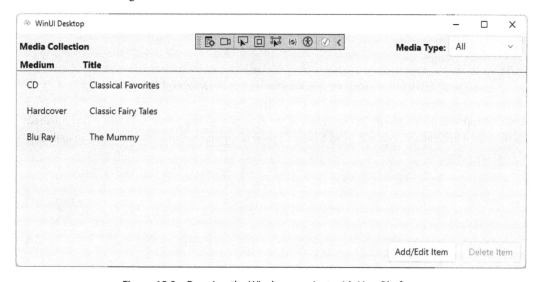

Figure 13.8 – Running the Windows project with Uno Platform

It looks exactly like the *Chapter 5* version of our WinUI application. If you try adding, editing, or removing items, everything should work as expected. Great work! That was pretty simple. Let's move on and try using the application on Android with WSA.

Running on Android with WSA

Running and debugging Android applications on Windows is fast and easy with WSA. The easiest way to install WSA on Windows 11 is to install **Amazon Appstore** from the Microsoft Store. You can get the app here: `https://aka.ms/AmazonAppstore`.

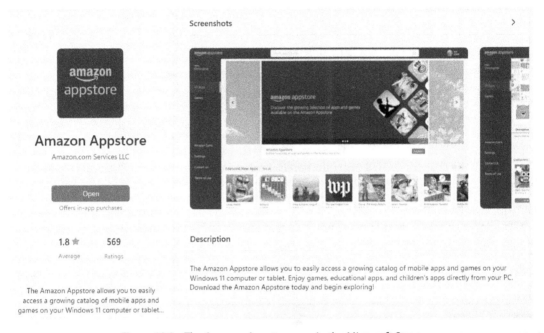

Figure 13.9 – The Amazon Appstore app in the Microsoft Store

Install the app and follow the prompts to install WSA as part of the process. When it has finished with the initial installation, you will need to restart your computer to complete the WSA installation and configuration:

Figure 13.10 – Completing the Amazon Appstore installation

After the reboot is complete, find the Amazon Appstore app in your Windows Start menu and launch it. You will see WSA start up first:

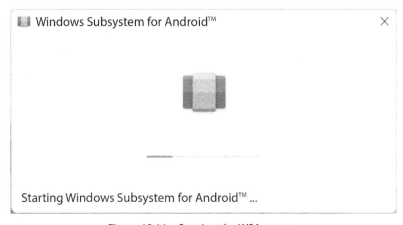

Figure 13.11 – Starting the WSA process

Keep Amazon Appstore running in the background to ensure your Android system remains active. You can minimize the window if you like. The other thing you will have to do to use WSA from Visual Studio is to ensure **Developer mode** is turned on. Launch **Windows Subsytem for Android** from the Start menu. This will open the WSA **System** settings page. Select **Advanced settings** from the left navigation panel to open the **Advanced settings** page:

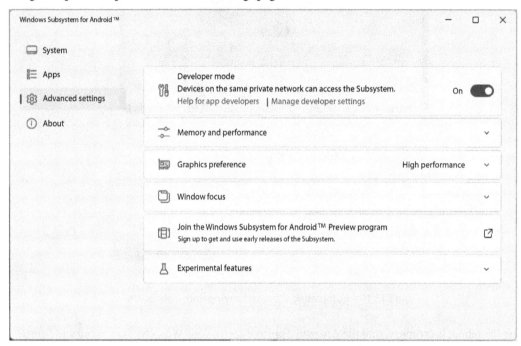

Figure 13.12 – The WSA System settings

If **Developer mode** isn't turned on, turn it on now. The last preparation step is to connect the **Android SDK** to the WSA for our debugging session. To do this, you'll need to find where your Android SDK is installed. It should be at this path if it was installed with your Visual Studio installation:

```
c:\Program Files (x86)\Android\android-sdk\
```

You will need to run the following command from a command prompt. Open a terminal or command window in the `platform-tools` subfolder of your SDK location. This is the command if you are running within **PowerShell**. I am using **Windows Terminal** with a PowerShell window:

```
.\adb connect 127.0.0.1:58526
```

If you get the `failed to authenticate to 127.0.0.1:58526` message, check whether there is a WSA pop-up dialog behind your other windows. Click the **Allow** button on there and you should now be connected to WSA to enable debugging in Visual Studio. You will need to run this `adb connect` command each time you start debugging with WSA.

It's time to run the Android version of our application with WSA. Update the startup project to be **UnoMediaCollection.Mobile**:

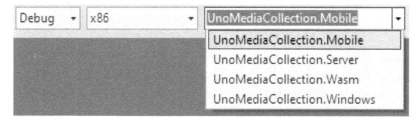

Figure 13.13 – Updating the startup project to run on mobile

If the WSA is still active, you should see **Microsoft Corporation Subsystem for Android** followed by an Android version number on the **Debug** button. Start debugging and wait a few minutes. Compiling, deploying, and running an Android application can take a bit longer than the Windows version. When the application launches, it should look something like this:

Figure 13.14 – Running the UnoMediaCollection application on Android with the WSA

Everything should function just as it did on Windows, but there could be slightly more lag in the UI, depending on the performance of your system. The cool thing about using the WSA is that you can resize your application's window to test the UI layout in different aspect ratios. Give it a try.

If you have an Android emulator configured in the Android SDK on your system, you can also try selecting that on the **Debug** button and running it there. It will look something like this on a traditional phone emulator image:

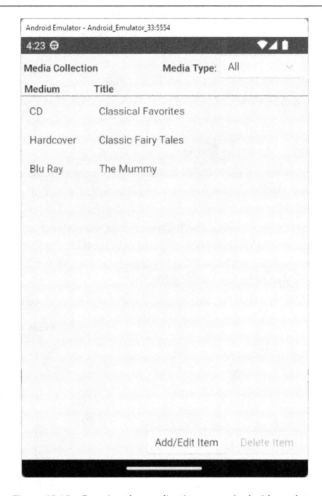

Figure 13.15 – Running the application on an Android emulator

We're up and running on Android. In many cases, switching platforms is as easy as changing the startup project. Let's finish up by trying our application on the web with WebAssembly.

Running in the browser with WebAssembly

In this final section, we will try running the application in the browser with WebAssembly. Uno Platform makes it easy to do, but like Android, the compilation and deployment can take a little time. That's because the entire application needs to run client-side within the browser. That means that in addition to deploying our application, all its dependencies (even a version of the .NET runtime) also need to be deployed.

This is one reason why the adoption of WebAssembly hasn't been as fast as many anticipated. The first-time load performance of these apps can be sluggish at best. Uno Platform published a blog post about optimizing WebAssembly performance with Uno Platform applications. If you plan to pursue this option, you should read this post: `https://platform.uno/blog/optimizing-uno-platform-webassembly-applications-for-peak-performance/`.

Change the startup project to `UnoMediaCollection.Wasm` and start debugging. You'll notice a command window launch in the background, hosting the web server that deploys the WebAssembly application. Next, a browser window will open. While the application is deploying and loading, you'll see a Uno Platform logo acting as a splash screen. When the application loads, it will look like this:

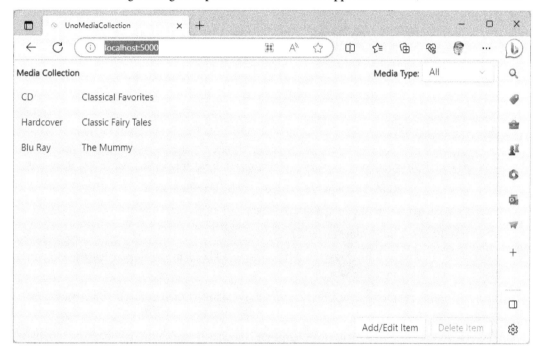

Figure 13.16 – Running the Uno Platform application in a browser with WebAssembly

Try using the application. It should function exactly as it did on other platforms. While a few of the visuals may differ from platform to platform, Uno Platform promises near-pixel-perfect applications on each supported platform.

If you would like to explore debugging further, there are some differences when debugging WebAssembly applications. The Uno Platform documentation has some great information on this: `https://platform.uno/docs/articles/external/uno.wasm.bootstrap/doc/debugger-support.html`.

That is all we will be doing in this section with WebAssembly and Uno Platform. Let's wrap up and review what we've learned in this chapter.

Summary

In this chapter, we learned all about Uno Platform. WinUI developers can take their Windows development experience and leverage it to build applications for every platform. While we focused on Visual Studio and Windows development here, with Visual Studio, VS Code, and JetBrains Rider, you can build your Uno Platform applications from any platform. We started with a basic *Hello World*-style application and imported the code and XAML from our WinUI project to create a cross-platform version of the application with very few changes. We also learned how you can leverage WSA to debug resizable Android applications on Windows without configuring an emulator. Finally, we ran our application in the browser with Uno Platform and WebAssembly. You're ready to try Uno Platform for yourself and test some of the other platforms that it supports.

In the next (and final) chapter, we will discover how to deploy WinUI 3 applications to the Microsoft Store, via **WinGet**, or with enterprise deployment options.

Questions

1. What are two deployment options when debugging Android applications with Visual Studio?

2. What are two application design patterns supported by Uno Platform?

3. What XAML schemas are supported by Uno Platform?

4. When was the first Uno Platform release?

5. What client-side web technology can .NET and Uno Platform developers leverage to run applications natively in the browser?

6. What two online resources does Uno Platform provide to test their controls and components in your browser?

7. What design tool can you leverage to design your Uno Platform applications before developing them in your favorite IDE?

14

Packaging and Deploying WinUI Applications

WinUI developers have several options to package and deploy their applications. Developers can create an account on **Microsoft Store** and upload a packaged app to be released for public consumption through **Microsoft Partner Center**. App packages can also be created to be distributed by organizations through **Microsoft Endpoint Manager** and **Microsoft Intune**, or sideloaded by individuals on Windows PCs.

In this chapter, we will cover the following topics:

- Discovering application packaging and **MSIX** basics

- Getting started with application packaging in Visual Studio

- Deploying applications with **Windows Package Manager**

- Distributing applications with the Microsoft Store

- Sideloading WinUI applications with MSIX

By the end of this chapter, you will understand the methods available to package and distribute your WinUI applications and how to use each of them.

Technical requirements

To follow along with the examples in this chapter, the following software is required:

- Windows 10 version 1809 (build 17763) or newer, or Windows 11

- Visual Studio 2022 or later, with the **.NET Desktop Development** workload configured for Windows App SDK development

The source code for this chapter is available on GitHub at this URL: `https://github.com/ PacktPublishing/Learn-WinUI-3-Second-Edition/tree/master/Chapter14`.

Discovering application packaging and MSIX basics

For most of this book, we have built and run our WinUI 3 applications locally. Now, it's time to learn the concepts of packaging and deploying WinUI applications and put that knowledge to use.

Why package your application? Well, an application package is the easiest way for WinUI applications and their dependencies to be installed in Windows. Today, when you run a WinUI project in Visual Studio, the **integrated development environment** (**IDE**) creates a package and deploys it locally. Packaging serves several other important purposes, outlined as follows:

- **Providing a clean uninstall**: A packaging system ensures that any files installed or updated with an application are removed or restored to their previous state when the application is uninstalled

- **Bundling dependencies**: The application package will bundle and deliver all your application's dependencies, optimizing disk space by sharing files across installed applications when possible

- **Facilitating updates**: Differential updates are optimized to only deliver files that require updating, based on the manifest of the original package and the updated one

- **Declaring capabilities**: By declaring your application's capabilities in the manifest, users know what types of access your app requires before they choose to install it

- **Verifying integrity and authenticity**: In order to install a Windows application on someone else's device, the application package must be digitally signed with a valid certificate from a **trusted signing authority**

If you are going to distribute your WinUI applications, the packaging format you will use is **MSIX**. What is MSIX? Let's find out.

MSIX

MSIX is the latest standard introduced by Microsoft to package applications. It is not only for Windows. The **MSIX SDK** (`https://learn.microsoft.com/windows/msix/msix-sdk/sdk-overview`) is an open source project that can be used to create application packages for any platform. You can use the SDK for Windows, Linux, macOS, iOS, Android, and even web browsers. We will focus on delivering WinUI applications to Windows users in this chapter, but you can learn more about the MSIX SDK on its GitHub repository at `https://github.com/Microsoft/msix-packaging`.

On Windows, the following platforms currently support the MSIX format:

- Windows 10, version 1709 and later, and Windows 11

- Windows Server 2019 **Long-Term Servicing Channel** (**LTSC**) and later

- Windows Enterprise 2019 LTSC and later

Earlier versions of Windows 10 required **APPX** packages, which were the predecessor to MSIX packages. However, all Windows 10 versions supported by WinUI 3 also support MSIX packages. Microsoft introduced MSIX packages in 2018 as an evolution of APPX, intending to fill the needs of APPX as well as legacy **Windows Installer** (**MSI**) packages. MSIX is an open standard, and as such, it can be used to distribute applications to any platform. MSI has been the standard to package and install Windows desktop applications since 1999. Installing Windows applications with MSI packages is supported in Windows 95 and later operating systems.

With the new MSIX packaging standard, **Universal Windows Platform** (**UWP**) applications delivered to Windows users run inside a lightweight app container. WinUI 3 applications can also be configured to run in an app container for additional security. The **Windows App Container** provides a sandbox for the execution of an application, restricting access to the registry, filesystem, and other system capabilities, such as the camera. Any capabilities that an application needs to access must be specified in the manifest file. Applications packaged to run in an app container and installed with MSIX have *read access* to the Windows registry by default. In this configuration, any data written to the virtualized registry will be completely removed if the application is uninstalled or reset. The same is true of data written to the virtual filesystem.

As documented on Microsoft Learn (`https://learn.microsoft.com/windows/msix/ overview#inside-an-msix-package`), an MSIX package's contents are grouped into *application files* and *footprint files*, as illustrated in the following diagram:

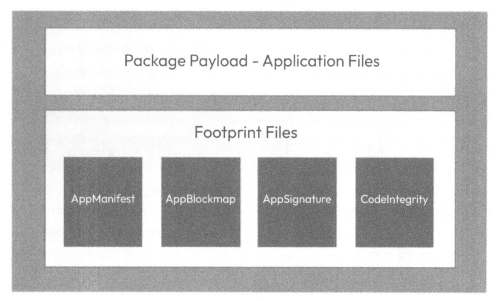

Figure 14.1 – The contents of an MSIX package

The application files are the payload of code files and other assets delivered to a user. The footprint files are the metadata and other resources that a package needs to ensure the application files are delivered as intended. This metadata includes the following:

- `AppManifest`: The manifest (`AppxManifest.xml`) includes information about the application's identity, dependencies, capabilities, extensibility points, and visual elements. This is generated from the `Package.appxmanifest` file in your WinUI project.

- `AppBlockmap`: The `AppxBlockMap.xml` file includes an indexed and cryptographically hashed list of the files in the package, digitally signed to ensure its integrity when the package is signed.

- `AppSignature`: The `AppxSignature.p7x` file in the package is generated when the package is signed. This allows the operating system to validate the signature during installation.

- `CodeIntegrity`: Code integrity is ensured by verifying information about the package in `AppxManifest.xml`, `AppxBlockMap.xml`, and `AppxSignature.p7x`.

The application files in the package will be installed to `C:\Program Files\WindowsApps\<package_name>`, with the application executable found at `C:\Program Files\WindowsApps\<package_name>\<app_name>.exe`. Note that you can't directly execute this EXE file, and access to the `WindowsApps` folder is restricted by Windows. Data created by the application during and after installation will be stored under `C:\Users\<user_name>\AppData\Local\Packages\<package_name>`. All the application files, dependencies, and data will be removed when the application is uninstalled.

Now that we know the background and history of MSIX, let's review a few of the tools available to developers and IT pros.

Reviewing MSIX tools and resources

Before we start using MSIX to package our own application, we will review a couple of other available tools and resources, as follows:

- **MSIX Toolkit**: The MSIX Toolkit is an open source collection of MSIX tools and scripts maintained by Microsoft on GitHub: `https://github.com/microsoft/MSIX-Toolkit`.

- **MSIX Labs**: Microsoft maintains a set of hands-on tutorials for developers and IT pros interested in leveraging MSIX, to package and distribute their applications: `https://github.com/Microsoft/msix-labs`.

- **MSIX Packaging Tool**: The MSIX Packaging Tool is an application to repackage classic applications in the MSIX format. Existing EXE, MSI, and **Application Virtualization (App-V)** installation packages can be converted to MSIX packages with the tool via its interactive UI or command-line tooling. It is available on the Microsoft Store at `https://apps.microsoft.com/store/detail/msix-packaging-tool/9N5LW3JBCXKF`.

- **MSIX videos**: Microsoft Learn has a series of introductory videos on MSIX packaging here: `https://learn.microsoft.com/windows/msix/resources#msix-videos`. This is a great way to get started on your MSIX journey.

- **MSIX community**: **Microsoft Tech Community** has a group of discussion spaces dedicated to MSIX packaging and deployment. Join the community and get involved here: `https://techcommunity.microsoft.com/t5/msix/bd-p/MSIX-Discussions`.

These tools and resources will assist you in your journey while learning the ins and outs of WinUI application deployment. It is important to remember that MSIX is an area of continual investment by Microsoft. It is the go-forward strategy and recommendation to package all applications. WinUI developers don't need to have a deep understanding of MSIX. You will only need a basic knowledge of MSIX and the properties that are relevant to our applications. Before we get hands-on, we'll briefly discuss the concepts of **packaged applications**, **package identity**, and **app containers** in Windows.

Packaged applications and application identity

There are a few deployment concepts that are specific to the Windows App SDK. Let's cover the basics here before we start to package and deploy our own applications.

One of the most important concepts to understand is packaged applications. The concepts we have discussed so far apply to packaged WinUI applications. These applications are packaged and installed with MSIX, they have package identity, and by default, they are **framework-dependent**. We just touched on some important concepts in that sentence; let's start by examining package identity.

All packaged applications, whether they are WinUI, UWP, or some other desktop Windows application type, benefit from package identity. Package identity is the unique identifier used by Windows to distinguish and validate the identity of your application. There are some Windows App SDK features that are only available to applications with package identity. The new Windows App SDK notifications APIs that we used in *Chapter 8*, *Adding Windows Notifications to WinUI Applications*, are available to any packaged application because those apps have package identity. For a current list of other features that require package identity, see this Microsoft Learn topic: `https://learn.microsoft.com/windows/apps/desktop/modernize/modernize-packaged-apps`.

Now, let's discuss packaged applications and **unpackaged applications**. We already reviewed some aspects of packaged apps. Most packaged apps are both packaged and installed with MSIX. However, there is a particular variation of a packaged application called a **packaged app with an external location**. These applications are packaged with MSIX, thus having package identity, but they are installed with a different installer mechanism. We won't deploy a packaged app with an external location, but you can read more about them on Microsoft Learn: `https://learn.microsoft.com/windows/apps/desktop/modernize/grant-identity-to-nonpackaged-apps`.

Unpackaged applications don't have package identity, so there are limits on the APIs they can access, as previously discussed. In most cases, you will only choose this route for legacy applications that don't require any of the features that require package identity and often require fewer restrictions on their capabilities, such as filesystem or registry access. UWP applications cannot be unpackaged, but WinUI applications can be.

The final concept to review is that of framework-dependent applications and **self-contained** applications. WinUI applications that are framework-dependent rely on the Windows App SDK runtime to be installed on the target machine. This reduces the size of your application's installer and allows apps to receive security bug fix updates during runtime, without each application updating. The downsides are having to check for the presence of the runtime during installation and the potential risk of users uninstalling the runtime after your application has been installed.

Self-contained deployments bundle the Windows App SDK runtime with the MSIX. This increases the size of the installer but provides complete control over the version of the runtime that the application uses. Self-contained applications also enable **Xcopy deployment**. You can copy the application and its dependencies from the project's output folder to any supported PC. Other than the package size, the primary downside to this option is performance. Self-contained applications are slower to load, and they use more system memory because their dependencies are not shared with other WinUI applications on the system. They are isolated to your application's process.

For more detailed information on these concepts, there are two excellent topics on Microsoft Learn:

- The *Windows App SDK deployment overview* (`https://learn.microsoft.com/windows/apps/package-and-deploy/deploy-overview`) discusses the pros and cons of self-contained deployment

- The *Deployment overview* topic (`https://learn.microsoft.com/windows/apps/package-and-deploy/`) dives deeper into packaged apps versus unpackaged apps

Now, let's get started and go hands-on, creating our MSIX package in Visual Studio.

Getting started with application packaging in Visual Studio

In this section, we'll see how we can package our applications with MSIX in Visual Studio. Visual Studio 2022 includes two WinUI project templates capable of creating MSIX deployment packages, outlined as follows:

- **Blank App, Packaged (WinUI 3 in Desktop)**: Creates a WinUI 3 project with a `package.appxmanifest` file to generate an MSIX package

- **Blank App, Packaged with Windows Application Packaging Project (WinUI 3 in Desktop)**: Creates a solution with two projects – a WinUI 3 project and a packaging project that contains the `package.appxmanifest` file

We will work with the completed **MyMediaCollection** solution from *Chapter 8*. You can either use your own solution from that chapter or download a copy from this chapter's GitHub repository at

https://github.com/PacktPublishing/Learn-WinUI-3-Second-Edition/tree/
master/Chapter14. Let's see how to generate an MSIX package for the application, as follows:

1. Start by opening the solution in Visual Studio.

2. If you want to review the manifest data for the project, you can open the `Package.`
    `appxmanifest` file and review the settings on each tab, as illustrated in the following screenshot:

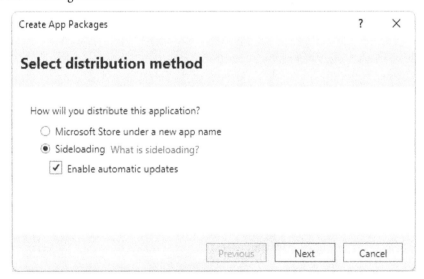

Figure 14.2 – Reviewing the application manifest

3. Then, right-click the `MyMediaCollection` project in **Solution Explorer** and select **Package
    and Publish | Create App Packages**. The **Create App Packages** window will appear, as illustrated
    in the following screenshot:

Figure 14.3 – The Create App Packages window

4. Select **Sideloading**, leave **Enable automatic updates** selected, and click **Next**. This is the MSIX equivalent of **ClickOnce deployment** (`https://learn.microsoft.com/visualstudio/deployment/clickonce-security-and-deployment`).

5. On the **Select signing method** page, remove the current certificate if one appears. You will see options to add a certificate from **Azure Key Vault**, the Store, or a local file, or create a new one, as illustrated in the following screenshot:

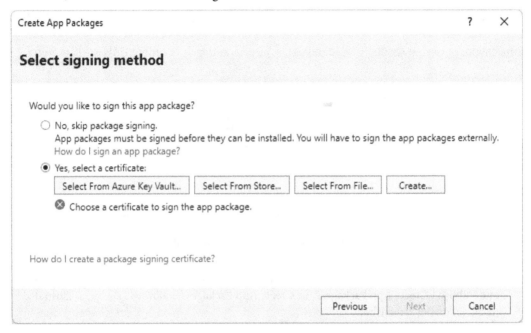

Figure 14.4 – Selecting a signing method for the package

6. We will create a self-signed certificate here. If you wanted to create a package with a certificate from a trusted authority, you would choose one of the **Select** buttons here to import the `.pfx` file. For this exercise, select **Create**.

7. Enter and confirm a secure password on the **Create a Self-Signed Test Certificate** dialog, and click **OK**. If you are prompted to overwrite an existing certificate, you can do that. Select **Yes** to continue. You will also receive a message about the certificate being imported to the certificate store for package signing. You can click **OK** on that message dialog.

8. When you return to the **Select signing method** page, the new certificate details will appear. Make sure you click the **Trust** button on the page to trust the certificate on your machine before continuing. Click **Next**.

9. On the **Select and configure packages** page, there are options to change the version number, generate an app bundle, or add, remove, and change solution configuration mappings. There is also a checkbox to include public symbol files with your package. Leave all the defaults and click **Next**.

10. On the **Configure update settings** page, an **Installer location** path is required. For applications where you will install a workstation on an internal network, you could enter the network path to the package here. For our test purposes, we will enter a local path, as illustrated in the following screenshot. For an application to update correctly on other machines, the same local path to the installer would need to exist:

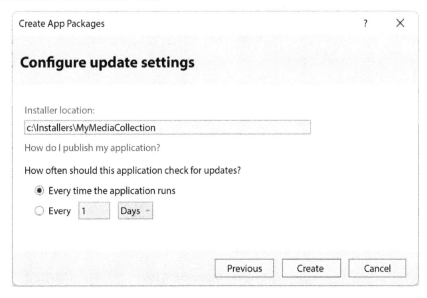

Figure 14.5 – Configuring update settings for the package

11. Click **Create**. The solution will be built, and the package will be created. When it completes, click the **Copy and Close** button to copy the installer to your selected installer location.

12. Open the `MyMediaCollection_1.0.0.0_x64_Debug_Test` folder to see the generated MSIX file, as illustrated in the following screenshot:

Name	Date modified	Type	Size
Add-AppDevPackage.resources	9/23/2023 10:48 AM	File folder	
Dependencies	9/23/2023 10:48 AM	File folder	
Add-AppDevPackage	7/21/2023 6:29 PM	Windows PowerShell Script	37 KB
Install	7/21/2023 6:29 PM	Windows PowerShell Script	14 KB
MyMediaCollection_1.0.0.0_x64_Debug	9/23/2023 10:43 AM	Security Certificate	1 KB
MyMediaCollection_1.0.0.0_x64_Debug	9/23/2023 10:43 AM	MSIX File	41,563 KB
MyMediaCollection_1.0.0.0_x64_Debug.msixsym	9/23/2023 10:43 AM	MSIXSYM File	32 KB

Figure 14.6 – The MSIX package created for MyMediaCollection

13. Navigate to the `MyMediaCollection` parent folder and double-click the `index.html` file to install the package. It will open the file in your default browser and present you with options to install any of the configurations selected during packaging. Note, in the following screenshot, I packaged the application a second time, so the version number has been automatically incremented to `1.0.1.0`:

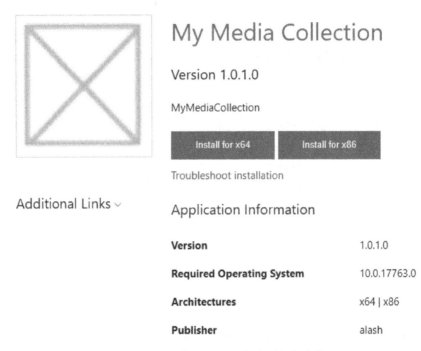

My Media Collection

Version 1.0.1.0

MyMediaCollection

| Install for x64 | Install for x86 |

Troubleshoot installation

Additional Links ⌄

Application Information

Version	1.0.1.0
Required Operating System	10.0.17763.0
Architectures	x64 | x86
Publisher	alash

Figure 14.7 – The installation page for MyMediaCollection

14. If you try to install the package on the same machine where it has already been installed and run, you will be prompted to update the application. Continue to install or update the application on your system.

Creating a package with Visual Studio is how most IDE users will choose to generate their installers. There are also tools to create MSIX packages and bundles at the command line, which are described in the Microsoft Learn documentation: `https://learn.microsoft.com/windows/msix/package/manual-packaging-root`.

Now, let's look at an alternative distribution method, Windows Package Manager.

Deploying applications with Windows Package Manager

Windows Package Manager, also referred to by its command name **WinGet**, is an open source command-line package management tool from Microsoft. In this section, we will cover how to use the `WinGet` command to install published packages and the steps to add your own MSIX packages to the **Windows Package Manager community repository**, which can be found here: `https://github.com/microsoft/winget-pkgs`. This is where `WinGet` finds available packages to install. The Microsoft Store is one of the package sources available to `WinGet`. So, if you plan to publish your application to the store, it is not necessary to also publish it to the WinGet repository.

Let's start by reviewing the steps to add a package to the community repository.

Adding a package to the community repository

To make your applications available to Windows users with the `WinGet` command, they must be published to Microsoft's Package Manager community repository or the Microsoft Store. Any application published to the community repository can be discovered and installed through the `WinGet` command in Windows.

> **Note**
>
> This method of distribution is inherently less secure than distribution through the Microsoft Store. In theory, anyone with access to the public repository could extract the package and de-compile your application.

To add your existing MSIX bundle to the repository, we will need to make it publicly available, create a WinGet manifest, and submit a GitHub **pull request** (**PR**) to have the manifest added to the community repository, as follows:

1. Start by pushing the contents of the installer folder we created (`C:\Installers\MyMediaCollection`) to a public URL. To do this, you could create a static website in Azure. This Microsoft Learn topic walks through the process: `https://learn.microsoft.com/azure/static-web-apps/get-started-portal`. This would require a GitHub or Azure DevOps repository to host the files to be deployed.

   The files can be made available on any public URL. Another option is to host the files in **Azure Blob Storage** (`https://learn.microsoft.com/azure/storage/blobs/storage-blob-static-website-how-to?tabs=azure-portal`). We will choose this option.

2. After the **Storage account** application resource has been created in Azure, open the account overview, and use the **Static website** page to enable this option. Enter the `index.html` filename that we'll upload as the index document name. After you save the file, the **Primary endpoint** field will appear, as seen in the following screenshot:

Figure 14.8 – Setting up a static website in Azure Blob Storage

3. Click the **$web** link on that page to navigate to the portal page, where you can upload files to the static web app folder.

4. Click **Upload**, and drag and drop or browse for your files. Upload all of the files and folders to the `C:\Installers\MyMediaCollection` folder.

Once your package is in the cloud, you are ready to create your manifest file for the community repository. The file is created in the **YAML** format. YAML files are the current standard for **DevOps** workflows.

For detailed instructions on creating a manifest and links to learn more about YAML, check out this Microsoft Learn topic: `https://learn.microsoft.com/windows/package-manager/package/manifest`:

1. Name your YAML file `YourCompany.MyMediaCollection.yaml`; the contents should look something like this:

```
PackageIdentifier: YourCompany.MyMediaCollection
PackageVersion: 1.0.0.0
PackageLocale: en-US
Publisher: Your Company Name
PackageName: My Media Collection
License: MIT
ShortDescription: My Media Collection helps you get your media
collection organized.
Installers:
  - Architecture: x64
    InstallerType: msix
    InstallerUrl: https://mymediacollectiondeploy.z20.web.
core.windows.net/MyMediaCollection_1.0.0.0_x64_Debug_Test/
MyMediaCollection_1.0.0.0_x64_Debug.msix
```

```
    InstallerSha256:
    712f139d71e56bfb306e4a7b739b0e1109abb662dfa164192a5cfd6adb24a4e1
    SignatureSha256:
    e53f48473621390c8243ada6345826af7c713cf1f4bbdf0d030599d1e4c175ea
ManifestVersion: 1.0.0
```

2. To get the `Sha256` information for your `.msix` file, you can use this command:

    ```
    certUtil -hashfile
      C:\Installers\MyMediaCollection\
        MyMediaCollection_1.0.0.0_x64_Debug_Test\
          MyMediaCollection_1.0.0.0_x64_Debug.msix SHA256
    ```

3. Then, test your manifest with WinGet. To install WinGet, you can install the **App Installer** app from the Microsoft Store at `https://apps.microsoft.com/store/detail/ app-installer/9NBLGGH4NNS1`.

4. After the application is installed from the store, test the syntax in your manifest with the following command:

    ```
    winget validate <manifest-file-name>
    ```

5. Then, test installing the app from your manifest with this command:

    ```
    winget install -m <manifest-file-name>
    ```

6. If your tests succeed, you're ready to submit a PR to the community repository. Use the following path structure when you submit the PR. Your `publisher` name must be unique. If you have an account on **Microsoft Partner Center** to publish apps to the store, you should use the same publisher name here. `package` is the name of your application:

    ```
    manifests\<letter of
    alphabet>\<publisher>\<package>\<version>\<filename>.yaml
    ```

> **Note**
>
> If you're unfamiliar with the GitHub forking and PR workflow, the Package Manager documentation has more detailed steps: `https://learn.microsoft.com/windows/package-manager/package/repository#step-3-clone-the-repository`.

After the PR has been approved and merged, any users with WinGet will be able to install your application from the command line. Let's see how to use WinGet next.

Using WinGet for package management

WinGet is the command-line client for Windows Package Manager. If you are familiar with other application package managers, such as **Chocolatey** for Windows (`https://chocolatey.org/`)

or **Homebrew** for macOS (`https://brew.sh/`), WinGet will feel familiar to you. A package manager allows you to install, list, and update applications on your operating system and to script the installation of multiple applications, such as when you're setting up a new computer. In this section, we will see how to use WinGet to install **Windows Terminal**, Microsoft's modern command-line app, built with WinUI!

> **Note**
>
> To read about how the Windows Terminal team created the application with WinUI, check out this blog post: `https://devblogs.microsoft.com/commandline/building-windows-terminal-with-winui/`.

Let's now look at the steps:

1. You already have the App Installer preview installed, so open **Command Prompt**.

2. Test WinGet with the following command:

    ```
    winget -?
    ```

    The WinGet help and available commands should appear in your **Command Prompt** window.

3. Now, run the `search` command to find the application we want to install, as follows:

    ```
    winget search windowsterminal
    ```

    You will see two results, as illustrated here:

```
PS C:\Installers\MyMediaCollection\MyMediaCollection_1.0.1.0_x64_Debug_Test> winget search windowsterminal
Name                      Id                                  Version        Source
---------------------------------------------------------------------------------------------
Windows Terminal Preview  Microsoft.WindowsTerminal.Preview   1.17.10234.0   winget
Windows Terminal          Microsoft.WindowsTerminal           1.16.10261.0   winget
PS C:\Installers\MyMediaCollection\MyMediaCollection_1.0.1.0_x64_Debug_Test>
```

Figure 14.9 – Performing a search with WinGet

> **Note**
>
> You may have to agree to the Microsoft Store *terms of transaction* before continuing.

4. To get more information about the package, use the `show` command, as follows:

    ```
    winget show Microsoft.WindowsTerminal
    ```

This will return the following from the application's manifest:

```
License: MIT
License Url: https://github.com/microsoft/terminal/blob/master/LICENSE
Privacy Url: https://privacy.microsoft.com
Copyright: Copyright (c) Microsoft Corporation. All rights reserved.
Copyright Url: https://github.com/microsoft/terminal/blob/master/LICENSE
Release Notes:
  This release of Windows Terminal addresses a crash in self-elevation.

  Huge thanks to @jboelter for fixing it in 1.17 (#14637).
Release Notes Url: https://github.com/microsoft/terminal/releases/tag/v1.16.10261.0
Tags:
  cli
  cmd
  command-line
  command-prompt
  console
  developer-tools
  powershell
  ps
  shell
  terminal
  utilities
  wsl
Installer:
  Installer Type: msix
  Installer Url: https://github.com/microsoft/terminal/releases/download/v1.16.10261.0/Microsoft.WindowsTerminal_Win10_1
.16.10261.0_8wekyb3d8bbwe.msixbundle
  Installer SHA256: ba6fc6854e713094b4009cf2021e8b4887cff737ab4b9c4f9390462dd2708298
  Release Date: 2023-01-27
PS C:\Installers\MyMediaCollection\MyMediaCollection_1.0.1.0_x64_Debug_Test> |
```

Figure 14.10 – Viewing manifest information for a WinGet package

5. Then, enter this command to install Windows Terminal:

    ```
    winget install Microsoft.WindowsTerminal
    ```

    You should see a message that Windows Terminal was found and installed on your PC. If you already have Windows Terminal installed, you could try another app such as `Microsoft.PowerToys` (you can find out more about **Microsoft PowerToys** at `https://learn.microsoft.com/windows/powertoys/`).

That's all there is to using WinGet. Because it is a command-line tool, you can build scripts that install all the software you need to get a new PC or **virtual machine** (**VM**) up and running. Get more information about scripting with WinGet on Microsoft Learn: `https://learn.microsoft.com/windows/package-manager/winget/#scripting-winget`.

Let's move along to our final section, where we will learn about distributing applications in the Microsoft Store.

Distributing applications with the Microsoft Store

We have seen how to deliver WinUI applications to users through packages that can be sideloaded and with WinGet. There are a couple of other distribution channels available to Windows developers – **Microsoft Intune** for enterprise application distribution, and the **Microsoft Store** for consumer apps.

A deeper dive into **Microsoft Endpoint Configuration Manager** and Intune is beyond the scope of this book, but if you are interested in learning how to distribute **line of business** (**LOB**) applications through them, you can read this Microsoft Learn topic: `https://learn.microsoft.com/windows/apps/publish/distribute-lob-apps-to-enterprises`.

The Microsoft Store is the consumer app store for Windows users. The store accepts submissions for free and paid apps. Additional monetization options such as in-app purchases, sale pricing, and paid apps with a free trial period can also be configured.

In this section, we will cover the basics of submitting a free application to the store. If you want to learn more about monetizing your app, you can start here: `https://learn.microsoft.com/windows/apps/publish/publish-your-app/price-and-availability`.

Let's see how to submit **MyMediaCollection** to the Microsoft Store.

Preparing a free application for the Microsoft Store

In this section, we will use Visual Studio to prepare and submit the **MyMediaCollection** application to the Microsoft Store. The Microsoft Store is the primary delivery outlet for consumer applications. Before you start this process, you will need to have a developer account on the store. Let's do this now, as follows:

1. First, visit the sign-up page for the Microsoft Store (`https://developer.microsoft.com/microsoft-store/register/`) and click **SIGN UP**.

2. Sign in with a Microsoft account, and select the country or region where you or your company is located.

> **Note**
> This account will be the owner of the Store account and cannot easily be changed. If you create a Store account for an organization, it is recommended to use a separate Microsoft account that is not tied to any individual at the organization or company.

3. Choose **Individual** or **Company** as your account type.

4. Enter your publisher display name. This is the name that will be seen by users on your public application store listings, so choose this carefully.

5. Enter your contact details – this information will be used by Microsoft to contact you if there are any issues or updates with your store listings. Click **Next** to continue and enter payment information.

6. Pay a one-time store registration fee. Microsoft charges a small fee the first time you register for an account on the store. This helps to prevent fraudulent and malicious accounts from being created. In most countries, the fee is approximately *$19 US Dollars (USD) for individuals* and *$99 USD for a company account.*

    The full listing of fees by country is available here: `https://learn.microsoft.com/windows/apps/publish/partner-center/account-types-locations-and-fees#developer-account-and-app-submission-markets`.

7. When you are finished, click **Review**.

8. Review the details for your account and the app developer agreement, and click **Finish** to confirm your registration. Payment will be processed at this time, and you will receive a confirmation email.

Now that you have an account on the Microsoft Store, we can proceed to submit our first app, as follows:

1. Return to Visual Studio and right-click on the `MyMediaCollection` project in **Solution Explorer**.

2. Select **Package and Publish | Create App Packages**. This process starts out the same as when creating a package for sideloading.

3. On the **Select distribution method** screen, select **Microsoft Store under a new app name**, and click **Next**.

4. On the **Select an app name** screen, ensure the Microsoft account linked to your store account is selected, and enter your desired application name in the **Reserve a new app name** field. Click **Reserve** to check whether the name is available. Each app name must be unique across the Microsoft Store. The app name will appear in your list of apps, as illustrated in the following screenshot:

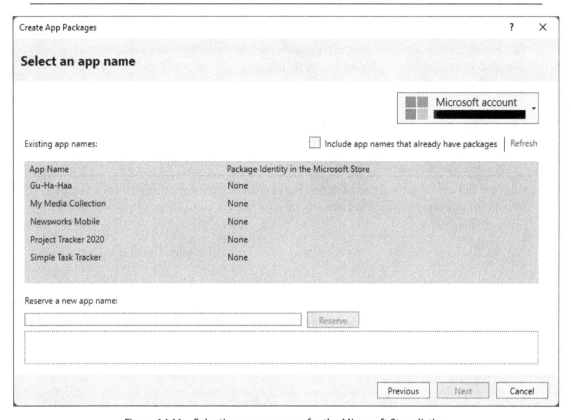

Figure 14.11 – Selecting an app name for the Microsoft Store listing

5.   Select the app name in your **Existing app names** list, and click **Next**.

6.   You can leave the default values on the **Select and configure packages** screen unless you want to update the version or the solution configuration mappings. Click **Create** at the bottom of the screen, as illustrated in the following screenshot:

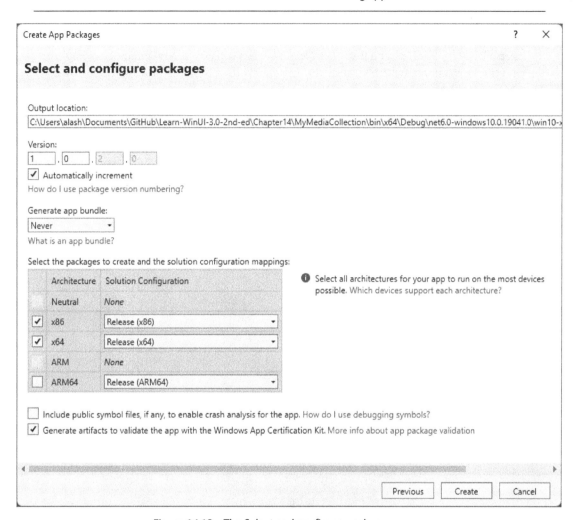

Figure 14.12 – The Select and configure packages screen

7. Visual Studio will build your project and prepare the package for the store. It will also do some validation of your app manifest data. If you receive any errors during packaging, fix them and try again. If you feel your submission is ready to go after reviewing the submission checklist (`https://learn.microsoft.com/windows/apps/publish/publish-your-app/create-app-submission#app-submission-checklist`), you can check the **Automatically submit to the Microsoft Store after Windows App Certification Kit validation** checkbox on the **Finished creating package** screen. This will submit your package to the store upon a successful validation run.

8. Click the **Launch Windows App Certification Kit** button. When the certification kit launches, keep all the tests selected, and then click **Next**. The tests will take several minutes to complete, and the application may launch several times during the validation process. The following screenshot illustrates the **Validating App** progress:

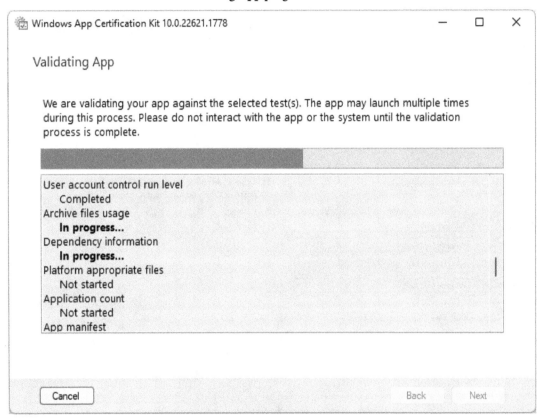

Figure 14.13 – The Microsoft Store application validation in process

9. The process should provide a **PASSED** result on the **View Final Report** page. Upon completion, you can click the **Click here to view the results** option to see which tests passed or failed. All failures should be addressed before continuing with the store submission. These tests will be run during the Microsoft Store approval process, and any failures here are likely to cause the submission to be rejected. For details on the tests and corrective actions that can be taken for failures, you can review this Microsoft Learn topic: `https://learn.microsoft.com/windows/uwp/debug-test-perf/windows-app-certification-kit-tests`.

When you have a validated application ready to submit to the store, you can continue the process. Let's walk through how to submit a WinUI application through the Microsoft Partner Center website.

Uploading a package to the Store

In this section, we will walk through submitting a package created by Visual Studio to the Microsoft Store using the Partner Center dashboard. To do this, proceed as follows:

1. Start by logging in to the Partner Center with your Microsoft account at the following URL: `https://partner.microsoft.com/dashboard/home`.

2. Click **Apps and Games**, and you will be taken to the **Overview** page to submit apps and games to Windows and Xbox.

3. You will see a list of reserved app names and submitted apps on your account here. If you do not yet have an app name reserved, you can click **New product | MSIX or PWA app**. I am going to select **My Media Collection** from my apps to submit an initial version of this application. The following screenshot illustrates how you would start to reserve a new name:

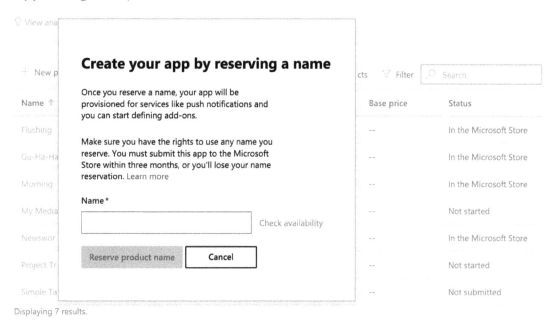

Figure 14.14 – Reserving a new name for your application

4. On the **Application overview** page for your selected app, click **Start your submission**, as illustrated in the following screenshot:

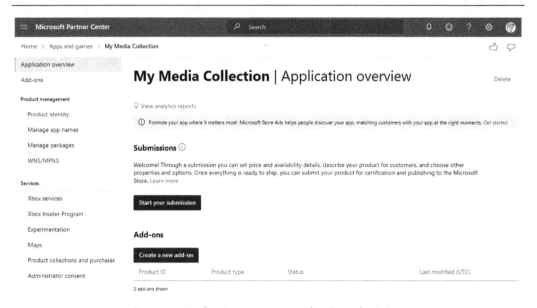

Figure 14.15 – Starting your new application submission

5.   Begin the submission by selecting the **Pricing and availability** section.

6.   We will keep all the default settings in this section, except for the **Base price** option. A selection must be made here. Choose the **Free** option or select a base price from the list. When you are done, select **Save draft**.

7.   Then, select the **Properties** section. Select a category and sub-category, if necessary, and enter your **Support info** data. Enter any relevant data for your app in the **Display mode**, **Product declarations**, and **System requirements** sections, and click **Save**.

The **Properties** section can be seen in the following screenshot:

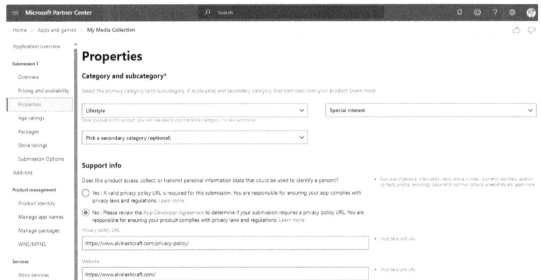

Figure 14.16 – The Properties section of the application submission

8. Complete the questionnaire on the **Age ratings** page and click **Preview ratings**. This page determines whether your app should be restricted to certain age groups, based on the data it collects or exchanges with other users. If everything looks good after generation, click **Save**, followed by **Continue**.

9. Select the **Packages** page. On this page, you can browse to your `.msixupload` or `.msix` file and upload it to the site for submission. Choose the compatible device families and click **Save**.

10. Then, select a language under the **Store listings** section. Supporting multiple languages and specifying them here makes it more likely that your application will be installed in different countries. Add an application description and at least one screenshot of your application. The remaining fields are optional, but the more you complete, the easier it will be for customers to find your app, and the more likely they are to try it. When everything is completed, click **Save**.

Some example language options are shown in the following screenshot:

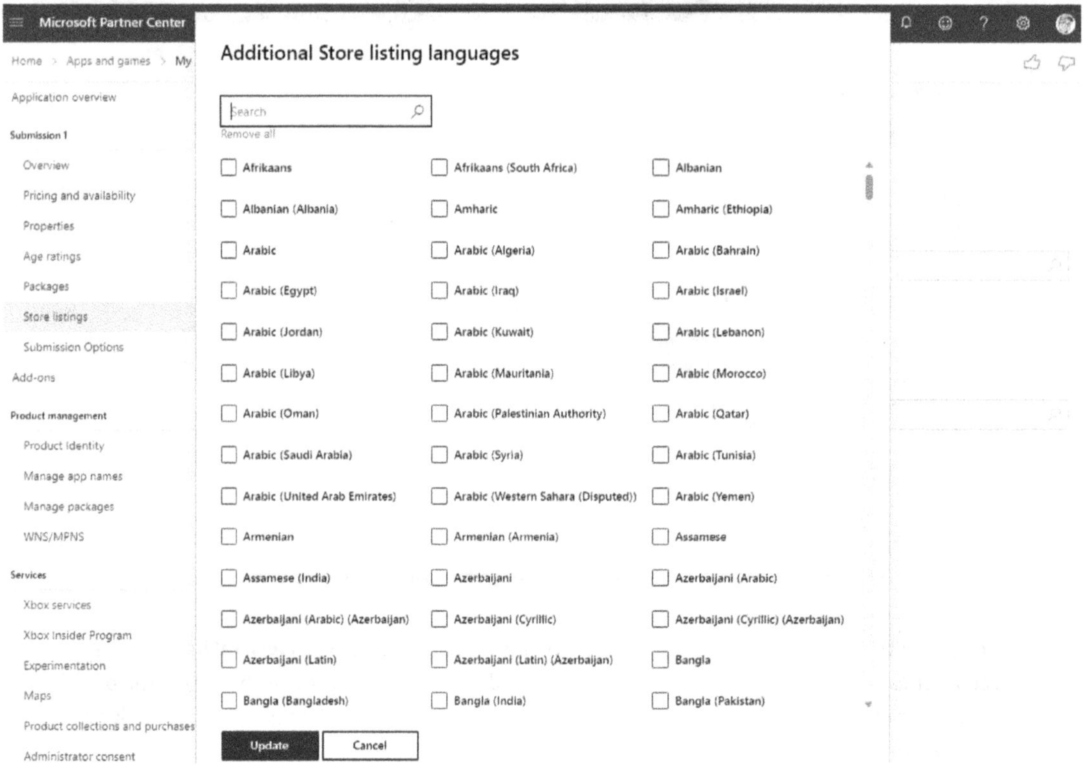

Figure 14.17 – Selecting languages for the application submission

11. Completing the **Submission options** page is optional. By default, your app will be published immediately after passing certification. I will select **Don't publish this submission until I select publish now** because I do not want this app to be available in the store until I make some additional changes.

12. Finally, click **Submit to the Store**. Your app will be submitted for certification. If it passes, it will be available in the Microsoft Store when you have indicated this on the **Submission options** page. If your app fails validation, you will receive a list of issues to address before attempting another submission.

Those are the basic steps to submit a new application to the Microsoft Store. For more detailed scenarios, and information about updates and add-ons, you can review the Microsoft Learn *app submission* documentation: https://learn.microsoft.com/windows/apps/publish/publish-your-app/create-app-submission.

Now, we will cover how to sideload applications in Windows with MSIX.

Sideloading WinUI applications with MSIX

In this section, we will create an MSIX package for a WinUI project and learn how to sideload it on Windows 10. When you sideload an application, you install it directly with the MSIX UI or PowerShell commands. This method of installation is important to understand, as it is frequently used by enterprises to distribute applications internally.

> **Note**
>
> You could also create a self-contained application package and use Xcopy deployment for distribution, but this method has some performance drawbacks, which we covered earlier in the chapter.

We are going to start by creating a package for sideloading.

Creating an MSIX package for sideloading

In this section, we will create a package for a WinUI project with Visual Studio. You can start by either opening an existing WinUI project or by creating a new, empty one. I have created a new project named `ProjectTracker`. Proceed as follows:

1. First, right-click the project in **Solution Explorer**, and select **Package and Publish | Create App Packages**.

2. On the **Select distribution method** screen of the **Create App Packages** window, leave the **Sideloading** radio button and the **Enable automatic updates** checkbox selected. Click **Next**.

3. On the following page, select a signing method. Select **Yes, select a certificate**, and click the **Create** button. Here, you will create a self-signed certificate. By using a self-signed certificate, any users who install the app will need to trust your package and import the certificate from the MSIX package. We will explain this process in the following section, when we sideload the package. Enter a name and password for the certificate, as illustrated in the following screenshot:

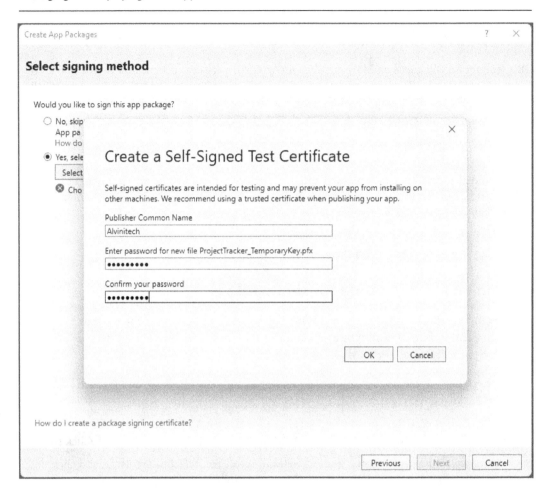

Figure 14.18 – Creating a self-signed certificate for the package

4.   Select **Trust** to trust the certificate, and click **Next**.

5.   Leave the default settings on the **Select and configure packages** page. Click **Next**.

6.   Enter the installer path. This can be a local file path or a network location. Click **Create**. Your project will compile, and the package will be created in the specified location.

Now that we have an MSIX package for our project, we're ready to sideload it. Let's walk through this process.

Sideloading an MSIX package

In this section, we will learn how to sideload a WinUI application with MSIX. We created a new MSIX package in the previous section. Navigate to the folder where the package was created inside your project's folder, and review the files in the package folder – named `ProjectTracker_1.0.0.0_x64_Test`, in my case. The following screenshot illustrates this:

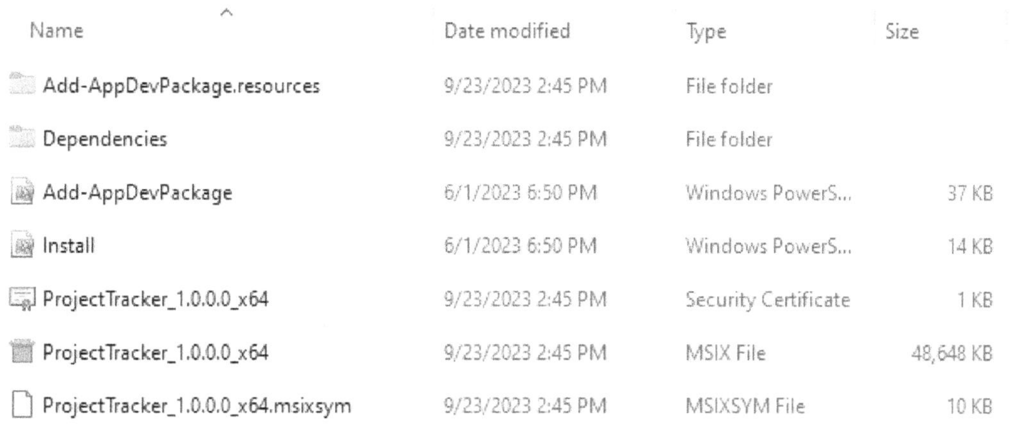

Name	Date modified	Type	Size
Add-AppDevPackage.resources	9/23/2023 2:45 PM	File folder	
Dependencies	9/23/2023 2:45 PM	File folder	
Add-AppDevPackage	6/1/2023 6:50 PM	Windows PowerS...	37 KB
Install	6/1/2023 6:50 PM	Windows PowerS...	14 KB
ProjectTracker_1.0.0.0_x64	9/23/2023 2:45 PM	Security Certificate	1 KB
ProjectTracker_1.0.0.0_x64	9/23/2023 2:45 PM	MSIX File	48,648 KB
ProjectTracker_1.0.0.0_x64.msixsym	9/23/2023 2:45 PM	MSIXSYM File	10 KB

Figure 14.19 – Reviewing the package files

Now, let's look at the steps to sideload the application:

1. To install this package on another Windows device, start by copying the `Project Tracker_1.0.0.0_x64.msix` file to the machine. This file contains all of the necessary information and files to install the application.

2. Then, we need to install the self-signed certificate used to sign the package. You can install it by running the `Install.ps1` **PowerShell** script, but you can also install it at the time it was created if you are installing it on the same machine. We will install it by right-clicking the MSIX file and selecting **Properties**.

3. Click the **Digital Signatures** tab, and select the certificate in the **Signature list** box, as illustrated in the following screenshot:

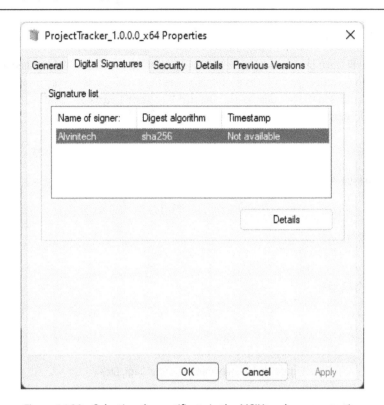

Figure 14.20 – Selecting the certificate in the MSIX package properties

4. Click **Details** to open the **Digital Signature Details** screen.

5. Click the **View Certificate** button. On the **Certificate** page that opens, click **Install Certificate**.

6. When completing **Certificate Import Wizard**, import the certificate to the local machine, and on the **Certificate Store** page, select **Place all certificates in the following store**, as illustrated in the following screenshot:

Figure 14.21 – Importing the package certificate

7. Click **Browse**, and select the **Trusted Root Certification Authorities** folder. Click **OK** on the dialog and click **Next** on the wizard.

8. After clicking **Finish**, the certificate will be imported. If all goes well, you will receive a message that the certificate was successfully imported. You can close the **Properties** page and continue with the package installation.

9. Now, double-click the MSIX package file. The installer will open a window with some of the application's manifest information. Click **Install**, and leave the **Launch when ready** checkbox selected, as illustrated in the following screenshot:

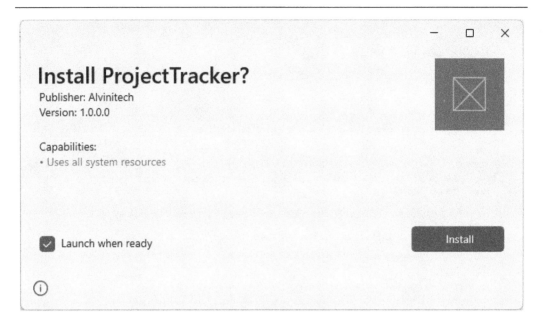

Figure 14.22 – Installing a trusted application from its MSIX package

The application will install and launch, and you're ready to go. Note that the package is trusted because we imported the certificate to the **Trusted Root Certification Authorities** folder.

This installation can be automated with PowerShell if the MSIX certificate is already trusted on the target machines. Use the Add-AppPackage command to install an MSIX package or MSIX bundle from a PowerShell prompt, as illustrated in the following command:

```
Add-AppPackage -path c:\Installers\ProjectTracker\
ProjectTracker_1.0.0.0_x64.msix
```

If you have several packages to distribute, you can create a custom PowerShell script to iterate over all of the MSIX packages in a given folder. For more information about PowerShell scripting with MSIX, check out the following Microsoft Learn topic: https://learn.microsoft.com/windows/msix/desktop/powershell-msix-cmdlets.

Let's wrap up and review what we have learned in this chapter.

Summary

In this chapter, we reviewed various methods of delivering WinUI applications to consumers. We learned the basics of MSIX packages and how to create packages to sideload our applications. We also covered the process of creating an account on Microsoft Partner Center to create application submissions on the Microsoft Store.

Then, we validated and submitted an MSIX application package to the Store. Finally, we learned how to manually sideload MSIX packages and how PowerShell can be leveraged to automate the sideloading process. These concepts will help you when you are ready to create your own WinUI applications for enterprise or consumer use.

This is the final chapter of our book. I hope that the concepts covered in each chapter will help you succeed in your quest to become a WinUI application developer.

Questions

1. What are some of the application installer formats that preceded MSIX?
2. Is MSIX only for UWP and WinUI apps?
3. In a WinUI project, which file contains the application manifest data?
4. Which command is used to install packages with Windows Package Manager?
5. How can you make your application available with WinGet?
6. What is the name of the online portal to submit applications to the Microsoft Store?
7. How many screenshots are required in a Microsoft Store listing?

Index

`Packtpub.com`

Subscribe to our online digital library for full access to over 7,000 books and videos, as well as industry leading tools to help you plan your personal development and advance your career. For more information, please visit our website.

Why subscribe?

- Spend less time learning and more time coding with practical eBooks and Videos from over 4,000 industry professionals

- Improve your learning with Skill Plans built especially for you

- Get a free eBook or video every month

- Fully searchable for easy access to vital information

- Copy and paste, print, and bookmark content

Did you know that Packt offers eBook versions of every book published, with PDF and ePub files available? You can upgrade to the eBook version at `packtpub.com` and as a print book customer, you are entitled to a discount on the eBook copy. Get in touch with us at `customercare@packtpub.com` for more details.

At `www.packtpub.com`, you can also read a collection of free technical articles, sign up for a range of free newsletters, and receive exclusive discounts and offers on Packt books and eBooks.

Other Books You May Enjoy

If you enjoyed this book, you may be interested in these other books by Packt:

Modernizing Your Windows Applications with the Windows App SDK and WinUI

Matteo Pagani, Marc Plogas

ISBN: 978-1-80323-566-0

- Understand the key concepts of the Windows App SDK and WinUI
- Integrate new features by creating new applications or by enhancing your existing ones
- Revamp your app's UI by adopting Fluent Design and new interaction paradigms such as touch and inking
- Use notifications to engage with your users more effectively
- Integrate your app with the Windows ecosystem using the Windows App SDK
- Use WinML to boost your tasks using artificial intelligence
- Deploy your application in LOB and customer-facing scenarios with MSIX

Building Modern SaaS Applications with C# and .NET

Andy Watt

ISBN: 978-1-80461-087-9

- Explore SaaS and understand its importance in modern application development
- Discover multi-tenancy and its impact on design decisions for SaaS
- Build, test, and deploy a database, API, and UI for a SaaS application
- Approach authentication and authorization like a pro
- Scale a SaaS application
- Employ C# and .NET to build SaaS applications

Packt is searching for authors like you

If you're interested in becoming an author for Packt, please visit authors.packtpub.com and apply today. We have worked with thousands of developers and tech professionals, just like you, to help them share their insight with the global tech community. You can make a general application, apply for a specific hot topic that we are recruiting an author for, or submit your own idea.

Share your thoughts

Now you've finished *Learn WinUI 3*, we'd love to hear your thoughts! Scan the QR code below to go straight to the Amazon review page for this book and share your feedback or leave a review on the site that you purchased it from.

https://packt.link/r/1805120069

Your review is important to us and the tech community and will help us make sure we're delivering excellent quality content.

Download a free PDF copy of this book

Thanks for purchasing this book!

Do you like to read on the go but are unable to carry your print books everywhere?

Is your eBook purchase not compatible with the device of your choice?

Don't worry, now with every Packt book you get a DRM-free PDF version of that book at no cost.

Read anywhere, any place, on any device. Search, copy, and paste code from your favorite technical books directly into your application.

The perks don't stop there, you can get exclusive access to discounts, newsletters, and great free content in your inbox daily

Follow these simple steps to get the benefits:

1. Scan the QR code or visit the link below

https://packt.link/free-ebook/9781805120063

2. Submit your proof of purchase
3. That's it! We'll send your free PDF and other benefits to your email directly

www.ingramcontent.com/pod-product-compliance
Lightning Source LLC
Chambersburg PA
CBHW080610060326
40690CB00021B/4643